LONDON'S BURNING

True Adventures on the Frontlines of Punk, 1976–1977

Dave Thompson

CHICAGO
REVIEW
PRESS

An A Cappella Book

Library of Congress Cataloging-in-Publication Data
Thompson, Dave, 1960 Jan. 3-
    London's burning : true adventures on the frontlines of punk, 1976-1977 /
Dave Thompson.
    p. cm.
    ISBN-13: 978-1-55652-769-2
    ISBN-10: 1-55652-769-1
    1. Punk rock music—England—History and criticism. 2. Punk culture—
England—London. 3. Thompson, Dave, 1960 Jan. 3- I. Title.

    ML3534.6.G7T46 2009
    781.66—dc22

                                                        2008040527

Lyric Credits:
"I Ain't Gonna Be History"—lyrics by Alan Lee Shaw, reprinted by permis-
    sion of Alan Lee Shaw and EMI Music Publishing Ltd.
"Great British Mistake"—lyrics by TV Smith, reprinted by permission of TV
    Smith and Twist And Shout Music.
"The Great Beast" by Alan Lee Shaw. Lyrics reproduced by kind permission
    of Alan Lee Shaw.
"New Day Dawning"—lyrics by TV Smith, reprinted by permission of TV
    Smith and Twist And Shout Music.

Cover and interior design: Scott Rattray
Cover photographs: ©Jorgen Angel, iStock

Published by Chicago Review Press, Incorporated
814 North Franklin Street
Chicago, Illinois 60610
ISBN 978-1-55652-769-2
Printed in the United States of America

Contents

Preface

If I were asked to describe this book in one word, it would be *memoir*, albeit one without too much "me" in it. A *moir*, then. And I will state here and now that I have no claims to greatness during the period of which I write. I did make a couple of appearances on Independent Television's *Pop Quest* game show, sixteen years old with too much hair and a razor-blade pendant, but I crashed and burned in the semifinal because I couldn't bring myself to say "Chirpy Chirpy Cheep Cheep" on a national prime-time broadcast.

The author on the set of Yorkshire TV's *Pop Quest*, December 1976. *Author's collection*

Don't bother with the blackmail notes, though; I have both the photos and the tapes.

I neither published a fanzine (that would come later) nor played in a band; I neither draped myself prominently in the corridors of power, nor grinned inanely from the background of some iconic image. In fact, the only other photograph of myself from this period that I have ever seen shows the back of my head retreating down the King's

Road, Chelsea, while Johnny Rotten holds court outside Malcolm McLaren's Seditionaries store.* So much for making my mark on history.

What I did do was attend a lot of concerts—including probably 95 percent of the shows mentioned here—buy a lot of records, and save up a lot of memories. I was an observer who was lucky enough to witness some great things; I was a bystander who happened to bump into some remarkable people. It is those great things and remarkable people that take center stage here, and, if my own presence often fades into the background, then that's exactly as it should be. I was in the room, but others were on the stage, and it's their impressions and ideas that I sought as I was writing this book.

In among these recollections are woven a handful of my own personal adventures and experiences. They are not exhaustive; I was sixteen when the book begins and seventeen when it ends, ages at which life-changing events occur on such a regular basis that every experience, in some way, forged its own unique perspective. To even try and chronicle every thought and emotion that crossed my mind as I stood, one more time, at the back of the Roxy would be as pointless as it would ultimately be boring.

I note the things I'm glad I noticed. But some impressions are so universal that it would be redundant to reel them out, and others are so personal that it would be meaningless. At the end of the day, if you were there, I hope you'll remember how it felt to witness history unfolding; and if you weren't, you'll come away with a taste for what you missed.

Namely: Warm malt liquor, stale cigarettes, cheapo perfume, gob in your hair, someone's heel on your toe, and that awful sticky sensation you feel when you've spent too long crushed up in a crowd, sandwiched against somebody who ought to be wearing a shirt. The support band is rubbish and the main band stinks; you've got a long walk home; and you have to work tomorrow. Ah, good times.

---

*You can find it on page 322 of Jon Savage's *England's Dreaming*.

The thrill of buying a brand-new single, and rushing home to play it to death, while admiring the picture sleeve and absorbing all the credits. Sporadically throughout this book, playlists appear of each month's best new records. Gather them up and play them loud, and you'll have a sense of what it was like to be out soaking up the new sounds. There's a lot of reggae in there. I liked reggae. But you're welcome to replace it with something else. Chicago's "If You Leave Me Now" was very popular back then.

And, finally, attempting to blend in with a crowd of city slickers, to avoid the attentions of the bully boys on the other side of the road. Tribal warfare has always been a major part of British youth culture, ever since the first mods and rockers slugged it out on Brighton beach. But there was something especially feral about the fighting that erupted around punk, less a conflict of minority cultures than it was an outright declaration of war, straights versus weirdoes, old guard versus upstarts, the establishment versus a handful of rebels who dared to dream that life could be better.

The period covered by this book is relatively short: just thirteen months, from May 1976 to June 1977. But what tumultuous months they were, opening with Britain's first ever glimpse of the Patti Smith Group, and closing with the London coronation of Bob Marley and the Wailers, but in between scooping up such maniacal activity that it is difficult to believe that so much happened in so little time.

My own world was even smaller, bracketed by the twin barriers of my last days at school and first months of work, and an income level to match. Perhaps more than anything, that is what drew me to what became (but most certainly wasn't) punk rock; how I would have loved to spend my evenings flitting from one major rock event to another (if it's Wednesday, it must be Genesis). But I couldn't afford two or three quid a ticket, so I found my fun where I could, in the pubs that often waived admission in the hope that you'd spend your cash on drinks, and even if they didn't, asked for pennies, not pounds.

It was within those less than salubrious surroundings that I first saw, and met, the musicians whose stories are told in these pages, and whose music and friendship has remained alongside me ever since. Not all of them are household names, even after so many other books have come along to scour the archaeological debris of this thoroughly overworked seam; but even those who are now "famous" tell tales here that really haven't been heard, tales of kids no different from the rest of us, who had a dream to fulfill or an itch to scratch, or maybe just a yearning to clamber out of the crowd that was clustered by the stage, and get up in front of it instead.

It's the story of ambition and inspiration in the days before the Reality Fairy arrived to render her decision: *you* can be a star, *you* can be a cult, and *you* shall remain in perpetual obscurity. It was indiscriminate, it was unpredictable, and it was certainly, in some cases, unfair. But in fairness to the Fairy, and to any shattered dreams that she might be responsible for, I don't believe there is anybody in this book who does not still draw at least a portion of their living wage from making music (at least among those who are still in the position to do so). For them, "punk" may have offered an escape route from their basement rehearsal room, but they would have found a way out regardless of the prevailing climate. Which is another reason why this book closes where and when it does. In 1976, it was optimism that guided most aspiring young musicians. In 1977, it was opportunism. In 1976, we were creating a scene. In 1977, we were looking around and wondering who were all these strangers, and why did they all dress and sound the same?

Perhaps my main motivation to tell these stories, however, was the fact that I wasn't reading them anyplace else. The years 2007–2008 saw the bookshelves groan beneath the combined weight of more "thirtieth anniversary" punk rock histories than any one person could ever read—but I did read them because I wanted to discover whether what I thought I had experienced ever really happened.

Apparently not. Stories I recalled wandered off in new directions. People I remembered turned into somebody else. And records that I loved were redefined as rubbish. So I cast them all to one side and started again.

I have done my best in these pages to avoid time traveling. Lessons taught in 1976 were not necessarily learned until years, even decades, later. I can look back at a certain sequence of events and see how they might be connected. But hindsight is not a gift that I had at my disposal at the time, and so I have avoided it—not entirely, because sometimes, a point needs to be made to prevent you, the reader, from wondering what on earth is happening here. But other times, I made a deliberate decision to leave you in the same state of suspense that I found myself in at the time, in the knowledge that, by drawing your own conclusions, you will arrive at an answer that makes as much sense to you as the answers that I formed mean to me. Yes, it's fun to read of someone else's personal experiences. But how much more intriguing it is to experience them yourself.

So, a memoir without too much "me," a history of hopefulness, and a slice of life that will never be repeated, because the circumstances that created it can no longer exist, even if we overlook the unique social and economic conditions that were bubbling all around the mid-1970s. The music industry is too savvy these days— and too selfish. Rock 'n' roll is a career today, taught in colleges and fluffed up on the news. There is no sense of danger, or flying too close to the sun; just an army of publicists and personal assistants doing and saying whatever is necessary to keep their client in the public eye, while the music itself has so little pride that even the musicians now refer to it as "product," and to themselves as "brands," while the record companies sue the pants off their "customers" for not caring enough about the shareholders' bottom line.

Even the underground, the grassroots scenes that are the logical descendant of that which underlies this book, is more concerned with maximum exposure than with getting their rocks off or kicking out jams. And nobody even bats an eyelid if you swear on television, because they don't even call it swearing anymore. You're dropping the "F-bomb" instead.

No, the world that revolves in these pages has gone, good-bye, forever, and now it's down to those of us who were there to tell everyone else how it happened. Pete Townshend once told us "we won't get fooled again." This book is about the last time we paid him any attention.

Acknowledgments

I did not do all this on my own. Endless e-mails, phone calls, and all-night conversations jogged memories, rectified forgetfulness, and corrected misapprehensions. So thank you, first and foremost, to everybody who resisted the temptation to declare that they'd been interviewed enough about that-long ago era and responded to my call to arms:

Danny Adler, Gaye Advert, Attila the Stockbroker, Wayne County, Andy Ellison, Mick Farren, Dee Generate, Martin Gordon, Chris Goulstone, Mik Heslin, Brian James, Ivan Kral, Danny Kustow, Gene October, Andy Partridge, Andy Prince, Tom Robinson, Alan Lee Shaw, TV Smith, James Stevenson, Bernie Tormé, Cherry Vanilla, and Steve Wilkin.

To all those whom I either interviewed elsewhere, or just spent time casually talking to: Stiv Bators, Budgie, Hugh Cornwell, Michael Dempsey, Ian Dury, Bruce Foxton, Richard Hell, Gary Holton, Billy Idol, Tony James, Rod Latter, John Lydon, Joey Ramone, Sandy Robertson, Steve Severin, Siouxsie Sioux, Nils Stevenson, Richard Strange, Joe Strummer, Rikki Sylvan, John Towe, Chris Townson, Dave Treganna, Nik Turner, Twink, Ari Up, Tom Verlaine, and Larry Wallis.

To Jo-Ann Greene for the Rat Scabies and Glen Matlock interviews.

To Malcontent Pictures for permission to quote from the TV Smith documentary *Uncharted Wrecks of Wonder: The Story of the Adverts and TV Smith*.

And to Cassie Wilkinson, who accompanied me through most of the memories contained in this book.

Et aussi, Amy Hanson, Veronique Cordier, Jenny and James, Linda and Larry, Phil and Paula, Sue and Tim, Deb and Roger, Bob and Jane, Dave and Sue, Oliver, Toby and Trevor, Jenny W., Karen T., Anchorite Man, Bateerz and family, Chrissie Bentley, Blind Pew, Mrs. B East, JD, Mrs. Nose and family, Gef the Talking Mongoose, the Gremlins who live in the heat pump, Geoff Monmouth, Naughty Miranda, Nutkin, Steve Wright, a lot of Thompsons, and Neville Viking.

Cast of Characters

Alan Lee Shaw
Vocalist, guitarist, and songwriter with the Maniacs and Rings.

Alan Merrill
Frontman for teen sensations the Arrows, and the man who wrote "I Love Rock 'n' Roll." Now an ever-entertaining solo artist.

Andy Ellison
Vocalist with Jet and the Radio Stars.

Andy Prince
Bassist with Rikki and the Last Days of Earth.

Bernie Tormé
Ireland-born lead guitarist with the Bernie Tormé Band.

Bev
a.k.a. Sid Vicious. A Bowie freak I used to know. Later joined the Sex Pistols. Now deceased.

Brian James
Damned guitarist and songwriter, went on to the Lords of the New Church, the Brian James Gang, and more.

Cassie Wilkinson
The author's constant companion.

Cherry Vanilla
American singer.

Chris Miller
a.k.a. Rat Scabies, Damned drummer.

Dagenham Dave
The Stranglers' first and greatest fan. Now deceased.

Danny Adler
American-born leader of Roogalator, the greatest pub rock band of all, now leading the Danny Adler Band across the United States.

Danny Kustow
Lead guitarist with the Tom Robinson Band.

Dave Letts
a.k.a. Dave Vanian, frontman with the Damned.

Dee Generate
Eater drummer.

Gary Holton
Frontman with the Heavy Metal Kids, future actor. Now deceased.

Gaye Black
a.k.a. Gaye Advert, bassist with the Adverts.

Gene October
Vocalist with Chelsea.

Howard Pickup
Guitarist with the Adverts, now deceased.

Hugh Cornwell
Vocalist and guitarist with the Stranglers, now solo.

Ian Dury
Led Kilburn and the High Roads to glory. Later solo, now deceased.

Ian North
American-born leader of Ian's Radio.

Ivan Kral
Czech-born guitarist with the Patti Smith Group.

Jake
The man with the best bootleg cassette collection in town.

James Stevenson
Glam fan and guitarist with Chelsea. Later with Gene Loves Jezebel, the Cult, and the Alarm.

Joe
A friend of Cassie's.

John Towe
Drummer with Chelsea, worked in a music store with Howard Pickup, and later joined Generation X, the Adverts, ATV, Ian Mitchell Band, and more.

Larry Wallis
Former Pink Fairy, record producer par excellence and a great guitarist.

Laurie Muscat
a.k.a. Laurie Driver, Adverts drummer.

Linton
Rastafarian squatter and friend of Cassie's.

Margarita
Winston's girlfriend.

Martin Gordon
Bassist and songwriter with Sparks, Jet, Ian's Radio, and the Radio Stars, now turning out a succession of brilliant solo albums.

Mick Farren
Journalist and genius.

Ray Burns
a.k.a. Captain Sensible, Damned bassist.

Rikki Sylvan
Frontman with Rikki and the Last Days of Earth. Now deceased.

Rod Latter
Drummer with Maniacs and Rings, and later the Adverts.

Sandy Robertson
Journalist.

Steve Bruce
Of the immortal Cock Sparrer.

Steve Wilkin
Guitarist with Masterswitch, later recorded with Rikki Sylvan.

Tom Robinson
Vocalist with the Tom Robinson Band.

Tim Smith

a.k.a. TV Smith, vocalist and songwriter with the Adverts, now deep inside a magnificent solo career.

Twink

Ex–Pink Fairy, vocalist with Rings.

Wayne County

America's most shocking musical import. Now Jayne County.

Winston

Rastafarian squatter, Margarita's boyfriend, and one of Cassie's best friends.

1.

I Ain't Gonna Be History

MID-MAY 1976

SOUNDTRACK

"Angola"	The Revolutionaries (Disco Mix)
"Babylon Queendom"	Peter Tosh (Intel Diplo)
"Babylon Too Rough"	Gregory Isaacs (Belmont)
"Diverse Doctrine"	Ras Ibuna (Pittsburgh)
"Gloria"	Patti Smith Group (Arista)
"Have Mercy"	The Mighty Diamonds (Virgin)
"Hit the Road Jack"	Big Youth (Trojan)
"I'm Alright"	Jah Woosh (Attack)
"Jah Jah Bring Everything"	Jah Glenn (Eagle)
"Johnny Was"	Bob Marley and the Wailers (Island)
"MPLA"	The Revolutionaries (Disco Mix)
"One Step Forward"	Max Romeo (Island)
"Rat Race"	Bob Marley and the Wailers (Tuff Gong)
"Rockers No Crackers"	G. Washington (Student)
"Roots Music"	Jackie Bernard (Grounation)
"Runaway Girl"	U Roy (Virgin)
"Satta I"	Lizard (Black Wax)
"Tenement Yard"	Jacob Miller (Grounation)
"War ina Babylon"	Max Romeo (Island)

Don't know if I'm really gonna take it
Don't know if I'm really gonna fake it
Come on now, get in line
Put your life right on the line
You're only gonna end up ashes in a jar
Oh I ain't gonna be history
I ain't gonna be history

The Maniacs, "I Ain't Gonna Be History"

Less than twenty-four hours after they touched down in London, the Patti Smith Group was setting up in the studios of the BBC's *Old Grey Whistle Test*, and preparing, however unwittingly, to spark a revolution.

Their debut album, *Horses*, had just hit the British streets (it was already six months old in the United States), and clearly the Group was expected to give it a great big push. But Smith had never been very big on conforming to expectation; if she had, she'd never have gone onstage to read poetry to an electric guitar in the first place. *Whistle Test* viewers needed something more than *Horses*, because the Patti Smith Group was more than *Horses*.

Smith's guitarist, Ivan Kral, explained: "Patti had released a cover of Jimi Hendrix's 'Hey Joe' in New York, back when the group was just her, Lenny Kaye and Richard Sohl. We'd never played it before as a band; JD [Daugherty, drummer] and I had never played it, never rehearsed it. So when she said that was what we were going to play on *Old Grey Whistle Test*, it was exciting. We were in London, we were on TV, and we were walking a tightrope, playing an arrangement of a song we'd never played. Lenny and Richard knew what it was and where to go, JD and I concentrated on playing the proper notes. And, apparently, it caused a lot of fuss."

The Patti Smith Group performed two songs; first a passionate rampage through Smith's own "Land," with its knowing nods to

Oscar Wilde, Otis Redding, and, torn from that week's newspaper headlines, the disgraced English politician Jeremy Thorpe—the leader of the Liberal Party was currently embroiled in the kind of sex scandal that only the truly righteous ever get mixed up in, a dizzying panoply of hunky male models, murdered dogs, and fevered denials. It was an excellent performance, but if you'd already heard *Horses*, there were no surprises there.

But then she swung into "Hey Joe," a superstylized revision that slowed everything to the pace of a funeral dirge, Kral's guitar crying to the sky, Sohl's organ somber and stately, and Patti wailing and howling and crying, tearing down one of rock's most sacred cows, most sainted icons.

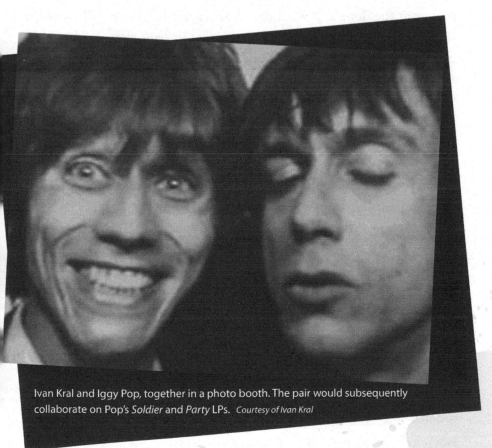

Ivan Kral and Iggy Pop, together in a photo booth. The pair would subsequently collaborate on Pop's *Soldier* and *Party* LPs. *Courtesy of Ivan Kral*

Jimi Hendrix was God back then. Six years after he choked his final breath, the British rock cognoscenti were still casting around for somebody to take his throne, and every hot new guitarist who as much as glanced at a wah-wah pedal would be instantly compared to the master. To even sniff in Hendrix's direction was a sin; to denigrate his playing or his performance was akin to the foulest blasphemy. And here was this scrawny Yank chick, Keith Richards's grandmother crossed with Bob Dylan's pet chicken, pecking his memory to pieces. Thirty years later, I have still to meet a Hendrix fan who appreciated hearing what she did to "Hey Joe." But I was blown away.

It was brilliant. It was soul stirring, it was magical, it was everything that you ever hoped you'd witness, every time you paid your money at the door and went to see another new group. Chills down the spine, goose pimples on the arm, tears in your eyes. Fuck whatever else was on the show tonight, fuck whatever local nonsense the music papers were hyping this week, and fuck the modern literary world's aversion to hyperbolic cliché. Because this was it. *This was the future.*

And why was that? Because, without even a glimpse of the show's host, the doubtless now-scowling Bob Harris in his comfy sweater and little swivel chair, the broadcast cut from Smith's defiantly dramatic restaging of the hoary old murder ballad to some crinkly monochrome footage of Hendrix kicking into the same song for the benefit of pop singer Lulu's late 1960s television show. There was no explanation, but you could hear it anyway, bleeding soundlessly subliminal out of the clip. *We apologize for the interruption in our service. We will now resume our scheduled predictability.*

It was almost four years since the last time something this cataclysmic had shaken Britain's most avuncular music television show, back in 1972 when the New York Dolls came over to pose and preen, and Harris dismissed them as "mock rock." Nothing more, nothing less. And the *Whistle Test* faithful sank back into their La-Z-Boys, safe in the knowledge that the aberration had ended.

Back then, they were right. A handful of watching kids might have disagreed with his dismissive sniff; might, as English R&B singer Graham Parker once hypothesized, have been "inspired into saying 'this is what we want to see, not bloody Osibisa.'"

But anybody who reckoned that Harris's put-down genuinely made a lasting impression on even a handful of viewers would wait a long time to see them do anything about it. The year 1972 folded into 1973, which became 1974, which begat 1975; and suddenly it was spring 1976, and the New York Dolls were ancient history. Four years is a lifetime when you're a teenager and the Dolls weren't even irrelevant any longer. They were forgotten. The Patti Smith Group, on the other hand, were here and now, and, with one single moment of musical defiance, they drew a line in the sand that the British music scene was never going to recover from, the line that divides icon from iconoclast.

Nobody was immune. At boarding school on the south coast of England, I was watching the show with the rest of the fifth form, and already planning the phone call I would be making to my parents the following day, convincing them to arrange for me to return to London for the weekend, so I could catch the Patti Smith Group in concert as well. I mentioned my plans to the friend seated next to me. He thought I was crazy. "What would you want to go see this pile of shit for?"

In Snaresbrook, East London, Steve Wilkin, guitarist with jazz-rockers Wired, experienced the same feral response from his bandmates. Just a year before, he and keyboard player Mike Taylor were working alongside pop-soul singer Linda Carr in her live backing combo, and that had been a big deal, a sign of just how high Wired might climb. Tight and professional and very, very serious, they had no time for this pseudo-arty nonsense and they were astonished that Wilkin should find it so exciting. "They became very agitated and defensively derisive. It offended their sense of musicianship. I could see their point, but the very fact that it produced such a strong reaction, rather than the usual indifference, stirred my imagination and got me scouring the classifieds for new people to work with."

Another guitarist, Mik Heslin, felt the same way. As resident lead poser with West London hard rockers Tarot, his first reaction was "What the hell's this?" He'd tuned in to *Whistle Test*, like so many others, in anticipation of a smorgasbord of extended guitar solos and thoughtful singer-songwriters. Instead, he got "a wiry thing with straggly hair and a large conk, doing something that sounded like poetry with a backing band that didn't seem to have a guitar virtuoso. *Boring!!!* It wasn't Be Bop Deluxe, it wasn't Sassafras, and it *certainly* wasn't Deep Purple!"

He kept watching, the wiry thing kept going, and suddenly he realized it was destroying "Hey Joe." "The word *sacrilege* went through my mind, but somehow it gripped me. Even when she went down on her knees with her guitar à la Hendrix phallus style, I was being won over. Damn, there was passion when she covered that song and there was something just new and different about the whole sound. I loved it!" The following day, he called his bandmates to outline his Smith-inspired ideas for a brand-new direction. "I was shot down in flames and we were never heard of again. Serves us right! Ha!"

Across the board, the people who got it *really* got it. Watching with all the controlled cynicism that hallmarked the best of his writing for the *New Musical Express*, journalist Mick Farren was astonished to find his jaw on the floor. Almost a decade earlier, Farren had led his own group, the Deviants, to heights of rebellion untapped since the heyday of Luddism. Smith's performance assured him that those ideals still existed.

"I thought she was doing for angry wannabe girl singers what Bob Dylan had done for me a decade earlier," he explained to me. "She was proving that passion, not dulcet pipes and perfect pitch, is what makes a rock singer." A month later, Farren would write the single most important manifesto of the year, a *New Musical Express* feature titled "The *Titanic* Sails at Dawn." In his mind, if not on paper, Smith's *Whistle Test* performance was one of the foundations that he built upon.

"The *Titanic* Sails at Dawn" was a beautifully opinionated distillation of all that Farren had seen happening on the UK live circuit over the past six months, and all that he envisioned might occur in the months to follow. It would be absurd to describe it as the catalyst for all that was swirling around the London underground at that time. But for a lot of Farren's readers, the absurdity was about to become reality. Forget Year Zero, this was Page Zero.

Away from the pubs and clubs and the sticky end of the *Old Grey Whistle Test*, British rock was enjoying some of its most super-showbiz events of all time. Rock was still meant to be the antithesis of "showbiz," to be the grubby, grimy, hyper-rebellious little monster that polite society kept walled up in the attic. But it was growing increasingly difficult to see how.

I saw David Bowie headlining one of his umpteen nights at Wembley, an ant cavorting on a brightly lit stage that looked a hell of a lot better in the photographs than it did from row ZZ.

I'd just purchased a ticket to see the Who headlining the Charlton Athletic football ground, introducing England to the age of the sports arena concert at a time when even the best-appointed soccer stadiums had as much acoustic beauty as a bucketful of sick. And I could have seen the Rolling Stones block-booking the vast emptiness of Earl's Court, an aircraft hanger wannabe designed for motor shows and boat exhibitions, before being carelessly hijacked for entertainment purposes. The first time a major rock gig was staged there, Bowie (again) in 1973, the audience rioted because the sound was so bad. I doubted whether it had improved since then.

Three bands, three sets of concerts, and three lots of ticket receipts that dwarfed several countries' national debts. It was all a very long way from whatever and wherever rock 'n' roll claimed to have started, and a far cry from anything it had threatened in its youth. This ain't rock 'n' roll, as Bowie could be paraphrased, this is mass consumption.

"There can be no question," Farren was now musing, "that a lot of today's rock is isolated from the broad mass of its audience. From the superstars with champagne and coke parties, all the way down to your humble servant spending more time with his friends, his writing and his cat than he does cruising the street, all are cut off."

Yet the answer to that conundrum was already at hand. "The best, most healthy kind of rock and roll is produced by and for the same generation. Putting the Beatles back together isn't going to be the salvation of rock and roll. Four kids playing to their contemporaries in a dirty cellar club might. And that, gentle reader, is where you come in."

In isolated pockets across the country, people watched Smith's performance with the same sense of personal commitment that Farren was calling upon, and a conviction that bordered upon disbelief. "Hey Joe" was a rebel yell, defiant and daring in the face of both the law (the song's lyric concerns a killer on the run) and received musical history. Public and critics alike were united. You just don't fuck with Hendrix. Patti Smith wanted to know why; and, now that she came to mention it, so did a lot of other people.

The day that the future Sex Pistols met Johnny Rotten for the first time some nine months earlier, he had been sloping down the King's Road in a Pink Floyd T-shirt, across which he had scrawled the words "I HATE" in shaky ballpoint pen.

It was, even Rotten's detractors would subsequently agree, an unequivocal statement, and one that would have endless repercussions. Just weeks off the release of *Wish You Were Here*, itself the landmark successor to the multizillion-selling *Dark Side of the Moon*, Pink Floyd had arrived at the level where nothing could hurt them, certainly not a few slashes of ink on a teenager's shirt.

But the repetition of the story did make people think and, as it continued to do the anecdotal rounds, so dawned the realization that a lot of other people hated Pink Floyd as well.

Not musically, perhaps, and maybe not personally. But what they had come to represent was a different matter: a corporate money-making machine, calculated purveyors of bottled emotion and cynical repression, a brand name no more or less pernicious than any high street retailer or soft drink peddler. Yeah, that was very easy to hate and, when you pursued the thought to its logical conclusion, and wrote off the past as just so many boring old farts, that, too, made an awful lot of sense.

Except, in May 1976, not too many people had even heard of Johnny Rotten, and fewer still cared what he wore. Right now, the Sex Pistols were best known as the unschooled yobbos that started fights with their audience, and whose manager ran a bondage store in Chelsea called Sex. Hence the name, the Sex Pistols. A little edgier than, say, the Woolworths Pistols, but it was difficult not to draw a similar conclusion from the smattering of press that the band had received so far. A mouthy marketing gimmick that compensated for its lack of musical ability by grabbing headlines with its fists.

The Patti Smith Group, on the other hand, had already proven all that they needed to. It was a year since *New Musical Express* journalist Charles Shaar Murray first heralded Smith in British print, and six months since he followed through with a second piece, "A Scuzz Odyssey," that introduced the rest of the New York scene that had birthed her. Opening sentiment—"The Ramones are quite ridiculous"; closing argument—we need to hear these bands. Talking Heads, the Heartbreakers, the Tuff Darts, and so many more. He made them sound so exciting as well. But none of them had records out at that time, none was more than a local blip on a faraway screen, white noise with the mute button on.

So we imagined what they must sound like instead.

The Ramones made the Archies sound like Black Sabbath on downers.

The Dictators, an unholy cross between the street smarts of Bruce Springsteen and the undiluted slobbering of the Stooges.

Television, all endless guitar solos and Shakespearean poetic thrust. Journalist Dave Marsh later dubbed them "The Grateful Dead of Punk," and he wasn't the first to draw that conclusion, but vocalist and guitarist Tom Verlaine shuddered when I mentioned it. "It's strange, I never even heard the Grateful Dead except when I was a kid, my girlfriend had their first record. I remember listening to it and I didn't know what to make of it at all, it reminded me of noodle pudding."

Blondie. Murray described them as "a crudd[y] garage band [fronted by a singer] with a voice like a plastic bath toy," and I cuddled up close to my Shangri-Las records. It's OK, I assured them. Nobody will ever be able to replace you.

We imagined so much, and it was only when the Patti Smith Group crossed the ocean in May 1976 that we realized just how far off the mark those imaginings could be.

Even more exciting, the desecration of "Hey Joe" was only the first shot in the rebellion that Smith was so joyously leading. Flip over her latest single, itself a complete revision of that hoary old Them chestnut "Gloria," and what did you find? The Who's "My Generation," taken at a faster pace than its makers could ever have dreamed of, and underpinned *not* by the increasingly disreputable dream of dying before they got too old (it was way too late for that!), but by a boisterous scream of defiant intent. "I don't need that fucking shit!" she sang in lieu of that familiar old war cry, "Hope I die because of it!" Or, as Smith breathed into the microphone onstage a few nights later, "I don't fuck much with the past. But I fuck plenty with the future."

2

The Great British Mistake

MORE MAY 1976

Britain in 1976 was obsessed with the past, a monolith that dominated every walk of life, and permeated every corner of culture. It was decades since the country had ruled over half the planet, but the golden days of Empire lived on whenever a politician opened his mouth to speak. It was decades again since the Second World War, but victory, too, was being rammed down our throats every day, by the men who fought battles for the freedoms we now took for granted (and relived them at every opportunity they were given), and the women who did their bit on the home front all war long, and who either couldn't, or wouldn't, comprehend that it was time to move on.

Occasional flurries of legislation tried to push the country into the modern era. A Royal Commission on Environmental Pollution was set up to halt the ecological devastation that had been taking place unhindered since the dawn of the Industrial Revolution; a Race Relations Act to promote equal opportunities for black and white; a Sex Discrimination Act to ensure that women received the same treatment in the workplace as men. All were long overdue.

But laws are only as effective as the people who are enforcing them, and if those people don't want to be bothered, then they won't be. No matter that the country had an ostensibly socialist government. Still it was governed by the same cultural mores that had been in place since the Victorian age, unwritten laws that insisted that a woman's place was in the home, that children were to be seen and not heard, that the only good black (or homosexual or Pakistani or Jew or whatever) is a dead one. And those were the laws that remained in force, among the High Court judges who let rapists go free because the victim's lifestyle shed "reasonable doubt" on her character; among the social services that consigned needy kids to children's homes staffed by abusers and pedophiles; among the police who went out rounding up immigrants, simply to keep the arrest statistics up.

So the polluters kept on polluting, the racists kept on rioting, the sexists kept on snorting, and, though there'd be the occasional show trial to prove the law had teeth, that's all it ever was. A show, because the miscreants would all be let off in the end. It sounds so overearnest (and impossibly teenage dramatic) today, but I'd wake up some mornings and feel like Winston Smith, hero of George Orwell's *1984*, looking around at a world of unrelenting grayness and conformity and asking, surely there must be something more to life than *this*? Winston Smith was tortured and ultimately executed for his discontent. But we were expected to grin and bear it. It was what the British people did.

Stoic acceptance only goes so far, though. There had to be some kind of alternative to living in the same run-down housing as your parents grew up in, to working the same dismal job as your grandfather worked, and to eating the same flavorless food every dull, featureless day. But when you turned on the radio, what did you get? The same music that you'd been hearing every day for years without end. *And that was "Honey" and before that "Windy," and right after the news read by a middle-aged man in a cardigan, "Spooky."*

Then you heard Patti Smith and you knew there *was* an alternative, there *was* some relief. Listening to her was like watching palaces fall and old documents burn, cities collapsing in great clouds of rubble, and an entire way of life being put to the sword. But it was not murder, it was a mercy killing, and, once the dust had settled, they would be rebuilt and replaced, by something new, something better, by something that *we* created, the youth of the day, the kids on the street, the brats who didn't want to clamber aboard Mick Farren's vision of the imminent musical apocalypse. "Hey Joe" was the demolition crew. We were the builders who would move in once it was finished.

"You put everything into the conviction that Patti couldn't go wrong," Ivan Kral thrilled. "She was just real. None of these shows were ever alike, every night was different, not just the set, but the poetry between songs. One of my most exciting moments was when she started doing poetry onstage, making it up between songs or during, just creating it on the spot. There was something incredibly romantic about it, and you don't fake that. There was nothing to hide behind, the excitement was knowing that we could fall over at any moment, and seeing the audience standing there asking 'who is this?' It's not the Jefferson Airplane, with the band and the sex symbol out front, it was just so original, and that's what I loved."

The Patti Smith Group had a mission, then. But they also had time to play.

Kral's first port of call was World's End in Chelsea, the bustling ribbon of shops and businesses perched on the grimier end of the King's Road, which mythology insisted still overflowed with the trendy boutiques and pubs that made it the heartbeat of Swinging London at the end of the 1960s.

I knew the area well. When my family first moved up to London in 1972, home became a dingy ground floor flat shared with my stepfather's ancient mother, and I still cannot remember one without thinking of the other. She had lived there for who knows how long, and her presence permeated not only the paint-peeling walls of the apartment, and the sour cabbage smell of the kitchen, but the entire neighborhood, because as far as the eye could see, every house looked and felt just as decrepit—filthy brick and battered plaster— draped in the shadow of Lott's Road power station.

It had been a fairly well-to-do area once, when it was built a century before. The rooms were high-ceilinged and spacious, with ornate ceiling roses and fixtures that were carved, not molded. But that was before rapacious landlords and greedy local councils descended upon the neighborhood, buying up everything as it came on the market, then cramming in as many sad souls as the sagging floorboards could tolerate. One day I asked granny when the street was last given a facelift. "During the war," she replied, when the Germans went after the power station, and took out a church and a few streets of houses instead. She spent most of the blitz hiding in a wardrobe because she didn't like the look of the nearest public shelter. Grin and bear it.

World's End was still grinning and bearing it, and once you'd been there for a while, you didn't even bother asking how or why it was ever landed with such an ominous name. If you did demand an answer, the pub of the same name rose proudly overhead, standing grimly sentinel over a dogleg in the road that might indeed have led to the end of the world but which, in the eyes of the tourist trade, was one more legendary sight to see.

Swinging London had stopped swinging years before, of course, and the handful of rugged veteran boutiques still clinging resolutely to those halcyon days had long since been joined by row upon row of more perfunctory outlets. The legendary Granny Takes a Trip was still there, its open door releasing so many shades of pungent incense that you had to wonder what else they might be smoking inside its dark corners, but it was a ghost of its former self. Just like the rest of the street, just like the rest of the country.

Still, Kral and Daugherty had no complaints as they walked the strip from one end to the other, past names and places they had only dreamed of ever seeing. Exotically named pubs like the Chelsea Potter, the Water Rat, the Man in the Moon, and the Roebuck. They passed Biba, fashion central (and a shoplifter's paradise) for the glam rock kids who used to descend upon the street every weekend in search of the latest accoutrements.

They saluted the Chelsea Drugstore, immortalized in song by the Rolling Stones ("You Can't Always Get What You Want"), where a mishmash of small businesses were bunched together in market style, and a tiny record stall seemed loaded with the most astonishing treasures. I blew an entire month's pocket money there one weekend, picking up French import copies of the first two Stooges albums, then went back the following Saturday to grab the new Pink Fairies. It was called *Kings of Oblivion*. LP titles rarely get better than that.

The Americans moved on. They browsed through ACME Attractions, a subterranean bazaar beneath the Antiquarius market, where a young Rasta named Donovan Letts ensured a perpetual rhythm of reggae music washed over an Aladdin's Cave of outlandish fashion. Fluffy jerseys, PVC trousers, rubber tops, and plastic bottoms, this was *not* your traditional London clothes store.

They passed Town Records, smack in the center of the dog's leg. In 1972, I bought my first-ever LP record there, Bowie's *Ziggy Stardust*. Nowadays, I spent more time in the basement, where a rack of used vinyl was guaranteed to produce a treat or two. A day or two after Mick Farren published "The *Titanic* Sails at Dawn," I found a copy of his first solo album there for 50p, scratched to hell and absent its cover. I figured its previous owner had junked it in protest over the words its maker had just written. I bought it out of solidarity with them.

Keep walking. There was a travel agent on that corner as well, and maybe . . . just maybe . . . a bank. I didn't have a bank account;

I wouldn't have noticed. And then you came to Sex, the unequivocally named storefront where Malcolm McLaren and his partner,
designer Vivienne Westwood, plied their peculiar trade in T-shirts
adorned with dangling penises and tributes to the Cambridge
Rapist.

Few people have ever forgotten their first time inside Sex, simply
because few people ever imagined that such costuming even existed.
True, you could walk through the red light alleyways of Soho and
catch the occasional glimpse of rubber and gas masks peeping round
the blank, anesthetized windows of the raunchier storefronts. But
even if you closed your eyes and dreamed really hard while listening
to the Velvets' "Venus in Furs," still your first sight of a genuine pair
of shiny-shiny boots of leather was going to come as a shock.

At an age when "kinky" meant having a poster of Charlotte
Rampling in *The Night Porter* taped up inside your school locker, in
a society that was genuinely, mortally, shocked and disturbed that a
pop group could call itself Sex Pistols, Sex itself was like a blow to
the brain with a bagful of butt plugs. Or it would have been, if we'd
only known what they were.

Row upon row of the most fabulously outlandish clothing, fetish
gear that had barely been adapted for public consumption, T-shirts
emblazoned with the most shocking images and symbols, nudity and
perversions made woven flesh, Sex was a buffet of fashionable
madness.

In years to come, Sex's output would be regarded as one of the
seminal artistic statements of the age, and Westwood feted among the
most liberated spirits to ever grace the rag trade. At the time, the staff
in the store spent as much time kicking out schoolkids who came in
to giggle, and fending off the attentions of the local police station's
obscenity squad, as they did dealing with regular customers—and
even they weren't always what they seemed. There was at least one
strain of clientele who dropped by not to purchase new clothes, but
simply to test-drive their latest fantasy outfit, and who would then

disappear again, leaving nothing more than a damp, sticky mess on whichever garments they'd taken into the changing room.

Kral was staggered—by Sex, by Biba, by everything. "I remember all the hair and the fashion and the shops, it was so exciting! Going to Kensington Market where everybody was blasting reggae music. Coming from New York, it was such a shock. New York seemed so quiet by comparison." The day of the first London show, at the Chalk Farm Roundhouse, Kral returned to the Portobello Hotel to show Smith his purchases, two pairs of twenty-six-inch-waist checkered pants, one in shades of red, the other black and white. She promptly hijacked one of them to wear on stage that evening.

Located in North London's slightly seedy Chalk Farm neighborhood, the Roundhouse was a loosely refurbished Victorian railway shed (and, for much of its lifespan, a Gilbey's Gin warehouse) that became, across the course of its late 1960s to early 1980s lifespan, perhaps *the* most important venue in London.

It wasn't the biggest, it wasn't the oldest, it wasn't the most prestigious. But it had an atmosphere like no other. When you breathed in, you tasted the same soot and oil that Jimi Hendrix, Jim Morrison, Hawkwind, and Man inhaled. And, when you looked into the darkest corners, the ghosts of old train drivers winked back at you, lined up alongside the hippies, greasers, and metalheads who, in turn, had called the Roundhouse home for so long.

Now they were to be joined by a new generation. Over the next couple of years, the Roundhouse would host historic shows by the Ramones, the Runaways, John Cale, the Adverts, Motörhead, the Clash, the Damned, Sham 69, and dozens more, until Sundays were not Sundays unless there was something going on at the Roundhouse.

The audience that awaited the Patti Smith Group was disparate. The following week, *New Musical Express* journalist Barry Miles (who "knew me when I was just a nobody," purred Patti) described the gathering as the "regular Sunday-night Roundhouse crowd, stoned and shaking sack-loads of dandruff over their Levis . . . a few fungoids and weirdoes who have come to check her out . . . [and] a large number of women delighted to have someone female do for rock what David Bowie did for males."

Someone else said the two gigs had not even been close to selling out before the *Whistle Test* on Tuesday, that the run for tickets had avalanched from there. Maybe that was true, maybe it wasn't. I had no problem picking one up, as soon as I got into London on the Friday. But the Roundhouse audience was no less polarized than the *Whistle Test* viewers were five days before, with half the crowd clearly there to cheer Smith's every gesture, and the rest happy to hope that the invader fell flat on her face. Because that's what you get if you jerk around with Jimi. And Van. And Wilson Pickett. And the Who.

Reports had already drifted over from the Group's first European show, in Paris, together with a cassette recording of the night, pressed into my hand by a friend who'd been there, with the murmured warning, "It's God-like."

It was, too, although not at first. Smith's voice was even more out-of-sorts than it normally felt; and, as early as "Kimberley," the second song of the night, the musicians sounded ever-so-slightly perfunctory. An error-strewn "Redondo Beach," a tentative (if pretty) "Free Money," and a lazy intro to "Privilege" were all punctuated by lengthy silences while the band did who-knew-what on stage . . . and then suddenly everything fell into place, as if Smith had just remembered who (and where) she was. And, from there on in, the performance was peerless. "Pissing in the River" pounded with laconic beauty, "25th Floor" blazed, "Ain't It Strange" hypnotized, and an unholy rap through what would one day become "Radio Ethiopia" astonished.

It was as if she'd suddenly decided to place *Horses* behind her, in favor of taking us on a tour of the albums she hadn't even made yet,

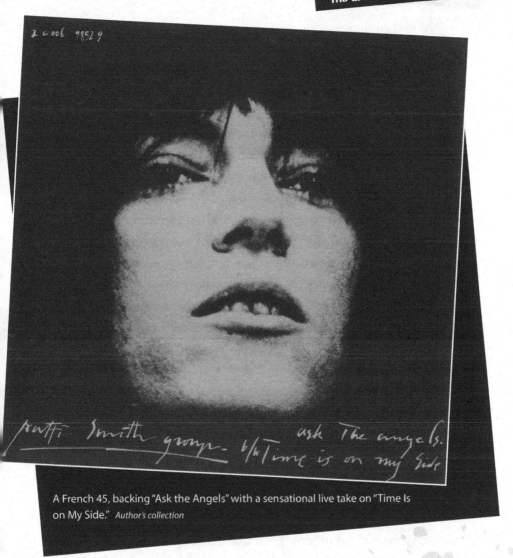

A French 45, backing "Ask the Angels" with a sensational live take on "Time Is on My Side." *Author's collection*

knowing that the audience would travel wherever she wanted them to go. She was chatting more, spooling out anecdotes that may or may not lead anywhere, stark contrasts to the now tightly coiled majesty of the music. By the time "Land" ripped into the room, the night was blazing so hard that the closing "Gloria" and the encore "My Generation" were almost unnecessary. Paris long ago got what it came for.

Now London was to taste the same magic.

The queue for the doors was moving quickly, and the smell from the tepee was better than usual as well. It was a Roundhouse tradition that dated back who knows how long; every gig, a bunch of longhairs would set up a tepee by the entrance, wherein they concocted, and then sold, steaming hot plates of—what? It was certainly vegetarian, and probably rather tasty. But it would require an incredible leap of faith to physically sample their wares, and it was only once you got inside the Roundhouse itself, walking into a wall of cannabis smoke that clung to your clothes and hung in your hair, that you suddenly realized how hungry you were. Secondhand munchies. Which somehow seemed to blend with the sound of secondhand Doors that was leaking out of the main room.

Describing Patti in the printed word, the earliest reports clashed Jim Morrison with Keith Richards, and then threw a blob of Dylan in on top. So, when you pushed through the crowd in the Roundhouse foyer, and the first sound you heard was a Ray Manzarek keyboard booming out of the auditorium, you panicked. The show had already started! Patti had already started!

And that is how I came to discover the Stranglers.

Over the next twelve months, I can safely say that I saw the Stranglers more times than any other band. Not through choice, mind you. Some nights you'd wander into a big gig and find they were the support act. Other times, you'd go to see one band and the Stranglers had replaced them. And other nights, there'd simply be no other show worth bothering with, so you'd end up at the Stranglers by default.

Did I ever actually like them, though? That's another question entirely.

By mid-1976, the Stranglers had been lurking around for a couple of years, emerging from a village close by the south-of-London city of Guildford (hence their original name, the Guildford Stranglers), and so inexorably pushing onto the capital's pub circuit that it was hard to even open the gig guide without seeing their name somewhere.

They were, by their own admission, "awful." Singer Hugh Cornwell once confessed that "we had good songs, but we were terrible," and he was half right. They were definitely terrible. In later months, the Stranglers would be driven by Jean Jacques Burnel's predatory bass lines, while organ stormed stentoriously around the edges. Right now, they were still searching for that equation, and marking time instead with piping ripples of tentative keyboards, through which every other instrument struggled to be heard, and the vocals were no more than a scratchy irritant.

They'd certainly got their name around, though. The mainstream music press ignored the band completely. But the women's libbers hated them without even hearing them play. A Stranglers poster, graphically depicting the handiwork of the Boston Strangler, had a moment in the tabloid sun in March, and a lot of onlookers formed their opinions of the band there and then.

Combine that with the murmured allegation that three of the four musicians were old enough to be your parents (drummer Jet Black was reliably forecast to be in his late thirties, while keyboard player Dave Greenfield had—wait for it!—a moustache); add to *that* the insistence that their audience was largely comprised of parolees and pariahs, bad-tempered bikers, and rent-a-thug football hooligans, and word of mouth alone was sufficient to steer most faint hearts far from their orbit.

There was no avoiding them tonight, though, even if the muddy rumble that was already shaking the old wood-and-brickwork structure boded as badly for their reality as it did for their reputation.

Glam rock idol Alan Merrill, taking a break from his day job with the Arrows, caught the Stranglers that night. When we talked about them later, he did his best to be diplomatic. They were a new band, he conceded, "and very rough sounding." But then he tired of pussyfooting around. "But they weren't rough in a good way. They sounded like a bad imitation of the Doors."

"I can't believe I'm listening to this." Arrows frontman Alan Merrill onstage, but maybe still remembering the Stranglers.
Courtesy of Alan Merrill

Which was a strange way of damning anyone, considering the high-altitude sainthood to which Jim Morrison had ascended since his death, and the fact that Patti Smith was now winning praise from a very similar comparison. But the rumble wasn't disagreeing as it pounded into every stomach in range without ever resolving itself into anything remotely approaching music.

There were probably more people still in the foyer than there were out on the dance floor, which was fine because it meant there'd be more choice of where to stand. Or sit. A few people were eyeing the rickety stairs that led up to the banks of seats that semicircled the balcony, themselves packed with refugees from the onstage cacophony. Some people began to mount them, but I was made of sterner stuff. Fuck that, no. It's Patti Smith. If her *Whistle Test* performance taught me one thing, it's that I didn't want to sit for Patti Smith.

Inside, the noise of the band was relentless, just as tuneless as I'd suspected. A tiny knot of Stranglers fans was gathered around the stage, and everything I'd heard about them, too, was true—the guys all built like a row of brick shithouses, their girlfriends as ugly as a hatful of arseholes.

They were defiant in their enjoyment of the Stranglers as well, although you felt as though they had toned down their legendary belligerence. For, as vociferous as the fan club might have been, the rest of the crowd was twice as furious, and it *hated* the Stranglers with a passion. Everywhere, faces were contorted in rage and disgust, and *wheeeeeeeeeeeee!*, there goes the first flying beer mug.

Hugh Cornwell stepped forward, placed one foot on the missile, and crushed it slowly into the wooden stage. It was a gesture that would have been a lot more effective had the mug been made of glass, not plastic, but no matter. The point was made.

Knee-deep in organ and rat-worshipping lyrics, the opening song finished, and the Stranglers didn't even pause for the applause that they knew they'd never receive. "That was called 'Down in the Sewer,'" came a voice from the stage. "This next one is called—"

"Fuck off!"

"Where's Patti?"

"Fuck *off!*"

More plastic beer glasses, but the Stranglers ignored them. A tight little rocker called "Grip" was in there somewhere. Later on, one of the brick shithouses told me a guy from Patti Smith's record label, Arista, was so impressed by the song that he offered the Stranglers a record deal on the strength of it. Nothing ever came of it, though, presumably because he then heard the rest of their repertoire. "Bitching." "Peasant in the Big Shitty." "I Feel Like a Wog."

"Piss off!"

"We want Patti!"

"You're shit."

The Stranglers didn't care. They introduced a song that may have been called "School Ma'am," and the bassist proceeded to strangle himself, half Alice Cooper, half Donald Nielsen, and the violence seething off the stage was both visible and palpable, oozing in discomforting waves across the dance floor.

"Where's Patti?"

"*Fuck off!*"

But the Stranglers still didn't care. "Thank you very much. This next song is called 'Tits.'"

Silence. For the first time since the Stranglers took the stage, the venue fell as quiet as the grave. The song is called "Tits"?

Tits. When Sparks wrote a song called "Tits" (and dropped it into the cleavage of their last album, *Indiscreet*), it was kinda funny, kinda wry, kinda avant-garde, because that's what Sparks were. But when the Stranglers came up with the exact same title, people were still trying to figure out just how self-righteously offended they wanted to be when the first (and only) verse swung in, and it was so utterly, absolutely, delightfully foul that who could resist joining in? Come on everybody, all together now: "She's got thirty-six–twenty-four–thirty-six hips . . . that was the size of her tits."

And they did it. It looked impossible; no, it *was* impossible. But the Stranglers didn't simply leave the stage to a roar of applause; there was still a gaggle of kids singing "Tits" to themselves when Patti came on fifteen minutes later.

She probably never had another introduction like that.

Smith was mesmerizing. Notwithstanding the checkered pants she'd borrowed from Kral, she was dressed for the album cover, but she was giggling and laughing, applauding the audience that was applauding her before she'd even sung a note, bouncing up and down on the stage like a schoolgirl unwrapping her very own pony.

The set was much the same as the Parisian tape; most of *Horses* and more besides. "Redondo Beach," "Free Money," "Land," "Kimberley," a sad "Louie Louie," a sweet "Pale Blue Eyes," and the lurching, compulsive, hypnotic dub of "Ain't It Strange." "Ah mooooove in anothah di-men-shun!" Smith crooned, and a voice to the left shouted back "So do I," as the entire room melted into a shifting, flowing mass, half skanking, half shaking their heads, until there were so many people grinding languorous hips against my leg that it was either the sexiest rhythm ever, or there was something more than water in the lager pumps tonight.

I spotted Alan Lee Shaw and Rod Latter, collectively the Maniacs, standing close by, as entranced by the magic as the rest of us, but laughing as well. Shaw, six foot plus of brawny blond brilliance, caught my eye and gestured toward the drunken figure that was trying to raise itself off the floor, and failing. Joe Strummer, singer with the 101ers, so exhausted from the effort of shouting Patti's name that his legs finally collapsed from beneath him. Onstage with his band, Strummer was cool, calm, and collected, the kind of rockabilly rock star that you wished you could see more often. But in the heaving maw of the Roundhouse, he was just another acolyte, thrilled to discover that the Patti Smith Group were as great as everyone hoped they would be.

Chrissie Hynde was there as well, a journalist with the *New Musical Express* and, apparently, a would-be musician. The Maniacs ran into her backstage and chatted briefly, hoping to convince her down to one of their shows. Unfortunately, Shaw confessed, "Rod and I were very pissed and must have said something vaguely sexist or whatever, because she stormed off, giving the distinct impression

The Maniacs, Alan Lee Shaw (left) and Rod Latter, 1976.   *Courtesy of Alan Lee Shaw*

that we were a bunch of pricks. Which, by that time, I think we probably were."

Somebody shouted for "Gloria," and Smith shouted it back at them. Someone laughed when she picked up her guitar; she laughed with them and feigned incompetence. Or maybe she wasn't feigning, because when you've got Lenny Kaye and Ivan Kral in your band, why would you even need to learn to play? Especially when you can make far more noise by unplaying. Keith Relf, lead vocalist with the Yardbirds, had died two days ago, electrocuted by his own guitar. Smith dedicated the next song to him, and howled out feedback over her instrument's yowling. Then it was into the closing salvo. "Gloria" ended the set, "My Generation" opened the encore, and the entire room gave voice to its savage denouement.

Another rap ended the night, short and sweet and to the point. "Everything comes down so pasteurized . . . everything comes down sixteen degrees . . . tick tock, tick tock, tick tock, FUCK THE CLOCK!" Then it was bang into a triumphant "Time Is on My Side," and Smith knew, in that instant, that it was.

"One of my favorite memories of being in rock 'n' roll, actually physically performing it, was the first night at the Roundhouse, when we did 'Time Is on My Side,'" Smith recalled years later. "I looked down and there's all those kids, English kids, they have this look about them you know, from documentary movies they look the sons of miners or something. There was so much real feeling, you know. They projected to me, like, honesty and some of them were crying, they were. Singing along, they were without shame. That's very important. That's how I judge an audience. If they're without shame and let themselves go."

Nobody could have predicted it that night, but an entire generation was about to let itself go.

3

We're Going Down the Pub

MID-MAY 1976

By 1976, a convoluted succession of family drama and tragedies saw my home shift across London, from World's End in Chelsea, to the butt-end of the universe. Edmonton was (and presumably still is) one of those working-class North London neighborhoods that both time and the city planners forgot, a straggling ribbon of leftover businesses wedged in between the marginally more cosmopolitan towns of Tottenham and Enfield, and which culminated in a concrete shopping center that ironic planners, constructing the high-rise utopia of their 1960s dreamland, elected to title Edmonton Green.

The shops lay on the first level or two; above them soared the tower blocks that presumably housed all the people displaced by the new development, vast foreboding edifices that I never had cause to enter for at least another three years, until I launched a short-lived career as a pirate radio DJ, at a station whose command center lay halfway up one of the towers. As dismal within as it was drab without, I was only mildly surprised to discover that, while the buildings looked like shit, they smelled of piss. I wondered if the residents ever got used to that.

Edmonton had been hopping once. The Sundown theater on the corner of Angel Road had entertained the Who, the Wailers,

Hawkwind, and many more in recent years, but that was then. Now it was a cinema, specializing (at least in my memory) in lightweight comedy movies spun off from the big television shows of the day. *Man About the House—The Movie. Steptoe and Son—The Movie. Till Death Us Do Part—The Movie.*

I recall a discotheque running in one of the back streets, in those peculiar days before disco itself took off. The only song I remember hearing there was "Hi Ho Silver Lining," but I didn't go there very often. A few of the pubs offered "live entertainment" as well, but I didn't go there either. You've heard one drunk singing "Danny Boy," you've heard them all.

But Edmonton wasn't simply dead, it was all but escape proof as well. So cut off from the rest of the city that even the London Underground gave it a wide berth, Edmonton was serviced by nothing more than a handful of slow-moving buses and an overground rail link into Liverpool Street, the most easterly of London's major railroad terminals, and so far off my own beaten track that it took another half hour to get anywhere from there.

London was magnetic, nevertheless. Of course, I was only there for three months of twelve, boarding school life devouring the rest of the calendar. But as soon as I'd got my geographical bearings (and worked out my escape route into the city), I was scouring the gig guide in the *New Musical Express*, searching for shows to go to— then checking out the record reviews to complement my discoveries.

1974, 1975, 1976. Glam rock still dominated the charts, and my record collection overflowed with spangles, satin, and tat. Bowie, Bolan, Gary Glitter, Cockney Rebel, Sparks, Roxy Music, 10cc. Not all of them fit the most precise definition, but they all served their purpose, and set out some fascinating jumping-off points as well. From the jukebox jive of classic T Rex, I found my ears bending toward the Pink Fairies and Hawkwind. Bowie hatched a fascination with Iggy and the Stooges and Lou Reed and the Velvets, who in turn brought John Cale, Nico, and Kevin Ayers into play.

I discovered Peter Hammill and Van Der Graaf Generator, and then saw them reborn when I caught the Doctors of Madness one night, four towering slabs of over-made-up pretension, howling doom-laden despondency over a screaming violin. The *New Musical Express* warned that they were "even uglier than the Glitter Band," but in an age when the interminable rock epic ruled, the Doctors tore the rule book to shreds by taking pretension to its furthest extremes, and then kept going from there, a musical beast squeezing out of glam rock's urethra, on its way to who knew where.

Most of what I saw, though, was pub rock, the faintly disreputable-sounding umbrella title coined for a generation of bands spawned, indeed, in the pubs and clubs of London.

Their emergence was an object lesson in adaptability, and further fuel to the fires Mick Farren had written about. Throughout the early to mid-1970s, the rock concert circuit in Britain languished firmly in the thrall of a handful of promoters, each one jealously guarding its stable of big-name attractions by allowing management and record companies alone to filter in a steady trickle of "up and coming" acts. If a performer didn't have those initial contacts, then the chances of breaking into even the lower echelons of the conventional touring circus declined accordingly.

So they went for the unconventional layers instead, to the network of pubs that pocked British cities, and which always needed someone to entertain the punters. In the past, they'd relied on informal weekend talent shows, strippers, impressionists, and drunken Irishmen. Now they booked bands. And, so long as the drinkers kept on buying drinks, they'd keep on booking them.

There was very little musical unity to pub rock. The Hammersmith Gorillas were a snarling garage band, but Kilburn and the High Roads played updated Cockney music hall. Kokomo and Chilli Willi and the Red Hot Peppers forged a tight funk groove, while Ducks Deluxe and Bees Make Honey went country, tinged with pop. I remember when bluesy-soul singer Graham Parker first emerged on the scene, with his sidemen comprised of former members of Brinsley Schwarz. He was mortified to find himself lumped in with the pub rockers, and even more aghast when he decided to check out one of his bandmates' old recordings. "I was amazed to find out it was some sort of soft wimpy country rock! I thought, 'What the fuck has this got to do with what I'm doing? I don't get it! People are calling me Pub Rock, what is this?'"

Dr. Feelgood would become pub rock's first unassailable superstars, in 1975. Spiraling out of the oil-refining wasteland of Canvey Island, on the edge of East London, the Feelgoods fired a solid battery of short, sharp R&B, the mid-sixties Rolling Stones if they'd found speed instead of acid. Totally retro in their wedding suits, they were tight, aggressive, and looked so tough they could beat you up from fifteen yards without even spilling their drinks. "Hiroshima in a pint glass" is how the *New Musical Express* once described them, but even that was an understatement. The Feelgoods probably didn't even drink from pint glasses, they chewed their beer straight from the hops, and that included Wilko Johnson, a solid teetotaler.

Johnson mimed machine gun attacks while he played; Lee Brilleaux sang with the growling savagery of a laryngitic jungle cat, and the rhythm section thought it was the San Andreas Fault. At their best (and for two albums/three years, the Feelgoods were always at their best), they unleashed a sonic firestorm that established them among the most popular live attractions in the country, without even one hit single to sustain them.

So far as I was concerned, there was just one band on the scene that could live in the same room as the Feelgoods. That was Roogalator, a band I caught so often that they felt like personal friends, even before frontman Danny Adler, a mass of angles trapped behind an accent that screamed his native Cincinnati at you, ever said hello to me.

Roogalator was one of those bands that appears out of nowhere and grabs the world by its throat. They played their first-ever show

Roogalator and friend squeezing into a typical English urban garden.
Courtesy of Danny Adler

in September 1975 and, within weeks, the music press was hammering on their door. The *New Musical Express* spread the band across its center pages in December, asked, "Is this the future of rock 'n' roll?" and then confirmed, "They aren't just the most important thing to come out of Britain in years, but out of anywhere at all."

Other journalists shared the excitement. It wasn't just the way the music sounded, harsh and angular chunks of sound fluttering between bedrocks of funk and rock. They looked great as well, just as Adler had planned. "At that time, everybody had long hair and was stoned, and I was really pissed off with playing with people who couldn't keep time, so I cut my hair, and started shopping in second hand stores, dressing like a 1950s spiv. Wilko [Johnson of Dr. Feelgood] did it, Paul Riley [Roogalator's bassist] did it, and I did it. It was a great contrast with all the boring hippie tie-dye stuff. We saw ourselves as a transition between being serious musos and something new, sharp, and exciting."

Roogalator's roots drew deep from Adler's own experience on the Cincinnati R&B club circuit of the late 1960s, and a short-lived stint with Elephant's Memory—with atrocious luck, the biggest Beatles fan in the band quit just before John Lennon turned them into his backing group. But Roogalator's energies twisted those so-American rudiments to conjure, in their stead, such an English-sounding agitation that even their best-known number, "Cincinnati Fatback," could as easily have been written in Canterbury.

Record companies prostrated themselves at Roogalator's feet; and everywhere Adler turned, an endless procession of would-be managers, agents, and fairy god–A&R men told them, "You're the biggest thing since Springsteen, and we'll sell Roogalator pajamas."

Nick Lowe, bassist and songwriter with Brinsley Schwarz, adored the band. "On their night, [they] were really sensational. They were like Captain Beefheart with a funky weird groove. Danny called it 'Roogalation' and nobody else has ever come up with a better word for that groove." Lowe's record label, United Artists, was sniffing around the group, calling them in to record a clutch of incendiary demos, and the coronation rolled on.

"They don't look deadly at all," mused *Sounds*. "But the moment [Adler] opens his mouth, all doubts are instantly incinerated. He has a strong, emotive, all-American voice and the songs he sings are tough strings of street talk with melodies that fuse all the major idioms in a way you only take for granted when it's signed Jaime Robbie Robertson or Lowell George."

And then it all came tumbling down. Wilko Johnson was one of Adler's closest friends, and arranged for Roogalator to tour with the Feelgoods when they returned from their first American visit in early 1976. "Wilko loved us," Adler smiled. "Lee wasn't so sure, we were a bit too subtle for him, but Wilko was really good to us. He gave us a bunch of PA stuff, we used to hang together."

But a countrywide journey around the theaters of the land was a step too far for an act that had only been playing together for three months, and had never set foot on any stage larger than a dishrag. By the time the package hit the final shows at the Hammersmith Odeon, it was obvious even from the back row that something was amiss. Songs that had stolen my heart in the pubs sounded vague and echoey in those vast expanses, while the band seemed like midgets, not because of my distance from the stage, but because of their own disconnection from the boards they were treading. It was one of the biggest disappointments of my early gig-going life, that show, but it was years before I finally plucked up the nerve to ask Adler what went wrong.

"It was too much too soon," he mourned. So many little things had niggled as the tour rolled on, little things that proved just how unprepared Roogalator were for the leap into the big time. But the final straw came at Hammersmith, stepping out onto the biggest stage Roogalator had ever graced and discovering that Adler's guitar lead wasn't long enough for him to walk more than a quarter of the stage. "I suddenly realized that I was out there with no trousers on. It was like trying to dig a thirty-foot trench with a toothbrush."

Nerves and poor sound read the last rites, and UA's decision to pass on the demos banged the final nails into the casket. Although Roogalator continued to gig, by the time they resurfaced in mid-May to record a session for BBC radio deejay John Peel (which, in turn, became their debut single), Adler and keyboard player Nick Plytas alone remained, alongside a brand-new rhythm section.

"We were still hot," Adler reflected, "I could play the band through. We played the Marquee the week after we recorded the Peel session, and it was a really storming gig." The Peel session was broadcast days later and it justified every last word ever written about Roogalator. The problem was, those words were written six months before. The world had moved on a lot since then. Now it was the Sex Pistols who were in the ascendant and Adler, watching them from the 100 Club bar, knew it.

The Boy Looked at Johnny

STILL MAY 1976

Why didn't I go back to school on the Monday? Honestly, I don't remember. Maybe they told me I didn't need to hurry, although that's unlikely; I'd already skipped classes once that month, to see Bowie at Wembley, and I can't imagine them inviting me to do that again. Maybe my stepfather pulled an extra string and landed me a bonus of a couple of days holiday, although that doesn't seem very likely, either. Or maybe I just missed the train, and kept on missing it until Wednesday rolled around. Either way, I hung on in London for a few days after the Patti Smith Group gig and so, it transpired, did they.

They spent their time exploring the city. Smith and guitarist Lenny Kaye caught the Rolling Stones at Earl's Court, and shamelessly enjoyed the experience. "I screamed and carried on," she laughed. "Me and Lenny incited the kids to riot." Then, when somebody suggested they pile on down to the 100 Club on Oxford Street, to catch Malcolm McLaren's latest managerial enterprise, there seemed no reason to refuse. They knew him from his short-lived sojourn managing the Dolls, and they were adamant, if this new band was as deliciously stylized as the Dolls had been, they had to be worth a laugh. Plus, there was the assurance that, with the story of their habitual audience baiting now taking on a life of its own, every time you caught the Sex Pistols might well be your last chance. Because one day, someone would hit them back.

The Pistols were little more than six months old at the time, and already their penchant for violence was paying dividends, even if most of their achievements so far were based on opportunism more than anything else. Their very first live show, outraging a college audience gathered to watch rock 'n' roll revivalists Bazooka Joe at St. Martin's College in November 1975, only came about because the college was located just across the road from the Pistols' rehearsal space in Denmark Street, which was handy for student Glen Matlock. It meant that rather than sit around despairing while his bandmates destroyed another favorite song, he could head off for class instead.

It also meant that when he heard there was a gig going on there, he could nip across the road and call the rest of the Pistols to arms. Drummer Paul Cook recalled, "There was this group playing and we said 'Can we come over and support you?' They said yeah, so we went on and it was really loud, deafening. And we were going really mad, because this was our first gig and we were all really nervous."

The set list that the Sex Pistols had rehearsed for weeks was suddenly written in a foreign language: "None of us knew what we were doing." They stumbled through covers of the Who and the Small Faces, and there was not a murmur of applause. For twenty long minutes they thrashed desperately around, until finally, blessed relief. Somebody pulled the plug on them. The Sex Pistols' first gig ended in a silence almost as confused as the noise that it replaced. Johnny Rotten later boasted, "The college audience had never seen anything like it. They couldn't connect with where we were coming from because our stance was so antipop, anti-everything that had gone on before." In fact, all they saw was a gaggle of stage-frightened noise merchants.

The Pistols had found their feet since then, but the players still rode their luck. Opening for Eddie and the Hot Rods at the Marquee in February, their first appearance at that most hallowed of London venues, they asked ever so nicely if they could borrow the headliners' monitors, then broke them and went home without even saying sorry. The Hot Rods took their grievances to the media, and the Pistols' attempts at explaining were completely drowned out. But guitarist Steve Jones still sounded almost apologetic when he admitted that the Pistols had never used such high-tech marvels before, and their destructive fury was, in actual fact, frustration at finally being able to hear themselves play, and realizing what a mess they were. "We didn't mean to smash them. We just wanted them to shut up."

The Rods were hot right then. A furious R&B firestorm, still kids and playing with all the untrammeled assurance of arrogant youth, they were newly signed to Island Records, and already burning up the distance that lay between them and the like-minded Dr. Feelgood. The best of the Rods' repertoire was still the cover versions, old chestnuts like "Gloria," "Satisfaction," "Get Out of Denver," and even "Woolly Bully," stripped back to their bare chassis, then amped up to breakneck speed and passion. But their originals were creeping into view, too, storming slabs of disaffection with titles like "Teenage Depression" and "Horseplay (Weary of the Schmaltz)" and, best of all, the epic drama of "On the Run"—"the boy should be pitied," cried vocalist Barrie Masters, "but they got me committed."

It was said that if you could leave a Hot Rods gig without sweating off twenty pounds, then you obviously went to the wrong show, and a lot of people wound up doing just that because the queue at the front door grew so long every night that half of it was doomed to be turned away disappointed. One evening, legend insisted, the Rods had packed seven hundred people into the Marquee, a venue that realistically could hold barely half that. I wouldn't know about that; it was too hot to even start counting. But I do remember that the crowd was so tightly packed, and the temperature so way beyond bearable, that the money in my pocket turned to mush within minutes, and my train ticket home looked like it had just gone thirteen rounds with a washing machine.

The February show was less densely populated, but it promised to be just as energetic, and the guest list had long since been pre-booked by the music press. If anybody noticed the support act's name on the posters, they didn't pay any attention.

By the time the Rods took the stage, however, it was they who were being ignored. Not by their own fans, who kept a barrage of abuse going throughout the Pistols' still-ramshackle set, then cheered the headliners like returning heroes. They were ignored by the pop cognoscenti, the pen-pushing scribes who arrived to witness the Rods' ascension to glory, then discovered there was a better party going on backstage. Journalist Neil Spencer's review in the next week's *New Musical Express* summed the whole affair up best. "Don't look over your shoulder, but the Sex Pistols are coming." The Rods didn't even get mentioned.

The Sex Pistols mastered the art of the monitor as successfully as they mastered every other task that the concert environment set for them. But a two-page spread in *Sounds* at the end of April went out of its way to avoid naming any of the songs in the Pistols' live reper-toire, which meant it was still the same old routine of "Substitute," "Stepping Stone," "Whatcha Gonna Do About It," and "Don't Gimme No Lip Child," mixed in with a handful of undistinguished, sub–Hot Rods originals. *Melody Maker* likened the Pistols' inepti-tude (favorably or not, it was hard to tell) to an attempt to become the new Stooges, and you couldn't help sensing that if Johnny Rotten didn't talk such a wonderful game of media baiting, the press would have lost interest long ago.

I arrived early at the 100 Club for the same reason a lot of kids do—in the hope of meeting one of the bands as they hauled their equipment in, and gaining free entry in the guise of helping them out. It didn't work tonight—the Pistols already had an entourage the size of a small dance floor—so I paid for my entrance with the rest of the audience, and then found a comfortable wall to lean on while I waited to be impressed. I'd read a lot about the Sex Pistols by then, but this was the first time I'd seen them.

It would not be the last. It wasn't a gig in any conventional sense. True, there were people with instruments on the stage, and a handful of the noises they made did eventually resolve themselves into something approaching a tune. You could even recognize the occasional cover that they played. But it was the magnetism, not the music, that rooted you to the spot, the sheer bloody nerve of four guys getting up there to play without looking like they'd even rehearsed in six months. Unless this was the rehearsal? It was ragged, it was ugly, it was discordant, and it was amateurish. But even as my distaste buds rebelled, my mind folded back to what Mick Farren had written just a month before. *Putting the Beatles back together isn't going to be the salvation of rock and roll. Four kids playing to their contemporaries in a dirty cellar club might.*

Were the Sex Pistols what he had in mind?

Johnny Rotten recognized Patti Smith before she was halfway down the 100 Club stairs, ahead of anyone else in the room. One moment he was singing/shouting/slurring another Pistols number into the microphone, the next he was embarking upon a chorus of "Horseshit, horseshit, horseshit."

Smith loved it, but, as Ivan Kral later wearily admitted, she was used to it as well. Back in New York, singer Wayne County's arsenal of outrageous routines included one that saw him don his own spot-on variation of Patti's customary onstage outfit—white shirt, black tie, and jacket slung over one shoulder—and launch into a full-scale stream of consciousness rap about masturbation and Jim Morrison that built and built until it finally reached its climax. "Wildebeest! Wildebeest!"

Rotten was not so inventive. He quickly returned to the script as the Pistols played on, volume compensating for the lack of variety in the set, while the audience shifted awkwardly, most of them hanging around the back of the room, wondering when the fights would kick off. It didn't matter if, as a spiteful branch of the grapevine was insisting, the much-vaunted fisticuffs that broke out at their gigs were only ignited when McLaren discovered a journalist was present. It was still more of a spectacle than you would be privy to at other shows.

Somebody—I don't know who, but they didn't look impressed—pointed out Siouxsie Sioux, the dominatrix-clad queen of a gang of fashion horses known to themselves as the Bromley Contingent, *über*-followers of the Pistols machine, who were fast garnering as much notoriety as the band itself. Someone else nodded pityingly toward a beanstalk by the stage, leaping up and down on the spot and clearly in danger of crashing through the ceiling. Muted by the din of the band, you could lip-read their contempt nevertheless. "Look at that idiot."

I looked. I knew him. Bev . . . John Beverley . . . lived in Finsbury Park, close by the station where I swapped my bus ride for the tube. A total Bowie nut, which is why a mutual friend introduced us, he enjoyed nothing better than a lager-fueled argument over which of the master's songs was the best. Neither, at the time, did I. But whereas I was willing to change my opinion, depending upon what kind of mood I was in, Bev was unyielding.

"'We Are the Dead'?" I would suggest.

"Fuck off! 'Rebel Rebel.'"

"'Drive In Saturday'?"

"'Rebel Rebel.'"

"'Cygnet Committee'?"

"I said, Fuck off!" And so it would go on until Bev fucked off, usually lured away by one or other of the pimply weasels who'd renamed him Sid, but who themselves were also named John: Wardle, who was sufficiently pear-shaped to be rechristened Wobble; Gray, who was anonymous enough that his surname already suited him; and Lydon, who was now up onstage with the Pistols, flashing

Sid Vicious's favorite Bowie single! *Author's collection*

the teeth that first gave him his *nom de guerre*. Sometimes you wondered what Bev saw in them. He hated it when they called him Sid, he hated it even more when they added the surname Vicious. And it was pretty obvious that his main attraction to them was to see how many outrageous stunts they could prompt him to rush into, simply by reminding him what a "great laugh" he was, and letting his overdeveloped need for attention to take over.

But he never shrugged them off, and you saw less and less of Bev these days, and more and more of Sid Vicious. One day, a few worried friends prophesied, Bev would vanish altogether and Sid would take over completely. Tonight, for sure, Sid was in total control, bouncing up and down on the dance floor, grinning wildly at the noise that his mates were making, and utterly oblivious to the fact that whatever rhythm he was hearing in his head was inaudible to everyone else in the room. Somebody said it looked like he was riding a pogo stick. Somebody else thought it looked like fun. The next time you saw the Sex Pistols, half the audience would be doing it.

The New Yorkers looked on in amazement. "The Pistols were very loud," Kral laughed afterward. "So loud that you couldn't even hear the songs begin or end." But still he found something to take away from the performance. "I thought the lead singer was extremely original. His delivery, his speech, it was nothing I'd ever heard before, that really working class London accent. There were Manchester bands I'd heard that I couldn't understand, but there was something in Johnny Rotten that was the most fascinating thing. You could see the way he was holding the mike in a certain way, mimicking various different people. But he was definitely original. His delivery was so great."

I spotted Greg Shaw standing by the bar. I'd been in awe of the man ever since I read a few paragraphs about him by Charlie Gillett, published in a slim volume of essays and chart statistics called *Rock File*, back in 1972. This particular article was called "So You Wanna Be a Rock 'n' Roll Writer," and the fact is, I did. So I devoured Gillett's words of wisdom, and when I read what he wrote about Shaw, Californian creator of a fanzine called *Who Put The Bomp,* I was hooked. "*Who Put The Bomp* is probably the most entertaining fanzine, certainly the only one that can be unreservedly recommended to any music enthusiast regardless of his particular interest." An envelope containing a complimentary copy of *Who Put The Bomp* issue 12, highlighting the Seeds and the Standells, and a brief note from Shaw saying hi, was the very first piece of mail I ever received from America, after I wrote to the address that Gillett supplied, asking for further details. Two years later, I had the opportunity to thank Shaw in person.

It turned out that he was in town with the Flamin' Groovies, the band he'd been managing ever since they realized that a fan was going to do a lot more for them than the besuited zeroes who normally performed those duties. They were in the midst of recording a new album in Wales, with producer Dave Edmunds at the helm; I cannot recall whether they were at the 100 Club as well, but I wouldn't have paid them much attention if they were—"Shake Some Action," the song that would enshrine them as legends in my mind, was still to be released, and whatever else I'd heard by them, the *Grease* EP maybe, or the album *Slow Death*, had not impressed. Shaw, however, was enthusiasm and excitement personified, the first person I'd ever met who behaved in the same way that certain records occasionally made me feel, as though every musical note he'd ever heard was the most enthralling thing in the world.

He was spellbound by the Sex Pistols, and would emerge from the evening convinced that he'd seen . . . not the new messiahs. But, at least, a workable resurrection of the kind of bands he'd believed were God-like a decade or so ago. "Their brand of revolt, though far from spontaneous, has much in common with the 1964 Mods," he wrote in a review for *Phonograph Record* magazine a few days later, a line of thought that he happily elaborated on in person.

"I didn't hear anything I'd not seen before. It was the same great sloppy rock 'n' roll that you could trace back to the Who and the Kinks and the Yardbirds when they were first starting, and playing exactly the same venues as the Pistols were in. And from there, there's the Small Faces, the Count Five, the Seeds, the Stooges, the MC5, the Dolls, early Television, Eddie and the Hot Rods, you could play join-the-dots with them all, and it wasn't a matter of who influenced who, or who copied who, which is what the English press always seemed to get excited about. It was a matter of, give four guys a bunch of musical instruments and tell them they're a band, and this is what they're going to sound like before they've figured out how to play properly. Which is the most exciting sound, and the most exciting period for any of them."

Hot Rods vocalist Barrie Masters, backstage at the Marquee. *Author's collection*

Mick Farren's *Titanic* was sailing.

After the show, Shaw went looking for the Pistols to ask whether there was any possibility that he could release something by them on his own Bomp label. He'd formed it a couple of years earlier, specifically to release some Groovies numbers during one of that group's label-less stints; and, over the next twelve months, a handful more 45s had emerged. But he had missed out on far more talents than he'd taken—Blondie was one of the ones that got away—and he didn't intend to make the same mistake again.

It was close to twenty years later before I met up with Shaw again, but he seemed to recall meeting me, and he certainly remembered that particular evening. "I found Malcolm, who I already knew from when he was in the States pretending to manage the Dolls, and asked if we could work something out. But it was obvious, even though he never actually said no, that he had his sights set a lot higher than a label like Bomp, although I don't think there was another record label in the world that would have touched the Pistols at that point. His idea, and you have to hand it to him because he pulled it off, was to sell the band on the strength of their notoriety, and let the music fend for itself. Whereas, if he'd gone with Bomp, then the music would have been the only focus. Plus, I don't think they'd even recorded a demo at that point, and I certainly couldn't have afforded to record them."

Shaw was not the only astonished witness to that performance. Back in November 1975, Roogalator had had a gig at the Central School of Art in London, but the PA they'd booked hadn't arrived. They called around everybody they knew, and finally bass player Paul Riley remembered that Malcolm McLaren had one that they might be able to borrow.

Riley made the call, and was amazed when McLaren told them he'd bring it straight over. He wouldn't charge them for it, either. He just had one favor to ask. He had a band that he was trying to get off the ground. Roogalator could use the PA free if they let these Sex Pistols open the show.

"That's fine." Danny Adler saw nothing wrong with the arrangement. But Riley was horrified. "No way! You don't know these guys. They're *terrible!*" Just two nights had passed since the Sex Pistols' debut show, that ill-fated twenty minutes at St. Martin's, but already word of the debacle was getting around town. "They'll drive the audience away. We've got to make some more calls."

But they still couldn't find a free PA and finally returned to McLaren. Half an hour later, the Sex Pistols arrived, buzzing with nerves and haunted by the memory of that dreadful first show. They couldn't believe that nobody had applauded them. Not many applauded tonight, either, but at least they made it through their entire repertoire.

"I remember feeling like they were Rolling Stone wannabes," Adler sighed. "I felt a bit sorry for them, and they all came up afterwards, 'What do you think, Dan?' and I was like . . . 'Keep practicing!' Lots of mid-tempo eighths rhythms, very thrashy, and they all looked like scrawny baby chickens, those 1963 pictures of Brian Jones before his hair was long, all big Adam's apples and little scrawny necks."

Half a year later, the gap between the Sex Pistols and Roogalator had narrowed considerably. Adler was at the 100 Club that night, and even he had to admit they'd improved.

One of the figures at the back of the 100 Club stepped forward. Until just a few weeks before, Chris Miller was drummer with a prog combo called Tor (or Rot as he gleefully inverted their name). Now he was hanging with guitarist Brian James, whose own last group was called Bastard, and that summed up their sound to a tee. Their new group, the Damned, intended to follow in those footsteps: loud, chaotic, adrenalined, raucous, riotous.

Now these Sex Pistols seemed to be working from a similar point of reference, and Miller was intrigued. If there were two bands that'd come to the same musical conclusions, then maybe there were more. And, if there were more, then maybe something might come of it. Something new, something unique, something that spoke of what it was really like to be seventeen, eighteen, nineteen years old, and knowing that your life was already as good as over. Because, if enough people realized that, then they might be able to do something about it.

"There really wasn't anything else like us around," Miller related. "Nobody had heard a Ramones record at that point in England, it was barely out, and hadn't been imported. We'd seen the photographs of the Heartbreakers, Television, and people. You've got the look, but you interpret in your own way. And I think the difference was, the whole New York scene was based much more around art and poetry, Allen Ginsberg. Whereas in England, we really didn't have any money, we were signing on, life was in the literal sense, not the romantic one."

Miller couldn't remember the first time he saw the Pistols. But he never forgot his first impressions. "It was either at the Nashville or the 100 Club. They were the funniest group I'd ever seen. They were a cartoon; totally larger than life, animated, horrible little gits. People don't think that, they think the Pistols were some kind of devastating social comment. But they weren't, they were like this comedy thing, they were funny. At the time, everyone was into Supertramp and Eric Clapton and being able to play your instruments, and there they were, kids that weren't hippies with brightly colored clothes, that couldn't really play, being obnoxious to the audience. At that point in time, it was like an affront to all the musical tastes that was going on in England. It was hysterical."

Ivan Kral agreed with him. He stepped out of the Pistols show with his senses still trying to absorb what he had seen. "They were like nothing I'd ever seen before. There was nothing in New York at that time that was even remotely similar. There was no such anger, no such depression. You didn't have kids in New York whose parents were unemployed, they could always go back to their parents to be supported. In England, those kids were really out on their own, 'this is what's waiting for me when I grow up.' It was totally different. You could feel the frustration."

5

Back in the Garage with My Bullshit Detector

JUNE 1976

SOUNDTRACK

"After Tonight" — Matumbi (Safari)

"Babylon Kingdom Fall" — Prince George (Stud)

"Babylon Trap Them" — Danny Clarke (Wild Flower)

"Blitzkrieg Bop" — The Ramones (Sire)

"Chant Down Babylon" — Junior Byles (Black Wax)

"Gypsy Woman" — Milton Henry (Cactus)

"I and I Can't Turn Back" — Mickey Simpson (Total Sound)

"It Was Love" — Brent Dowe (Student)

"Let It Be Me" — Honeyboy and Winston Curtis (Jamatel)

"My Time" — Dennis Brown (Morpheus)

"Natty Don't Make War" — Little Joe (Melrose)

"Roots Rock Reggae" — Bob Marley and the Wailers (Island)

"Speak and Say" — Big Joe (Soul Beat)

"Spear Burning" — Burning Spear (Spear)

"Three Pan One a Murder" — Rupie Edwards (Cactus)

"Wolf and Leopard" — Dennis Brown (Observer)

"Wooly Bully" — Eddie and the Hot Rods (Island)

"Words of the Prophet" — Trinity (Prophet)

"You're All I Got" — John Holt (Caribbean)

The first time I met Gary Holton, sometime during the summer of 1975, I was wearing a pair of electric blue satin (or something like it) flairs, a T-shirt, and a Bay City Rollers scarf, homemade in a fit of ironic excitement after some schoolfriends and I broke into their show at the Bournemouth Winter Gardens. The Rollers were at the top of their game at that time; "Bye Bye Baby" had just given them their first UK number one, and press reports from the attendant British tour were dominated by one subject, and one subject alone. Girls! A Rollers gig, as my friend Jon put it, was "wall to wall talent. We should go and pick up some birds."

So we went, charmingly oblivious to the fact that—having clambered in through a conveniently open window, and found ourselves in a crowded women's bathroom—being the only men in sight was not necessarily the ticket to sexual abandon that we imagined it would be. The audience's hearts had already been pledged, to Les and Woody and Derek and Eric and Alan. (Osmonds fans, I discovered later, were a lot less loyal.) We returned to school disheartened and disheveled, with our ears still ringing from the screaming from the stalls. Carving up a piece of tartan fabric that I located who-knows-where, and painstakingly stitching on the Rollers name in individually hand-cut lettering, was probably an act of catharsis that I couldn't avoid. Although why I then chose to wear it to a Heavy Metal Kids show, I cannot imagine.

The Heavy Metal Kids were one of those bands that everybody seemed to have a soft spot for. The Kids emerged in 1973, wrapped in a Dickensian image of street urchin chic, and living larger than life whether they were performing onstage or simply hanging out backstage while someone else did the work (ligging, as the locals would put it). They made an immediate mark on a London club circuit that was furiously trying to tear itself away from the prevalent proggy fascinations and into a more musically honest arena. That turned out to be pub rock, but the Kids weren't dismayed.

As Holton cackled, "It's the performance that counts. That's what you're up there for. What you do offstage is boring, no one really cares. So what you have to do is make what you do offstage as exciting as what you do when you're on, or at least make people think that's what you're doing."

Fifteen years old, aspiring guitarist and glam fan James Stevenson was an early convert. He caught the Kids at Biba in August 1974, around the time their eponymous debut LP was released, and he carried their memory with him for years to come. "A very underestimated band. If they'd had short hair, they'd have looked like a punk band. They wore ripped jeans well before the Ramones."

Brian James, as he pieced together the Damned, was equally impressed. "The Heavy Metal Kids were great fun. Gary used to take the piss out of himself so much, and they kinda filled a little bit of a gap amongst all that pomp of the early 1970s. You had the hippie side, you had the glam thing that was taking itself so very seriously, and then there was Gary and his boys, just being silly." West Country art student Tim Smith agreed. "They cared about their look, wearing makeup on stage, dressing up special for gigs, which was the kind of stuff we were looking for. Silly lyrics, funny, energetic on stage."

I adored them, bought the first album on the strength of one single; saw them on the *Whistle Test* and wished I could carry off a haircut like Holton's—a broken bird's nest atop Keith Richards's head, after a few backward jumps through a hedge; and even toyed with adopting a Cockney accent like his, before realizing that Home Counties English didn't quite lend itself to such romantic distortions.

Now I was going to see them for the first time, and I must have arrived early because Holton spotted me across the empty venue the moment I walked through the door—the Nashville, I think, but maybe not. "Fuckin' 'ell mate, what *do* you look like?"

Cue chronic blush, cue mumbled response, cue undiluted hatred for the Bay City Rollers. But Holton wasn't finished. "'Ere, look," he called over to a tableful of friends. "It's Woody from the fuckin' Rollers." And then a laugh and a pat on the back. "What're ya drinkin'?"

"Cider, please."

"*Cider, please,*" he parroted back, exaggerating my own tones to BBC newsreader perfection. "Don't we talk posh. For a Roller." And so on, a barrage of good-natured mockery shot through with genuine affability, until I accepted that, so far as he was concerned, I would forever more be named Roller Boy.

A year had passed since then, the Rollers scarf had long since been retired, but Holton always asked after it when he saw me. Except, just recently, he didn't seem quite as observant as he used to. In years to come, I would discover that a recreational drug habit that he adopted just for kicks had, around this same time, become something more of a problem; it had stripped away a lot of what people used to love about Holton, and was transforming him into a moody, miserable, and, most of all, unreliable so-and-so. At the time, so hopelessly naive about the potential effects of hard drugs that I still thought they could make you look like Keith Richards, I merely assumed he was having a bad day. A bad day that had lasted for most of the year so far.

The year 1976 started well for the Heavy Metal Kids, but rapidly launched itself downhill. A spot on television's *Top of the Pops* had failed to push them forward, while their latest album, *Anvil Chorus*, tumbled as hard as their first. And now, just to make things worse, a bunch of new bands coming up had taken what the Heavy Metal Kids considered their forte, the streetwise swagger and "I don't care" demeanor, and were making the newspapers believe that it was something new and exciting.

The Kids spent a lot of their free time drinking at the Roebuck pub on the Kings Road; Holton even started a pool hall for bikers in one of the upstairs rooms. It was there, drummer Keith Boyce recalled, "that we started noticing these spiky haired blokes hanging about. Then it turned out all these guys who were about to be in bands like the Damned and the Clash, the Pistols, the Adverts, Chelsea, the Pretenders, Cock Sparrow, had all been coming to our gigs, because we were one of the only bands they could identify with."

He was right as well; in months to come, I, too, would start recognizing people onstage from the dance floor at Kids shows, and kicking out much the same effervescent energies that we'd once merely admired from ground level. Their name might be a stylistic misnomer, but the Heavy Metal Kids were punks before any of the rest of us.

These newfound acolytes did not initially impress the Kids. With Holton the inevitable ringleader, the group delighted in taking the piss out of the flourishing new look. Boyce continued, "We thought it was a bit of a laugh, as these guys all reckoned they were something really new and outrageous, or at least the press did, when in fact they were just playing rock 'n' roll with spiky hair. I mean, have you seen photos of Mick Jones and Johnny Rotten and all before they cut their hair? They were all well hippie, and listening to prog rock!"

Even more damning than the photographs of Rotten, though, was Gary Holton's first glimpse of the young man at work. Bug-eyed and wiry, leering and louche, Holton had long ago perfected his onstage impression of the psychopathic hunchback from hell, and he merely shrugged the first time someone told him that the Pistol had lifted a lot of his look. But then he saw the performance in the flesh and he was furious. He caught up with his doppelgänger in the Roebuck.

I wasn't there, and neither was Keith Boyce. But, he told me, "I heard Gary had a right go at Johnny. He told him to stop ripping him off, and a lot more, so people told me. For once, I heard that Mr. Rotten was speechless!"

He would quickly recover, of course, and Holton rarely bore grudges for long. The next time the pair met up, the Sex Pistol solemnly pinned a gold safety pin to Holton's lapel and mourned, "You've been ripped off, Holton."

The Pistols and the Kids continued to eye one another warily, but elsewhere the ice quickly thawed. The Damned, in particular, befriended the Kids very early on, and Boyce "had a lot of time for those guys. I think because, like us, they didn't take themselves too seriously. They also had a lot of energy and some good songs."

Yet, there was also something gnawing at the Kids for which even friendship couldn't compensate—the growing sense that, somewhere along the line, events had overtaken them. Weeks after that confrontation in the Roebuck, with their third album already in the can, the Kids broke up. Like so many of the groups that arose at the wrong end of the early 1970s, and then got lost in the shuffle of the developing new year, the Heavy Metal Kids were just a little too far ahead of their time.

So were Kilburn and the High Roads. The Kilburns (as they'd just become, truncating a name that they adapted from a road sign) were one of those rare acts that simply radiated charm and personality. But they stumbled on one crucial point. In an age when rock singers were growing more and more beautiful, frontman Ian Dury journeyed the other way entirely, and the only people who weren't mortally offended by his onstage approximation of a cripple were those who knew that it wasn't an approximation.

A childhood bout of polio had rendered Dury partially paralyzed, giving him a twisted body that allowed him to ape just one rock 'n' roll idol, Gene Vincent. Plus, he was into his mid-thirties, which meant he was already ancient by his audience's standards. But there was something so compelling, so dramatic, about his performance that nobody held his age against him. He was simply Ian Dury, and the idea of anybody deliberately setting out to emulate his stage presence was so absurd that even he didn't believe it the first time he saw it happen.

By mid-1976, though, the Kilburns—like the Kids—had reached the end of the road. For six years, they had suffered through any number of false dawns, records recorded and left on the shelf, hit singles prophesied and then abandoned to rot, lineups broken in and then broken up. Dury and keyboard player Chaz Jankel were already dreaming of a fresh start.

One final show was arranged to give the faithful their chance to say good-bye. The Walthamstow Assembly Hall was just a few blocks from the art school where the Kilburns started in the first place, and one of the few venues that you could catch a bus to from the top of my street. Which made it even more infuriating that I was a hundred-odd miles away at the time, with examination fever now beginning to bite. "Pass all your O-Levels, sonny," we were told, "and the world will be your oyster." Which was absolutely no consolation whatsoever.

The end of the Kilburns. The end of an era. Back in my dormitory that night, I played their one album, *Handsome*, three times straight through before somebody told me to turn it off. They wanted to listen to Uriah Heep instead.

But what did I really miss? A friend who did make it said the gig itself was desultory, that Dury looked thoroughly bored with proceedings, and the rest of the band were already wondering what they were going to do next. There was just one spark to shatter the gloom of the evening, another chance to catch the Sex Pistols (who, with the Stranglers, opened the show), and a rare chance to see Malcolm McLaren struck dumb.

"'Ere, I know that geezer!" Dury had only half an eye on the stage when the Pistols sauntered out to open the evening, but he sprang into animated life the moment Johnny Rotten draped himself round the microphone, and glared out into the crowd.

"You should do, it's you," someone shot back and, though that wasn't what Dury meant (he simply recognized the singer from the audience at countless past Kilburns concerts), that someone was right. From the stance to the stare, and all the way down to the razor-blade earrings that Dury had been wearing for years, the king Kilburn might have been looking into a distorted mirror, and it was hard to tell at first whether Rotten, too, was somehow disabled, the way his back humped and his head twisted, while his snarly vocals slurred from a mouth that clearly couldn't be bothered to open too wide.

Dury was furious. "They're taking the fucking piss." He twisted around. "Fred! Oi, Fred!" A man mountain materialized by Dury's side, a Korean War vet who now worked as Ian's minder, and together they bore down on McLaren, just as they'd bore down on

IAN DURY   SEX & DRUGS & ROCK & ROLL

The classic Dury pose, from his debut Stiff single. Safety-pin earring inserted as a tribute to the people who stole his razor-blade motif.
Author's collection

all the other chancers and dodgers who thought they could take a cripple for a ride. They sandwiched him between them, Dury fierce and belligerent on one side, Fred Rowe a broadsided behemoth on the other.

"So what's going on, Malcolm?"

"Yeah, what's this all about?"

"Come on, Malcolm, they're your boys," and so on and so forth until the legendary McLaren motormouth wasn't simply stilled, it started spilling out barely audible squeaks. "It's true!" Dury delightedly told everyone who asked. "Malcolm just stood there squeaking."

6

Finding Ways to Fill the Vacuum

JUNE 1976

Don't look over *your shoulder but the Sex Pistols are coming.*
Four months after journalist Neil Spencer penned those fateful
words, they had arrived. Barely a week went by without the
Pistols being namechecked in each of the music papers—*New
Musical Express, Sounds, Melody Maker, Record Mirror,
Street Life*; they'd barely even played outside of London and
already they were getting more column inches than a lot of the
superstars. There was a bandwagon rolling, and it was collid-
ing countrywide.

In Bolton, in the north of England, a Captain Beefheart fan
named Howard Trafford was so enamored by news of this dis-
ruptive new monster that he and his best friend Peter McNeish
promptly arranged to attend the next Pistols concert, even
though it meant traveling three hundred miles to do it. And
afterward, they knew what they had to do next. They'd often
talked about forming a band together. The Sex Pistols were
exactly the role model they'd been seeking. They changed their
surnames to Devoto and Shelley, and the Buzzcocks were born.

In the suburban dormitory of Bromley, Kent, Susan Ballion
was already metamorphosing into Siouxsie Sioux even before

she discovered a way of life that would ease the transition further. But she is adamant. "In 1974–75, there weren't a lot of lulls in the tedium. There was Roxy Music, but Bowie was past it, Lou Reed was—losing it. There was Sparks, thank goodness for them, and it was really important to see them on television, they were one of the few bands you'd see and say 'thank God there's something good on, in amongst all this idiocy.' But that was it." Then she discovered the Sex Pistols.

In Exeter, in the West Country, art student Tim Smith handed his girlfriend Gaye Black a bass guitar, and started planning the group they would form. The fact that she'd never played bass before was a minor obstacle to which neither of them gave a moment's thought.

In Shepherds Bush, West London, Dublin-born Bernie Tormé filled his days with whatever low-paying part-time jobs he could luck into, and his nights playing whatever was required by whichever band he'd managed to squeeze into most recently, Irish country acts and pub performers mostly, who'd keep him on board until the night Tormé's instincts got the better of him, and "The Mountains of Mourn" would be sliced in twain by the sustained squealing of his frustrated guitar. "I came to London because there was sod all happening in Ireland, apart from Horslips and Celtic rock, which I hated. I got there and Queen were the highpoint."

And in Presteigne, mid-Wales, a foundry worker named Daniel Kustow stopped worrying about falling into one of the vast, red-hot vats in which the aluminum was smelted, and started dreaming of wider-open pastures. "One of the other workers told me about a guy who fell into one of the molten aluminum vats. His arm and penis were totally melted." That was a hell of a price to pay for £25 a week. Even worse, Kustow's foreman reckoned the lad had all the makings of a great stoker, and he had a job for life if he wanted it.

Which was almost as great an incentive to get out as Tim Smith was granted, the day he started work at the local sweet factory, and was promptly given a pitying glance from one of the older hands.

Smith smiled back. "It's alright, I'm only here for a few months while I sort myself out."

The old man smiled back. "That's what I said when I started here." He knew, as this young whippersnapper would soon discover, that once you found a job, you clung to it for life. For dear life. Ambition was something that you dreamed of in your spare time.

Only now those dreams were beginning to nag. There was a time when an aspiring young muso would flick through the music papers and only imagine what it must be like to be "up there," strutting the stage, a master of his musical instrument, and the master of his destiny, too.

Imagination was as far as it got, though. Rock 'n' roll stardom was something reserved for the luckiest of the lucky few, usually the ones with parents rich enough to buy them all the gear, a manager bent enough to inveigle them into the limelight, and an education broad enough to have taught them how to make the system work for them. "Jesus, I'm twenty-one," Danny Kustow would despair at nights. "How can I ever become good enough to break into this music business, with all these great musicians like Pete Townshend and the like already in there before me?"

Plus, the music industry had battened everything down so tight that when it did feel the need for a new musical sensation, it just made one up. The biggest new attraction of 1976 so far was Slik, who may once have been a Glasgow pub act, but had now been transformed into the new Bay City Rollers by the same songwriting team that invented the old ones. And maybe Slik were happy, selling their souls for a number-one single. But not Devoto or Kustow, Smith or Tormé. They'd rather do nothing than do *that*.

Then they read about the Sex Pistols, and suddenly there was hope. A bunch of kids up onstage, kids like them, giving it energy, and waving a great big flag in the air. *Join us!* Suddenly, they felt that they could be up there as well. It didn't matter that they'd not heard a note of this new music. They knew they would like it regardless, because it's what they'd always wanted to see, a band just getting up and doing it, without having any of the traditional requirements or even abilities. Like it, or fuck off.

But, although the Pistols catalyzed the mood, they did not create it. Other groups, too, were toying with the notion of unconstrained savagery; reformed old timers like the Pink Fairies and edge-of-metal veterans like Motörhead, ex-Hawkwind bassist Lemmy's new band, catalyzed around the insistence that they were both the worst, and the loudest, group you had ever seen—or, at the other end of the chronological scale, a bunch of schoolkids called Cock Sparrow.

Based in Dagenham, on the far eastern fringes of London, Cock Sparrow mashed their cultural love of West Ham United football club with musical influences that strayed from the Small Faces to Slade and not much further. But it was working. They played wherever and whenever they could. Their earliest gigs were drafty church halls, or a spin down to the youth club, alternate Fridays at the nearby Trinity Community Centre, any place that would bung them a fiver. Their early repertoire revolved around covers, anything that they could work out a decent approximation of. But, as more and more originals began creeping into the set and their local reputation spread, they stepped out into the pubs.

"We started out playing covers, the Small Faces, Bowie, the Beatles," drummer Steve Bruce told me once. "We liked bands with a bit of attitude and aggression, Steve Marriott was a hero of ours. The Heavy Metal Kids, AC/DC, the New York Dolls, Alice Cooper."

Terry Murphy, the eternally open-eared landlord of the Bridge House in Canning Town, was Cock Sparrow's first mentor, hiring them whenever he had a vacancy on the bill, usually on a wet Wednesday night in front of two people, and handing them a fiver for their troubles. They invariably handed it straight back to him to cover their bar tab for the night.

Word spread. The Black Boy in Mile End; the Dagenham Roundhouse, where they opened for Motörhead there, Stray, and Thin

Lizzy. By early 1976 a friendship with Archie, the doorman at the Marquee, saw them begin to darken that venue's door as well. Archie championed Cock Sparrow at every chance he got, forever putting them forward as a potential opening act, until finally his employers couldn't take any more. The week after the Sex Pistols played the Marquee for the first time, Cock Sparrow made their own debut there, to an audience that included an astonished Malcolm McLaren.

Blown away by the confidence that oozed off the stage, the imagery that swept off the football terraces, the stamping, shouting noise of the band, McLaren invited himself down to one of their rehearsals, at the Roding pub in Manor Park, and invited Cock Sparrow to show him what they could do.

The Sparrows just stared at him. The man had obviously raided the weirdest wardrobe in the world. They'd never heard of Sex at that time, and wouldn't have been interested if they had. Neither were they especially taken with McLaren. Too full of himself, too wired, and weasel-ish. A middle-class art snob, slumming with the plebeians. They treated him to a mass of terrible songs, and expected that to send him scurrying away. Instead, he asked if they wanted to support his Sex Pistols when they played a strip club in Soho. Cock Sparrow turned him down, and it depends upon which of the band members is telling the story, but it was because either he refused to buy them a round of drinks, or they didn't fancy getting their hair cut.

Either way, the visit alerted them to one fact. "Suddenly," Steve Bruce celebrated, "we realized that we were not alone in our outlook and music." Weeks later, they would modify their name to the more street-smart Cock Sparrer and, cropping their hair because *they* wanted to, started blazing their own distinctive trail around the pubs and clubs. Two years before *über*-skinhead rabble-rousers Sham 69 declared that if the kids were united they will never be divided, Cock Sparrer were cultivating an audience that was so fanatical in its devotion to the band that the mildly curious couldn't even get in to see them play. The club would have been filled up long before.

"The scene already kind of existed," Chris Miller of the Damned confirmed. "It wasn't like 'oh wow, here's the Sex Pistols, I'm going to be a punk.' It was, 'Oh, here's one of the other groups that are kind of on the edge of what we're doing.'" And the roll call was growing every week, new acts forming or emerging from the wreckage of one or another, unknowns bursting out of the rehearsal room to thrash their guitars and trash their audience's expectations.

But what you didn't realize, unless you were haring around like a mad thing, trying to cram as many live shows into a week as you could, was that because they were all forming in isolation, they all developed in isolation, too. Not one of them put an ear to the ground and heard what else was going on. They just seized their own initiative and let it blossom from there.

"What was good about the Pistols was that there were many influences that came in, there was a whole wealth of things that made that one particular sound," Glen Matlock reflected. "We had a myriad influences, and that's what made it so good. When I met up with Steve [Jones] and Paul [Cook], the common ground was that we all liked the Faces, who at that time were on the wane, but were the total antithesis of all the tired glam things, the pomp rockers like Yes, they were out there having a laugh. That was our starting point. Then John came along, and he was into Can and Van Der Graaf Generator.

"That was what was good about it, there was this [place] where the two things collide, there was this kind of interface where these two things really shouldn't be going together. And once we reached that stage where we were writing stuff of our own, it quickly became apparent that we didn't particularly sound like anybody. Instead of trying to say, 'Oh no it should be like this,' we said, 'It sounds good, let's go with it.'"

Tim Smith would agree. His own last band, an art-college quintet called Sleaze, could point to the likes of Cockney Rebel, the Doctors of Madness, David Bowie, and Peter Hammill for inspiration. But Gaye Black was into Zappa, the Stooges, the Dolls, and Alice Cooper. The ensuing cocktail could not help but prove fascinating.

Before Smith had heard about the Sex Pistols, and realized that everything he'd ever thought about the music industry was wrong, there was no way out, just a succession of minor highs that made him feel as though he was getting somewhere. Sleaze recorded an album with a real BBC sound engineer overseeing the session. It didn't matter that they paid for the session themselves, and paid to have the record pressed as well. They'd stepped forward in an age when most groups perished unheard no matter how great they might be. Later, when Smith and Black began scheming their future, they were

Sleaze onstage, 1975, and flyer for an upcoming live show. *Courtesy of TV Smith*

plus
DISCO
NEWTON ABBOT
GRAMMAR SCHOOL
MARCH 14th
7.30 - 11p.m.

sitting in a bedroom with a cheap amplifier and a pair of even cheaper guitars, marveling at the heights they'd already reached.

Little victories. One evening, Danny Kustow hooked up with a bunch of local musicians who were playing a free show to a field full of hippies. "They really liked what we were doing. I remember humping my guitar between my legs and feeling it was seriously the most erotic, naughty, exciting, dirty, and sexy thing one could ever do. I was finally showing off, with my big phallus, my Les Paul guitar barking and screaming, and to have people come up to you after the gig saying they really got off on what we were doing, and getting to pull a beautiful woman and have pure unadulterated sex, all on the merit of having been onstage, it was nirvana for a very shy person like me."

How could he go back to the foundry after that? "It was such a dead, depressing, colorless existence. I used to dream all day about getting onstage with a guitar, I used to get through a tough day just playing guitar in my head."

There was one ray of sunshine on Kustow's horizon. Periodically, whenever finances and the urge took him, he would hitchhike to London to catch a Café Society gig. Tom Robinson, one of his oldest friends, was leading Café Society toward what might have been their own shade of glory had their luck only held out. Signed to Ray Davies's Konk label, praised by the handful of journalists who'd caught their show, Café Society were at least hovering on the edge of a breakthrough of sorts, and if Kustow couldn't snag the fame for himself, then he'd share a taste of Tom's.

Robinson told him about the Sex Pistols, how he'd gone to see them at the 100 Club and walked out after fifteen minutes because he couldn't stand the excitement any longer. Nobody else was aware of the fact, but Café Society died that night, and Tom Robinson's own band took its first breath. Kustow hung onto the words like a drowning man, and then went to see the Pistols for himself. It was a revelation.

"Songs like 'I'm a Lazy Sod' and 'Anarchy in the UK' totally said what I was feeling: 'Fuck off out the way, established bands; fuck off out the way, great musical technicians. It's our time now.' Even before I heard of the Sex Pistols, I was my own angry young man, but now I was discovering that I wasn't alone, and isn't it quite amazing that all of us nineteen-, twenty-, twenty-one-year-olds were all feeling the same anger, boredom, and resentment, the same seething anarchic fed-up-ness! With everything!"

Of all the people who had an interest in what the Sex Pistols were said to be doing, however, perhaps the most significant were four New Yorkers called the Ramones.

"Clearly Malcolm had told the Pistols a lot about the Ramones," Greg Shaw told me, "not because the bands had anything in common, because they really didn't. But in terms of impact and sound, that idea of aggressive speed and the sense that you were almost watching a cartoon show, that came straight from New York and early on, Malcolm was really worried about the Ramones, that they might make it big before anybody had heard the Pistols. As it was, it didn't matter, because there was room for both of them, but there was a concern."

"The first time we heard of the Sex Pistols, it was a picture in one of the English music papers," Joey Ramone recalled. He'd been dutifully picking up the UK papers for years, making the same pilgrimage to the same store every week to buy the *New Musical Express* and *Melody Maker*, sometimes stretching out for *Sounds* as well, and then taking them home to digest every word.

"I was always an Anglophile. I'd read about things in the English papers, and it would become my life's ambition to track down a copy. Even the things that nobody else liked." One day in 1972, he walked into a particularly hip record store, thumbed through the racks, and discovered a newly imported copy of Gary Glitter's debut album. Glitter's "Rock 'n' Roll" was all over the radio that summer, a primal thump and raucous chant that had already polarized his friends. It turned out to have polarized the store's employees, too. "They didn't want to sell it to me and, when I insisted, they chased me out of the store!"

He discovered the Sex Pistols in the same manner that he discovered everything else he loved, through the pages of the import press. "My first thought was that [they] were doing the same sort of thing as we were, and when we found out that Malcolm was involved, that kinda sealed it for us. There was a lot of ill will towards him in New York at that time, Richard Hell was especially annoyed, because he saw those same photos, the ripped T-shirts and the safety pins and things, and he knew that Malcolm had lifted the whole look from him. But we were curious as well, because Malcolm was always interesting, even when he was completely wrong about something, and what we were reading about the Sex Pistols was interesting as well, the fights with the audience and all that. Once we knew we were coming to London, I think we all decided that we wanted to hook up with the Sex Pistols and find out what was really going on."

McLaren shared the Ramones' impatience. As soon as he heard the Ramones were coming over, he marched straight over to promoter John Curd's office to demand that the Pistols be added to the bill. Curd refused, then threw his visitor down the stairs when a polite "no" wasn't demonstrative enough. An enraged McLaren responded by accepting a Sex Pistols booking for as far outside of London as he could, at the Black Swan in Sheffield. There was no way he was going to allow the two bands to go head to head in the capital, because there was no doubting who the winner would be.

7

Summer's Here and the Time Is Right . . .

EARLY JULY 1976

SOUNDTRACK

"Bring It on Home to Me"	Johnny Clarke (Caribbean)
"Bump & Skank"	Dillinger (Love)
"Crazy Kids"	Trevor White (Island)
"Don't You Lie to Me"	Flamin' Groovies (Sire)
"Gimme Me Gun"	Dr. Alimantado (Ital)
"Judgement on the Land"	Prophets (Prophet)
"Keys to Your Heart"	The 101ers (Chiswick)
"Legalise It"	Peter Tosh (Virgin)
"Mango Walk"	The Crown (Sound Tracs)
"Natty Kung Fu"	Dillinger (Forward)
"Pichy Pachy"	Junior Byles (Ja-Man)
"Pressure inna Babylon"	Dennis Alcapone (Ethnic Fight)
"Shark Out Deh"	Errol Holt (Jah-Man)
"So It Goes"	Nick Lowe (Stiff)
"The Barber Feel It"	Alimantado and Jah Stitch (Jackpot)
"We Should Be in Angola"	Pablo Moses (Penetrate)
"Who Has Eyes to See"	Errol Holt (Cry Tuff)

And, through it all, the sun kept on shining. The summer of 1975 had been hot, but this year was destined to be even hotter, not simply breaking but shattering temperature records that were set decades before. Lawns died and flowerbeds smoldered, sidewalks cracked and old folk croaked with them. Drought bit, and the water supplies to entire cities were cut off, to be replaced by standpipes at the end of the road, and the queues of ragged children who splashed in the puddles in their dirty underwear could have stepped out of a documentary on the Great Depression. In some places, it was said, you could fry an egg on the pavement. You probably wouldn't want to eat it, though. The street cleaners were on strike.

At first, people simply shrugged. A dry winter became a warm spring, but even when the sun broke out in earnest in early May, and London soared into the mid-eighties, nobody batted an eyelid. The rains would return soon enough.

Except they didn't. The end of May cooled a little, but June began picking up again and after a while, it started getting tedious. Another blue sky, another hot day, another fortune spent on suntan oil because an hour on the street would turn your pasty skin purple. Oppressive, too, especially at night, when your covers were kicked off before you even looked at them, and there wasn't a breath of air coming in through the window because the night was as still as the grave.

Deep in the heart of Shepherds Bush, Bernie Tormé had finally put a band together, a hard metal trio called Scrapyard, but it was so hot that it was hard to get excited about that. Every night, he and his girlfriend would crawl out through the skylight in the roof of their flat, and lie in the gutter that ran between the slate roofs. "We'd get covered in dirt and pigeon shit and never get a tan, just get burnt—it was the days of the ozone layer holes and mega air pollution. But at least there was something pretending to be fresh air up there."

It was even worse at street level, where merely setting foot on the pavement was like passing through a furnace, and a newspaper rolled up beneath your arm would be a dripping mass of pulp before you reached the tube station. By the time the Ramones arrived in London on the first day of July, even the sun-worshippers were begging for a reprieve.

The Ramones were not the sole stars of their first major London performance at the Roundhouse. They shared that honor with the Flamin' Groovies, revisiting the land of so many inspirations on the back of their greatest record yet, the pounding pop supremacy of *Shake Some Action.*

Half bootleg Beatles, half yowling Yardbirds, and 100 percent West Coast America from the tip of their Carnaby haircuts to the soles of their Cuban-heeled boots, the Groovies were making much the same sounds that they kicked off with in the 1960s. But this record was different; this one added Phil Spector to the brew . . . or, at least, the nearest thing to Phil Spector that you could find if you went to Wales, producer Dave Edmunds. Now they were coming to London, to play a show that would have sold out a venue twice the size, so vast was their reputation. Add the Ramones to the bill and it was the most eagerly awaited concert of the year. Or, at least, since Patti Smith came over.

Touching down in the middle of the night, jetlag was the Ramones' first taste of London—that and the furnace blast of the heat wave. Of course, it was nothing that a native New Yorker had not experienced every summer of his life. But London was wilting. No rain, no clouds, nothing but temperatures that routinely nudged the mid-90s every day, and didn't seem to let up at night, either. And, of course, the Brits don't have air conditioning.

Checking into their hotel in the hope of catching some sleep, the quartet instead found themselves walking round Hyde Park at four in the morning. Back to base for a few hours of disturbed slumber, and then out on the town again. They wanted to go record shopping, and Greg Shaw of *Who Put The Bomp*, back in town with the Groovies, knew exactly where to send them: Soho Market, on the edge of Leicester Square, home to the Rock On market stall.

Rock On was the best record store in town. Cheaper than the Vintage Record Centre, up on Caledonian Road, hipper than Record and Tape Exchange, out in Notting Hill Gate, Rock On specialized in oldies but stocked a bit of everything. Everything that was worth stocking, anyway. Owner Ted Carroll scoured the world for fresh delights, buying up collections that he heard of in the States, hauling in box loads from warehouse stashes around old British military bases. Gibraltar and Malta were happy hunting grounds, he said, and it felt strange handing over 50p for an old 45, knowing it had traveled halfway round the world and back, just to wind up in your own record collection.

The first time the Ramones came over, you couldn't buy a button for love or money. A month later, they were everywhere. *Author's collection*

Browsing amid the Teddy Boys and Rockers who comprised so much of the Rock On clientele (for where else were they going to find those old Elvis Sun 45s, mint Billy Fury on Decca, and the latest releases by their current crop of favorites?), DeeDee Ramone stood out a mile. Not because I recognized him, although he looked exactly like his photo on the front of *The Ramones* LP; not because he was American, with an accent that could warp sheet metal; but because he was the only person I'd seen in weeks who was still wrapped up in a leather jacket.

I said hello, juggling a handful of scratchy singles aside as he promptly thrust out his hand to shake.

"Ya want me to sign the album?" I'd only paid for it fifteen minutes before, but it wasn't so precious that I'd not already stained the jacket with sweaty fingerprints. He scribbled a barely legible "love DeeDee" over Joey's face, then pulled a Hot Rods 45 out of his own pile of records. "Now you have to help me. Tell me about this band."

They're great. Fast R&B . . . not as fast as you guys, but I think you'll like it.

"Cool." He grabbed two singles, "Writing on the Wall" and that so wild revision of "Woolly Bully."

Dr. Feelgood. Imagine the early Stones on speed.

"Cool." Three of them, "Roxette," "She Does It Right," "Back in the Night," silver print on jet-black labels. He studied them intently. British records not only looked better than American 45s, he said, but they felt better as well.

The Count Bishops. Dr. Feelgood on downers.

"Cool."

He squinted at the label. Chiswick—but you pronounce it Chizzik, not Chiz-Wick. The first truly adventurous independent label to be launched in the UK in years.

"Cool."

He grabbed two more on the same label, the 101ers, and a genuine rock 'n' roll classic, Vince Taylor's "Brand New Cadillac."

You should talk to Ted over there about them, it's his label.

"Cool."

We shopped on, then he headed back to the hotel, clutching £20 worth of vinyl. "You coming to the show tonight?" he asked as we parted.

Yeah.

"Cool."

The Ramones were playing two London shows, but the Roundhouse was the one that everybody talked about. It was July 4, the two hundredth anniversary of American independence. While the rest of their countrymen were at home slapping backs, the Ramones were abroad, giving the motherland a progress report. This is what we came up with once you left.

As it turned out, the Roundhouse was only the curtain raiser. There were too many Groovies fans in the room, and too many people shouting abuse at the inevitably opening Stranglers, for the Ramones to truly say they had triumphed. Sixteen songs in thirty-five minutes were no disappointment, of course, but the first words from the stage—"Good evening, we're the Ramones, and you're a loudmouth, you'd better shut it up"—were anticlimactic to say the least. Where there should have been a wall of Ramonic noise, there was, instead, chaos, a screaming row between DeeDee and the sound engineer, a cacophony of buzzing and the sound of roadies trying to fix things, a host of sonic gremlins who cavorted across the stage as though it was them we had come to witness, and the Ramones were simply an afterthought.

Almost six minutes elapsed before the concert finally got started, six minutes during which the audience entertained itself with the kind of catcalls you never expected to hear at a Ramones gig: cries of "Boring!" and a round of slow handclaps. Occasionally a handful of heroic souls would interrupt the mayhem with a chorus or two, "Blitzkrieg Bop" and "Beat on the Brat," but the wait crept interminably on, the New Yorkers watching in mounting dismay—until finally they could launch into the song they'd introduced so long before. And half an hour of passion, sweat, and disbelief later, with the deafening echoes of "Today Your Love, Tomorrow the World" still burning in our ears, it was over.

The real occasion, then, was the following evening's gig at Dingwalls, a far smaller venue just a brisk walk down the road, a late-night hangout that served alcohol till two in the morning, and kept the music loud until just as late. It was there that the New Yorkers' UK fan club would come out in force, not only to be seen, but also heard and, as the nearly midnight showtime drew closer, a time traveler could have picked any number of future musical movers and shakers out of the crowd. For now, however, they were just fans, just kids, just a couple of hundred people desperate to find out what a handful of journalists was raving about.

Traveling up from Deptford, in the southeast corner of London, a bank clerk named Mark Perry had already bought *The Ramones* on import, after being bowled over by journalist Nick Kent's review of the album in the *New Musical Express*. He was so impressed by the Dingwalls gig that he went home and started to write his own fanzine. *Sniffin' Glue* was not the first homemade musical magazine to document the UK scene, but that didn't matter. It was the first to pick up on what a few writers were already describing as punk rock, and the first to take a stab at quantifying precisely what this new genre's musical boundaries might be.

Martin Gordon, clinging onto the remains of a glam band called Jet, was there, marveling at the Ramones' manic energy. "They played twenty songs in about as many minutes," he gasped, and it was a lesson he knew he should take on board. Just a week earlier, recording demos for a second album that he seriously doubted Jet would ever release, Gordon's bandmates barely shrugged when he unveiled a new song that had very little in common with the group's standard fare of witty prog-shaped pop. Now, "Dirty Pictures" sounded almost prescient, a high-octane fanfare that barreled along so quickly that, even as Jet's latest suitors, Island Records, rejected the demo out of hand, Gordon and vocalist Andy Ellison were wondering whether there was a new sound, a new direction, and maybe even a whole new act bound up in that one song.

Johnny Rotten, Glen Matlock, and Sid Vicious filed in. The Stranglers were there, and so was Ian Dury, taking his place at the bar and indulging in a low-level glaring contest with Rotten. Fred Rowe lurked ominously at Dury's side, in case the eyeballing got too rough.

I spotted the Damned, the first musicians Nick Kent had played the record to once he'd cracked the shrinkwrap. "We thought the MC5 were fast until we heard the Ramones," quipped Brian James, but later, he agreed, the album was just the warm-up. Live, they were even faster.

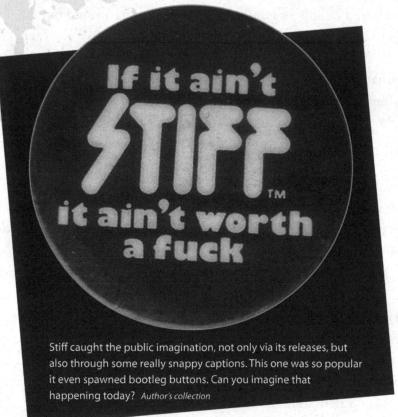

Stiff caught the public imagination, not only via its releases, but also through some really snappy captions. This one was so popular it even spawned bootleg buttons. Can you imagine that happening today? *Author's collection*

"Yeah, there were all these English kids, the ones that would become the punks, hanging out," Joey laughed when we talked about it a decade later. "The Clash, the Sex Pistols, the Damned, we didn't know that's what they were called, but we'd see pictures later and remember them, 'oh yeah, he was there, and he was. . . .' A bomb in that place could have changed the whole course of rock 'n' roll history!"

So could a little decorum. A year later, Malcolm McLaren was boasting that his Sex Pistols had succeeded in getting themselves banned from nigh-on every major venue in the land, and it was true. But it started at Dingwalls, first when one of the employees clocked Glen Matlock lobbing a plastic beer glass toward the stage, then when Paul Cook and Steve Jones fell into a scrap with the Stranglers' Jean Jacques Burnel. Dingwalls' management, siding with the seemingly innocent Burnel, promptly barred the Pistols from ever darkening the Dingwalls doorstep again. (They doubtless responded with some well-chosen words of conciliatory apology.)

It was little more than handbags at dawn, but the battle and the ban were to have long-standing repercussions anyway. McLaren, forever looking for new ways to up the Pistols' notoriety, seized upon the moment as an indication that, whatever this new musical scene might be, it had already split into two camps. There were the bands that didn't matter and those that did, which amounted to the Pistols, and anybody else who sailed alongside them: Siouxsie Sioux and her friends in the Bromley Contingent. The Buzzcocks. The Damned, whom McLaren had just agreed could open the Pistols' next 100 Club show. And the Heartdrops, formed when Joe Strummer quit the 101ers, and joined instead with the remnants of the London SS, the brilliantly named but hopelessly incomplete outfit that one of McLaren's associates, Bernie Rhodes, had kept rehearsing in a Paddington basement for much of the year-so-far.

They were all Ramones fans as well, but while the Ramones were filling the Roundhouse, the Heartdrops were playing their first-ever gig miles away in Sheffield, opening for the Pistols. A few months later, a friend of mine took great delight in reminding Strummer of that fact, even as the singer regaled a wide-eyed audience with tales of how he scaled the Roundhouse walls and broke in through a window, so desperate was he to see the Ramones.

There was one other group that McLaren was keeping his eye on, not because he'd heard them yet, but because he'd promised he would. They'd phoned him out of the blue one day, and made themselves sound so interesting that he told them to call him before their next show. They hadn't called back yet, but he was certain they would.

The Maniacs were one of those groups that everybody seemed to run into at some point, propping up the bill at another outer-London pub gig, but which few people would ever dare categorize. Like an angry Tyrannosaurus rex, the duo of vocalist/guitarist Alan Lee Shaw and drummer Rod Latter eschewed any accompaniment beyond that which they could thrash out themselves, or provoke from the audiences who watched them in amazement.

I first stumbled across them completely by accident, on one of those nights when the evening's entertainment is decided not by the quality of the band, but by the size of the admission fee. The Maniacs gig was free. There was no competition, although after I'd seen them, I knew I'd be looking out for them again, even if it did cost to get in.

Looking back on their teenaged years, most people would agree that it's hellishly difficult to say why *this* band made an impression on you, or *that* band didn't. You're fifteen, sixteen years old, for Christ's sake, which means you're barely even human yet, just a walking talking piece of sponge, absorbing everything as though it's the most exciting thing on Earth, and then filtering out the dross when you pause to take a breath.

Patti Smith mattered to me because she was tearing down a sacred cow, and the Pistols were impressive because they then proceeded to slaughter it. Groups like Roogalator, the Feelgoods, the Rods, and the Heavy Metal Kids were important because they were

Alan Lee Shaw onstage as a Maniac, white Strat and homemade Helter Skelter T-shirt at the ready. *Courtesy of Alan Lee Shaw*

so much fun, and the Ramones had an impact because they sounded like the best drugs were meant to make you feel.

But the Maniacs? Standing on the edge of the dance floor while they ran through their set was like standing on the edge of a cliff, while the wind tried to blow you over. There were only the two of them, but they kicked out a noise that fell halfway between an undermanned Velvet Underground and an overwhelmed MC5, and if the Ramones looked good in leather jackets, the Maniacs looked positively sinister when they slipped on the trousers to match. Plus, they were spraypainting slogans onto their T-shirts long before I saw anyone else doing it.

The Maniacs were relatively new to London, but they had already been making much the same sounds around their native Cambridge for a few years now, pausing only when Latter made a break for the big city to be with his girlfriend of the time. Briefly solo, Shaw fell into the orbit of Ken Pitt, David Bowie's old manager, and cut a single that the *New Musical Express* reviewed beneath the astonishingly prescient heading of "Pünke Rock." Unfortunately, the heading belonged to another record entirely and the review, of a Shaw original titled "She Moans," was more or less confined to the rejoinder, "I bet she does."

Still, not bad for an unknown oddity from the provinces, and in late 1975, Shaw followed Latter down to London. The drummer was single again, so the pair rented a flat together in Saltram Crescent, in Maida Vale, where £35 a week rent brought them a roof and four walls, dodgy plumbing, and a deadly electric system. But it was also the nerve center for their projected conquest of the music industry, or, at least, a base from which they could see where fortune would take them.

Latter was the trained musician, able to turn his hand to piano, guitar, and drums; Shaw was the self-styled "art student who could play the guitar and write songs and had a bit of arty vision." But they both possessed enough belief and blind determination to take their two-man show out on the road—belief, determination, and a shared wicked sense of humor.

The Maniacs had more front than Harrods and they stood out like a sore thumb. Latter stood up to play drums—a couple of copper timbales and a single cymbal; Shaw glowered over the microphone, and thrashed his white Stratocaster through a 1960s vintage thirty-watt Selmer amplifier. They mixed a handful of covers with a bunch of wiry originals. Lou Reed's "Waiting for the Man," "Sweet

Jane," and "Walk on the Wild Side," a *Who Live at Leeds*–shaped
version of "Young Man Blues" and a positively manic demolition of
"My Generation" all figured in the set. "I suppose," Shaw mused
one evening, "you could say we were somewhat exotic oddities."

While so many other people were still reading the music press,
and wondering whether they dared to take a chance, the Maniacs
were already pointedly seeking a fresh direction out of the stinking,
sinking rock mire of the day, an attitude that was more than enough
to land them a manager. The singularly named Des, Shaw explained,
was "an enthusiastic, but ever so slightly psychotic Irishman, which
was perfect because all the pub gigs seemed to have Irish or Scottish
landlords, so we really had a foot in the door."

Des was fearless and persuasive, and just what the Maniacs
needed at that point, a man with sufficient connections to land them
all sorts of weird and wonderful gigs, then hustle them into the late-
night venues, to drink and pose and simply be seen. One evening at
the industry hangout Speakeasy, Shaw found himself jamming into
the wee small hours with a totally incapacitated duo of rock veterans
Jimmy McCulloch and Tim Hardin. Des scored the band a residency
at the Windsor Castle pub on Harrow Road, and regular shows
across the capital—the Rochester Castle in Stoke Newington, the
Brecknock in Camden Road, the Greyhound on Fulham Palace
Road—and quickly they discovered another reason why what they
were doing was so valuable.

For some reason, the Maniacs always seemed to be booked to
open for acts whose name ended with the letters "er"—Stealer, Wid-
owmaker, Strider, Smiler, Rainmaker. It was, we were firmly agreed,
a conspiracy of hesitancy, an entire wave of bands emerging from the
hairy side of Pub Rock, and not one of them was confident enough
to name themselves with anything less than red-faced equivocation.
"Good evening, Neasden, we're called Heartbreak . . . er."

The Maniacs, on the other hand, were ferocious, confident,
already set on course, and when they heard about the Sex Pistols,

just the name of the band was exciting enough for Shaw. "Something subversive. Something different!"

He hadn't even heard the music.

Twenty-four hours after the Ramones scorched Dingwalls, he would. We all bundled down to see the Pistols and the Damned at the 100 Club, "and that was it," Shaw celebrated afterward. He'd seen the MC5 back in 1972, and every adrenalined emotion that he felt then came screaming back when he caught the Pistols and the Damned. "Raw energy! Chaos! Subversion! And that whole 'let's take things on and have a go' attitude. All these things really appealed in the drab old fag end of the plodding rock world of music at that time.

"Especially the Damned. They really had all the same frantic, chaotic assault as the MC5. Their sheer sonic attack was palpable, and it left you reeling. Fueled on cider and sulphate, and touched with an early Who-like madness and a real ability to play."

The Damned played for forty minutes, long enough to drive through nine of the songs Brian James was now writing from his flat in Birchington Road, just around the corner from the Maniacs' home-base. "Fan Club," built around a guitar line that would defy anyone to claim that these Punks couldn't play; "New Rose," clattering in on a cowbell straight out of "Honky Tonk Woman," but already fully formed and fabulous; "Feel the Pain," "1 of the 2," "I Fall."

A handful of cover versions were woven in around them: the Stooges' "1970" rechristened "I Feel Alright" from the only words in the song that most onlookers would know; an old Who B-side called "Circles," banged out with enough scratchy finesse that it could almost have been an original; and a delirious *Death Race 2000* remix of "Help," pounded through in such stark tribute to the Ramones that it wound up sounding nothing like them. Then it all wrapped up with "So Messed Up," living up to its title with such glorious dishevelment that, for a moment, the audience just stood and stared. But at last the applause got started, and the Pistols needed to be *really* hot that night to survive the inevitable comparisons.

The Damned always knew that they were going to be bagged up with the Pistols, once the media cottoned to them. "That's just the way the music press works," Brian James shrugged. Both visually and stylistically, however, the two bands were poles apart. You knew that the moment vocalist Dave Letts, now resplendent beneath his new name, Dave Vanian, appeared on stage. He was dressed as a vampire.

Hindsight kicks in. Big deal, people have been dressing like that for years. Haven't you ever been to a Cure concert?

Yes, but why do they dress like that? Well, these days it's because they've read too much Anne Rice. Back then it was because they'd seen Dave Vanian. There were a lot of different looks going around in the mid-1970s, but most of them were based around David Bowie's castoffs. Vanian, on the other hand, could have slipped into the Doctors of Madness with ease, so unique was his look, and so dedicatedly did he wear it. In fact, he eventually did join the Doctors, right before they passed away in 1978, and shortly after the Damned broke up for the first time, and that was truly a sight to behold, the Vanian vampire stalking the stage while bassist Stoner stomped in full Frankensteinian drag, and "Kid Strange" hovered on metaphorical bat wings . . . the Doctors were a horror show, the best theater that rock had seen in years, but the young Dave Vanian rode a very close runner-up.

"Dave's whole thing right from day one had been that he was some kind of a vampire bloke," explained Chris Miller, or Rat Scabies as he now was known. "The thing was, he was always like that, it wasn't something he put on just before he went onstage, it was the way he was when he got up in the morning, went to bed, working on the car. He was fairly committed to that look, that was why he was the cool guy to pick up on, and that's why we stuck with him, because everyone would say, 'Ah, look at him, he's funny,' but he really wasn't, he was probably the most genuine person I'd ever met, he really is a fucking fruitcake. Plus, he was a pretty good looking guy, he was pretty hot property."

Then there was Ray Burns, a blur of manic color and fuzz, hamming it up on the bass guitar that he seemed to be treating as the lead. A ritual at those early Damned shows revolved around Scabies leading the audience in a raucous chant of "the bassist's a wanker," and Burns would pirouette gleefully around the stage, already developing the persona that would soon see him renamed Captain Sensible, before Scabies took his own moment in the sun and began disemboweling his drum kit.

Add Brian James, an unholy collision between archetypal rocker and antisocial street urchin, who just happened to be the sharpest guitarist I'd heard onstage all year, and you had the Damned. Four distinct images, four distinct personalities. Taking the stage in their wake, and with Rotten alone having cultivated a "look," the Pistols resembled a bunch of plumbers.

Looks could be deceiving, though, and Alan Lee Shaw and Rod Latter were sufficiently impressed by the headliners that whatever else they'd had planned for the following day, they put it on hold. Instead they caught a bus down to World's End, sought out the Sex shop, and marched on in. Then they stopped stock-still and just stared. "It was like this is what we wanted, but thought would never happen."

Dumbstruck, Shaw and Latter wandered around the shop with their mouths hanging open. Echoing the observation made by many of the store's passing customers (at least, those without a trust fund to finance their wardrobe), Shaw noted that "it was very pricey and a bit too *über*-fashion statement for me." But "it was a cool place nonetheless." Finally, Latter picked up the pair of leather pants that would wind up physically rotting on his person, so often did he wear them, and the pair walked up to the counter.

Waiting to take their money, a vision named Jordan, breathtakingly bizarre with her teetering hair and electric-shock makeup, eyed them disinterestedly, and didn't even blink when Shaw asked for McLaren's telephone number. Neither did McLaren seem surprised when Shaw called him later that afternoon. He was hearing from a lot of bands (or would-be bands, or soon-to-be bands) these days, and Shaw was given the same response as all those others. "Call me when you're playing next, and I'll try to come down."

Shaw never made the call. For all the Maniacs' madness and for all their seat-of-your-pants edginess, in his mind the Maniacs were just too subtle, and not sufficiently thought-through enough to make an impression on McLaren. They made a noise, but not enough. True, Latter was gradually adding to his drum setup, and that made a considerable difference to their onstage volume. But Shaw was adamant: "It was as a band that our future lay. I didn't think we would impress as a duo. We needed to be a band!"

8

School's Out Forever!

LATE JULY 1976

If you weren't in London, you wanted to be, and once you got there, you wondered how you'd ever survived without it. "You could see live bands every night," my friend James Stevenson reflected. Where he grew up in Chiswick, there were several pubs that had live music all the time, "and I used to go and watch and learn. The John Bull in Chiswick High Road, the Cross Keys in Hammersmith; further afield, there was the Kensington and, of course, the Greyhound, which is where I went most. And the Nashville. I saw all the Pub Rock groups of the 75/76 period. Ducks Deluxe, Plummet Airlines, Kilburn and the High Roads, Hatfield and the North. Loads of them."

Imagine having all that on your doorstep. Permanently.

I didn't need to imagine; school holidays and the occasional weekender had already filled my head with the limitless vistas that would open to me once I escaped full-time education, and on July 23, I made my move. Bidding farewell to classmates with whom I'd spent the past five years, only a little bemused by the knowledge that I'd probably never see any of them again, I packed my bags for the very last time and took the train "home." Then, according to my diary, I headed out to the Marquee to see a band called FBI, establishing a gig-going pattern that would not only dominate my life for the next three or four years, but came to rule a lot of other people's. Including some who were even less familiar with the city, and all it had to offer, than I.

By mid-summer, Danny Kustow was traveling down as often as he could and, every time he visited the city, "it was like I'd died and gone to heaven," because every time, he'd hear another whisper about the groups that were suddenly appearing, and news about those that were still to come.

"I felt something big was happening in London, I felt a weird buzz and excitement, and a sort of funny premonition that I was going to be part of something big, and that something so powerful, pertinent, vital, and world changing was about to happen. I just felt my time was coming soon, that I had something huge to say, that I wanted to play my version of exciting rock 'n' roll.

"It felt like my whole generation were revolting, like we had had enough. It was 'our time' now, so move over all you boring fuckers. It was DIY. Anyone could pick up a guitar and write a song, we didn't have to be good musicians, or technically brilliant, it was as if we were all part of this shockingly sexy, naughty, anything-goes new society."

Tim Smith, too, felt his senses reeling as he stepped off the train at Paddington and saw London unfolding before him.

His first few visits cast him as a tourist as much as anything else, visiting friends and then scouring the gig guide in search of the next evening's entertainment. He didn't always choose correctly; not every band he saw was completely overwhelming. But even the bad ones were certainly different from anything he'd seen in Devon. Then, armed with his impressions of another crop of musical hopefuls, it would be back to Gaye Black and Exeter to continue their relentless plotting. "It was an exciting moment in your life. We *were* going to move to London, we *were* going to form a band, we *weren't* going to work in any more crappy jobs."

Finding a flat when you live two hundred miles away is not easy, of course. As often as they could afford the train fare, Smith and

Black would head up to London for the weekend to stay with friends, look through the classified ads in the papers and tour the letting agencies. Finally they found a place, a one-room attic flat on Agate Road, Hammersmith, a few corners away from the main thoroughfare, Goldhawk Road. They moved their belongings up by train and then walked them through the streets to their new home.

It was scarcely a palace. They were offered the flat on what was termed a holiday lease, a legal loophole that allowed landlords to circumvent the protections woven into the housing laws and evict their tenants whenever they wanted to. Not that too many people would have been queuing up to take over the tenancy, even with the housing situation as bad as it was. At the height of that summer, when the pair moved in, the room rarely sweltered at anything less than a hundred degrees.

By winter, on the other hand, the water would be freezing in the utility sink. Rain dripped down through the light bulb, the bathroom was shared with the house's other tenants, and their most regular visitors were the gas board, who would come round to affix a condemned sticker to the dilapidated old gas meter. The entire household would then have to wait for the landlady to come round and turn it on again. One year, they had to go an entire summer without a hot bath.

First impressions of London were chaotic. Smith grew up in a village with just 2,000 inhabitants, and now he was seeing that many people at a single gig. "Life was overwhelming and London even more so, but I found it less unsettling to come and live there, than I did when I was visiting, because I was there for a reason and I never forgot that. Gaye and I were this unit and we had this us-against-the-world mentality that does see you through unsettling times. Because it was unsettling."

Occasionally, he would grab his acoustic guitar and head out to the subways that littered King Street in Hammersmith, busking to the commuters as they rushed for their tube trains. "I'd be singing 'there's a killer in yer subway' ["Bombsite Boy"]. People didn't give me much money." He did get some advice, though, from the policeman who suggested he use the money he raised to purchase some singing lessons. Smith looked into the guitar case where passers-by tossed their offerings. He had earned 10p.

Evenings were spent at gigs, or going over the songs that Smith was now furiously writing. From the outset, there was no question that Smith would be the sole songwriter; Black confessed to having written one song, or at least part of one, but that was the limit of her ambitions in that direction. "I was working in this horrible, revolting factory [and] they had this sign on the wall saying 'draw to your attention that we've got mice here and we have got rat inspectors . . .' and I thought up this song, 'look after all the rats and strangle all the fucking cats.' That's the first part. So I thought I'd better shut my mouth."

There was some debate over what they should call themselves once their band came together. For a while, One Chord Wonders led the pack, after one of the earliest songs Smith had written, the story of an imaginary group whose musical limitations were reflected in their name but believed they had something to say regardless. It was never intended as autobiography, but Smith suspected it might become one anyway. It was back to the nomenclatural drawing board.

He hatched the Adverts as a band name around the same time as he settled upon a stage name for himself. Smith was the ubiquitous surname in the land; the TV that beamed the ads into your home was the most common piece of electronic furniture in the country. TV Smith was born.

All this time, the pair was watching as new acts burst into view, or catching up on the ones they'd missed out on so far. The first gig they ever attended as Londoners was the Stranglers at the Nashville, a few streets away on the North End Road. If they walked there, which they usually did, they'd have the money for a beer or two.

Gaye Advert during rehearsal. *Courtesy of Gaye Advert*

Throughout that long summer, every Tuesday until the end of August, the Stranglers ruled the Nashville, transforming themselves beyond all recognition as they did so. Or maybe my ears had just grown accustomed to what would be thrown at them. They were playing faster, sharper, more aggressively. Songs no longer rolled in on a wave of somber organ, before the rest of the band plodded in to pound everyone into a state of submission. They had intros and outros, while exuding the same kind of menace that you normally associated with a bar full of Hell's Angels. They were good, and they knew it.

"A lot of people knocked the Stranglers for not being punk, or not having the songs," TV Smith marveled. "But they were killer. The energy, the stage presence, fantastic stuff." They also became friends and grew so accustomed to seeing Gaye and TV at their shows, talking about the still theoretical Adverts, that they started adding them to the guest list. And when they realized that none of them knew Black's real name, they gave her one of their own. She was now, and would remain, Gaye Advert.

The ringleader of the Stranglers fan club, self-appointed but big enough to make sure that no one would challenge him, was Dagenham Dave. He was a Manchester lad, but had moved south, to Cock Sparrer territory, long enough ago that his native accent had already been deadened a little; it was Hugh Cornwell who rechristened him, and the Stranglers loved the guy. Other people, though, considered him a character to avoid . . . precisely the kind, in fact, that the Stranglers' reputation had warned about all along.

Sober he was fine, friendly and polite. But drunk—and he got drunk a lot—he could pick a fight in an empty room, and he could usually count on winning. Especially when the Stranglers' honor was at stake.

There were moments when he believed in the band more than they did. When the Arista label's interest cooled, it was Dagenham Dave who talked the Stranglers through the doubts, then talked them through all their other problems, too: their falling out with the Pistols, and the fact that a lot of kids were following the McLaren lead in dismissing them; the media's continued refusal to give the Stranglers space, when it seemed that any halfwit with a guitar and a snarl was now guaranteed a review in one of the papers. He talked them through a lot, and he fought their corner like a champ. All through the summer, through every stinking gig in every three-quarters empty club, Dave had been there for them, cheering his heart out even when everyone else in the room was either booing or silent.

He loved the group to distraction and beyond. He was smart, and he had an eye for details that most people weren't even aware existed. Generous, too. At a time when the Stranglers were barely earning £30 a night, he would treat them to meals before and after shows. He made sure they never lacked a bed to sleep in either; he and his girlfriend Brenda lived in a hotel in Sussex Gardens, in Bayswater, and if a band member was ever stuck for a place to crash, Dave would come to the rescue. The rest of the audience could hate their guts, but Dagenham Dave would always be there for them—at least until he wasn't.

In many ways, he reminded me of Sid Vicious, a nice guy who couldn't distinguish the person he was from the world in which he was suddenly living. I would never have said we were friends; for a start, I still wasn't wholly convinced by the Stranglers, and mainly went along to keep one of my friends company. But Dave spent as much time scrutinizing the audience as he did watching the Stranglers, and I suppose he just started to recognize me. Or my trousers. Those electric blue satin flares hung around for a long time.

Just like Sid, sometimes he'd be fine, a friendly nod, a few words exchanged before the band went on. Other times, though, when there was a crowd around, or when he thought he had a point to make, the best you'd get would be a flicker of a smile and a moment's recognition, before the public persona reasserted itself with a scornfully bellowed "Whatcha lookin' at, yer cunt?" Then his friends would smile, and I'd go on my way thinking "cunt yerself," because we were all too young to understand what was really happening, and too innocent to see how the story might end.

Sid wound up cold and dead in a New York hotel room, with an armful of smack and a murder charge hanging over his head; Dave ended his days stuck in the mud at the bottom of the River Thames, after throwing himself off Tower Bridge, the final act in a tragedy that went something like this.

Dave would have given anything to see the Stranglers make it big. But they needed to do so on his terms. As soon as other people, other influences, started to step into their lives, his relationship with the band changed.

The Stranglers were becoming popular. Their repertoire had set-tled down, rooting out the slower, softer songs, and going hell for leather with the aggressive grind. "Ugly," "London Lady," "Down in the Sewer," "Bitchin'," "Grip." Audiences began to respond not with rage and insults but applause and adoration. Suddenly, Dave wasn't the only person rooting for them when they went out to play, and he didn't like that.

It was the arrival of the Finchley Freds on the scene that proved the final straw, a gaggle of rough and rabid followers whom the Stranglers picked up when they played the Torrington pub one night that fall, and who quickly became as familiar a sight at the shows as Dave.

Dave hated them. Yeah, they were fans, but that's all they were, just a bunch of chancers who latched on to the Stranglers because they could see that their star was rising. Where were they when entire pubs full of strangers turned their backs on the stage, and walked out of the room? Where were they when the beer glasses flew and the microphones went flying?

There were a few weeks where a Stranglers gig seemed somehow incomplete if you didn't, at some point, catch sight of Dave furiously eyeballing one Fred or another, and numbers never phased him. Nei-ther did the growing perception that the Stranglers themselves seemed to be treating him with a little more scorn than they used to, laughing when somebody put him down, or making remarks that they knew would annoy him. The bigger the Stranglers became, the more insecure Dave felt. Finally, on the last day of November, he snapped.

The Stranglers were headlining the 100 Club and the Finchley Freds had descended *en masse*. They were loud, they were boister-ous, they were shouting for songs, talking with the musicians, show-ing off their familiarity for the rest of the crowd.

Too much familiarity. Dave was completely loaded that night, out of his skull on an incapacitating cocktail of dope and Special

Brew. Suddenly, he launched himself into the crowd. One, two, three . . . he was fighting seven of them at once, and the Freds weren't exactly saplings themselves. It was an absolute bloodbath. From the stage, the Stranglers could only watch in horror; in the audience, Malcolm McLaren stared aghast. This wasn't an act, and this wasn't part of the show.

For all his past differences with the Stranglers, McLaren had been friends with their manager for a long time, and was considering offering the band some gigs with the Sex Pistols. He changed his mind somewhere between Dave's wading into a phalanx of Freds, and his being carried out again, with two cracked ribs and a chipped bone in his face.

Dave went downhill fast from there. He remained part of the Stranglers' inner sanctum, but that had grown so large that what was it really worth? The band visited him when he came out of the hospital, and he celebrated with them when United Artists signed them. His voice was loud on the Nashville gig that UA taped with an eye toward releasing it as the Stranglers' first album; and, when the tapes were rejected as too rough for public consumption, Dave was given an open invitation to drop by the studio where they had now become ensconced. Arguing with producer Martin Rushent over the way the record should sound, and even returning after he was banned from the building, for a while he was his old self again.

But his girlfriend, Brenda, left him, and the Stranglers still seemed distant. So, on February 9, 1977, drunk again, he took himself down to Tower Bridge, and threw himself into the Thames. Apparently, his body was stuck in the mud for a couple of weeks before it was finally discovered. A few weeks after that, a new song turned up in the Stranglers' repertoire. It was called "Dagenham Dave." Magnanimous in victory, the Finchley Freds, or the Finchley *Boys* as they now preferred to be known, never failed to give it a rousing reception.

*　　*　　*

July 23, 1976. School was out. Now what? I was reasonably confident that I'd be walking away with at least five of the six O-Levels I'd sat. (Metalwork was the exception, but with no plans to make my career in spot welding, I didn't lose too much sleep over it.) The results would not be delivered for at least another month, so there really was no sense in trying to pick up a job until then. Not, I had already convinced myself, that there would be much point in looking even afterward.

Unemployment was murderous that summer of 1976, topping a million for the first time since the outbreak of World War Two. News reports talked of school-leavers being flung onto the scrap heap before they'd even been offered the chance to show what they could do. Sixteen- and seventeen-year-olds queuing outside the so-euphemistically named job centers in the hope that they might be the lucky one who was invited to sweep a warehouse floor. College and university graduates lying about their qualifications—*Who me? Nah, never took an exam in me life, guv*—in the hope of appearing thick enough to land a job flipping burgers. But there weren't many of those around, either. In the days before a McDonald's or Wendy's sprouted up on every street corner, the fast food industry in England amounted to a handful of Wimpey Bars, and they could scarcely dent the statistics.

So I did what every other school-leaver was doing: put on my best clothes, combed my hair, and headed down to my neighborhood Labour Exchange, to sign on the dotted line, pledge to seek work in any shape or form, and then sit back to await my twice-monthly benefit payment. "Young and broke and on the dole." It quickly turned into the ubiquitous cliché of the age, but it was no less the real for that.

"One of my first memories of London in early 1976 was catching the number six bus from Kilburn Lane to Lisson Grove Labour Exchange in Marylebone, to sign on the dole." It was the first thing Alan Lee Shaw did after he moved to London, the first thing I did, the first thing TV Smith did, the first thing Danny Kustow did. And so long were the lines and downcast the faces that it was hard to imagine that you'd ever stop doing it; that your entire life could ever break away from the semimonthly ritual of shuffling down the queue in order to place your signature on the dotted line, alongside a pledge that we all still remember, more than thirty years later. *There has been no change in my circumstances since I last claimed at this office.*

What did I get in return for submitting to this routine? A sixteen-year-old school-leaver received an unemployment check (a Giro, for the Girobank system through which benefits were paid) of £6 a week. That, it was decreed, was sufficient not only to keep body, mind, and soul together, but also to meet all those other expenses that the last decade's worth of schooling had somehow forgotten to mention would now be invoked.

The fact that I could no longer travel half-fare on buses and trains. The fact that my stepparents suddenly started demanding that I chip in for the household expenses. The fact that even looking for a job usually meant standing in a phone box with a pile of loose change . . . loose change that I could scarcely afford . . . making call upon call upon call, only to be told that the vacancy had gone. The fact that admission to soccer matches had doubled overnight.

Things would get worse. Travel forward another three or four years, and the dark days of 1976 would seem glorious by compari-son; by 1982, unemployment had all but doubled. And in March 2001, a *Daily Telegraph* headline would celebrate a recent decline in the statistics with the words "Unemployment Rate Hits Level of 1976," without even pausing to remember just how dire that rate felt at the time. So yes, things would get worse.

The difference was, in 1976, it was a new sensation, and nobody knew how to react. By 1982, it was just the same old same-old, and it barely even made the news any longer. But there's another thing to remember. By 1982, youth culture—the section of the population that remained hardest hit by the deprivations of the day—had long since come to terms with its lot. In 1976, the situation that most kids found themselves in was not merely without precedent, it seemed to be without remedy as well.

Exactly forty years before, faced with a similar collapse in work and opportunity, 207 men from the northeastern city of Jarrow marched the three hundred miles to London to protest their lot—the Jarrow Crusade bore with it a petition of over twelve thousand signatures, all demanding that the government of the day do something to alleviate the suffering. They reached Downing Street, home to the prime minister, on October 31, one month after setting out. The prime minister, Stanley Baldwin, refused to even meet with them. He was, he said, too busy.

Nothing had changed. James Callaghan, prime minister since the resignation of the elected Harold Wilson in March 1976, apparently had little interest in the state of the country's youth; he was, in any case, embroiled in a humiliating struggle to convince the International Monetary Fund and sundry other world banking organizations to bail the country out of the financial black hole it had spent all decade digging itself into, while the pound went into freefall, crime and homelessness rocketed, and the trade unions bunkered in for all-out war.

I was lucky. At least I did have a roof above my head, and a dole check to fall back upon. Other people didn't. Homelessness was endemic, squatting—taking illegal possession of a vacant or derelict house, and trying to turn it into some sort of home—was rife; and if the law tended to turn a blind eye to most established communities, particularly those in the poorer parts of the city, it also turned a blind eye to whatever the property's owner might do to reclaim his land.

Football hooliganism was at its violent peak, and entire neighborhoods became no-go areas as rival armies of supporters converged on one another. Some were more notorious than others; Tottenham Hotspur, just up the road from where I lived, were relatively innocuous, the bulk of their supporters more of an irritant than a threat. But still the local High Road could be transformed into a war zone on the occasions when a more volatile crowd descended—fellow Londoners Arsenal and West Ham, northerners Leeds and Manchester United—and pitched battles had been known to extend from the border with Edmonton, a mile to the north, to the Seven Sisters Road, close to two miles south.

But football hooligans weren't the only murderous miscreants who flourished amid the crumbling remains of the city, lurking in the alleyways where the streetlights had all burned out, or hanging out among the bombsites that still recalled the war, and which were only gradually beginning to be reclaimed. Some regions collapsed into violence because there was nothing else to do. "Old ladies are being mugged on their way to church and that's a shame," the Stranglers' Hugh Cornwell understated during an interview with *Record Mirror*. He didn't mean to sound so lackadaisical about it, but sometimes it was difficult not to. Unless a beating was especially heinous, and there were some good black eyes to show for it, it barely merited a mention in the local paper.

"It's England, isn't it?" shrugged Rat Scabies. "In England, they fight to entertain themselves. The band's boring, let's have a fight instead. Drink too much beer, go outside, be obnoxious, and start a fight. That's what they've been doing for hundreds of years." Fight, or attack, or mug or whatever. It was *years* since the first skinhead gangs marched around the streets chanting "Someone's gonna get their head kicked in tonight," but their younger brothers and sisters had learned the same words, and they believed it was their birthright to keep up the family tradition. Once again, the police usually let them get on with it.

It could have been worse. The firemen could have gone on strike, as they did the following autumn, and the parched, drought-dried tinderbox would truly have exploded. Or the dustmen could have downed tools for a few weeks, as they would the year after that, and you could have gassed the dole queues from the stench alone. But, again, "worse" is a subjective theme. Neither of those events had taken place; neither entered into anyone's equation. Things already seemed to have hit rock bottom. And the relentless sunshine just illuminated that.

In months to come, and for years thereafter, it would become extraordinarily fashionable to claim that this nightmarish confluence of social collapses spawned what we now know as punk rock. Particularly among journalists. The musicians themselves rarely talked, or even thought, in such terms; at best, they were reflecting what they saw taking place around themselves, but isn't that the function of any remotely aware artist? There was certainly no mass consciousness coalescing to protest the manifold injustices of the day, no grimly tenacious master plan to bind together the forces of change.

Even the songs that we now regard as biblical testimony of some vast political awareness—the Sex Pistols' "Anarchy in the UK," the Adverts' "Bored Teenagers," and the Clash's "1977" among them— were conceived as observation, not prophecy, and they certainly were never intended as polemic; that *would* come later, as other writers seized upon the notions they derived from the music papers, and purposefully set out to dramatize the national crisis. Right now, it was enough to simply document one's own world, and if you sensed it disintegrating, then that was what you wrote.

Composing the "Great British Mistake," one of the earliest songs he wrote for the Adverts, TV Smith mused, "I think, as a teenager, you grow up excited about change and moving forward, but you see a world, or at least a country, around you that refuses to change. That was more or less the starting point for the song"—a song the bitter disillusion of which might as well have been adopted as a national anthem for our entire generation.

> *The great British mistake was looking for a way out*
> *Was getting complacent, not noticing*
> *The pulse was racing, the mistake was fighting*
> *The change, was staying the same*

It couldn't adapt so it couldn't survive
Something had to give, the people
Take a downhill slide into the gloom
Into the dark recesses of their minds . . .

"Great British Mistake"

BORED TEENAGERS.

We've talking into corners
Finding ways to fill the vacuum
And though our mouths are dry
We talk in hope to hit on something new

Tied to the railway tracks — it's one way to revive
But no way to relax.

We're just bored teenagers
Looking for love, or should I say emotional rages
Bored Teenagers
Seeing ourselves as strangers

We talk about the whys and wherefores
Do we really care at all?
Talk about the frailty of words
Is rarely meaningful

When we're sitting watching the 'planes
Burn up through the night like meteorites

We're just bored teenagers
Bored out of our heads, bored out of our minds.

TV Smith's handwritten lyrics to "Bored Teenagers," destined to
become one of the anthemic rally calls of the entire era. *Author's
collection*

At the same time, however, the raw material for a universal call to arms was certainly in place, within the seething mass of disaffection and frustration that would ultimately find its voice in the stumblings of a new generation of teenaged musicians. Everywhere you went, you heard the same thing, the belief, as Hugh Cornwell murmured darkly, that "a lot of very intelligent people around today are getting fed up. Something's going to happen soon."

Right now, though, those musicians had no more idea of what they were fermenting than the people who were watching them, or even the people who were purportedly managing them.

An earlier generation, burned by the burnout of 1960s idealism, may have dreamed that someone, somewhere, could rekindle the flames that had long since been extinguished, but so what? Rock and truly radical political expression have seldom made comfortable bedfellows, and those performers that broke the mold in the 1970s—people like Mick Farren's Deviants, Hawkwind, and the Pink Fairies—did so from so far below the commercial radar that, even when success did come calling (as when the Hawks scored a UK number two with "Silver Machine" in 1972), it was the idealists who were corrupted first, not the idolizers.

Again, for anybody looking to draw conclusions from the events that did ultimately cause 1976 to shape the landscape of the decades to come, it is only the sweet fortunes of hindsight that allow even a vague hypothesis to take shape. For the people on the ground, in the frontline, at the sticky end of the pointed stick, 1976 was the same as 1975 was the same as 1974 was the same as 1973 and so on ad infinitum.

There were still no more than three channels on the telly; the programming still ended around midnight with the rousing chords of the national anthem. Some shows were still being broadcast in black and white. The pubs closed at eleven, public transport all but closed down at midnight—there was a handful of night buses in London, but the scheduled timetable was optimistic to say the least, just as there was a handful of late-night drinking holes, for people with the money and the connections to get in.

Comparisons to the world of today, with all its conveniences and extravagances, are meaningless. Hindsight might view the mid-1970s through a monochrome lens, but life was *not* gray, it was *not* flat, and it was *not* grim. A lot of people had a lot of fun in the 1970s, just as they'd had fun in all the decades that preceded them. The big difference between "then" and "now" was that people were making their own fun then, as opposed to waiting for some multimedia conglomerate to package it up and deliver it to their door. Because if they didn't, they would probably go insane.

Or even turn into their parents.

9

Snuffin' ina Babylon

AUGUST 1976

SOUNDTRACK

"Babylon Burning"	L.A.D. (Love)
"Between the Lines"	Pink Fairies (Stiff)
"Bur O Boy"	Junior Byles (Ethnic Fight)
"Country Style"	Dillinger (Jay Wax)
"Final Solution"	Pere Ubu (Heathen)
"Keep It Outta Sight"	Nick Lowe (Dynamite)
"Leftist"	Revolutionaries (Disco Mix)
"Little Johnny Jewel"	Television (Ork)
Live at the Marquee EP	Eddie and the Hot Rods (Island)
"Love Jah & Live"	Jah Woosh (Kiss)
"MPLA"	Tappa Zukie (Klik)
"Natty Pass Through Rome"	Prince Jazzbo (Black Art)
"One Step Forward"	Max Romeo (Island)
"Self Defence"	Dr. Alimantado (Ital)
"Sufferers Time"	Heptones (Black Art)
"Ten Against One"	Big Youth (Negusa Negast)
"Train Train"	Count Bishops (Chiswick)
"Whip Them Jah"	Dennis Brown (Flames)

Basking in the relentless heat, the sound systems had been pumping all year. From tip to toe of the Portobello Road, the gaily colored ribbon of market traders and antique stores that links Ladbroke Grove to Notting Hill, their insistent offbeat hung heavy in the air, rising above the babble of Jamaican patois and West London slang, blending with the traffic on the Westway overpass to create a sound that was the area's very own.

The summer cooked on. There was rain in the forecast for most days now, but still old people were dying in their homes from heatstroke and thirst, and young people were fighting in the streets from boredom and bad temper. But if you listened really closely, the word was that things were only going to get harder. For next year was 1977, the year when the two sevens clashed; and, according to one of Rastafarian figurehead Marcus Garvey's more apocalyptic prophecies, that was not likely to be a good thing.

Not that anybody seemed certain precisely what it portended. Back home in Jamaica, one interpretation dourly insisted that the day the two sevens clashed (July 7, 1977—which was actually four sevens, but no matter), the mere hardships with which so many people lived would give way to general doom and destruction. But another believed Garvey was anticipating the day that the black man would throw off all the shackles of his past, and a third hopefully suggested that if black people could survive the 1970s, they could survive anything.

Such uncertainty did not dull the fear, however, and when Jamaican singer Joseph Hill chose the prophecy to title the debut album by his group Culture, the foreboding spread even further to become a promise of unrelenting Armageddon that gripped Britain's West Indian population as fervently, and fearfully, as it did Jamaica's.

Jamaica was still staggering through the firestorms of the 1976 election campaign, the most violent explosion of civil unrest in the island's history, and reggae music—the voice of the people—had been growing correspondingly militant amid the flames that lit up the streets. Once, the average Briton considered reggae to be the

It had probably been five years since anybody last saw skinheads roaming the streets of England. Then reggae star Judge Dread (right) released this album, and suddenly the little sods were everywhere again. Seems he wasn't the last of them after all. *Author's collection*

property of such lewd lyricists as Lloyd Charmers and Judge Dread (a white Englishman, but still the biggest-selling reggae artist in the country), with their raunchy rhymes and knuckle-close humor. Or else it was the slow-dancing swing of John Holt and Ken Boothe, both of whom had scored British number ones over the last couple of years with sweetly rhythmic ballads that even your granny could love. That sort of song was still out there, of course. But it had been joined by a louder voice, a more strident cry.

Reggae in 1976 was Max Romeo demanding "One Step Forward" before declaring "War ina Babylon," it was Dennis Brown begging "Whip Them Jah Jah," Johnny Clarke proclaiming his "African Roots," Junior Murvin lining up "Police and Thieves." And across Britain, where the immigrant Jamaican community found its focal points in the underprivileged underbellies of the country's biggest cities, those same principles of righteous rebellion would inevitably get drawn into the stew. Babylon must burn.

It wasn't only the Jamaicans who felt this way. Reggae first infiltrated the British music scene in the early 1960s, when the Mods of Carnaby Street fame danced to the imported sounds of Laurel Aitkin, Derrick Morgan, Prince Buster, and the Skatalites. It grew from there. An entire generation of white Britons coming of age in 1976 had been raised on the sounds of Desmond Dekker, Dave and Ansell Collins, Bob and Marcia, and producer Lee Perry's Upsetters; had spent its pocket money on the supremely budget-priced series of *Tighten Up* compilations; had all learned to dance the Moonstomp and do the Reggay. By the time Bob Marley made it over in 1975, to be anointed King of Reggae by a spellbound English press, he already had a constituency larger than a lot of British bands could ever dream of attracting, and a royal court that spread far beyond the handful of other artists namechecked in the papers.

Barry Biggs, Big Youth, Jah Whoosh, Junior Byles, Keith Hudson, Augustus Pablo, King Tubby—many of the names that dominated the weekly chart published in London's *Black Echoes* magazine were the same as those championed in the dance halls of their homeland. And then there was Tappa Zukie.

Zukie was all but unknown in Jamaica when the Klik label picked up his *Man Ah Warrior* album and gave Britain one of the most memorable records of the age. The tracks on that record were almost three years old at the time—Zukie recorded them on his first visit to London in 1973, and had long since returned to Kingston. Now he was back, and the title track from his latest album, *MPLA*, was looming over the sweltering summer like a premonition that knew it was about to come true.

"MPLA" was an enormous seller, effortlessly crossing from Jamaican roots to Anglo white markets even before Patti Smith brought Zukie up onstage with her at the Hammersmith Odeon in late October. On a *Black Echoes* reggae chart that already abounded with heavy-duty Sufferers' tunes—Junior Murvin's "Police and Thieves" was number one, while Derrick Morgan's "Under Heavy Manners" and Prince Far I's "Zion Call" were close behind— "MPLA" thundered and rumbled past all of them.

But Britain was producing its own superstars as well, led off by Dennis "Blackbeard" Bovell's Matumbi, one of the very first British reggae concerns to truly grasp a local identity and, in so doing, give voice to an audience that had hitherto remained utterly disenfranchised: black Jamaicans who were born in Britain. In the past, British reggae bands were playing Jamaican music in a British society. Now they were playing British reggae.

Matumbi formed in 1971 as a backing group for singer Tex Dixon, but quickly became the accompaniment of choice for any number of visiting Jamaican performers.

A couple of years spent with the then-dominant Trojan label served them poorly, however, while there was further disruption when Bovell was jailed on that most ambiguous of charges, "incitement to cause affray."

His actual crime was to be present at the Carib Club on Cricklewood Broadway the night Sir Lord Koos and the Sufferers' Hi-Fi launched a sound clash. Twelve people—quickly dubbed the Carib Twelve—were arrested, and many more beaten when the police launched an unprovoked raid on the club; described as a ringleader, Bovell was hit with three years in jail, and served six months before the sentence was overturned.

Released, Bovell immediately led Matumbi into a new mood. Their next release, the sweetly swaying lover's rock of "After Tonight," became the biggest-selling British reggae single of 1976. Further hits followed, and fresh bands arose in Matumbi's revitalized wake.

North Londoners Black Slate broke out with "Sticksman," a seething masterpiece that took its title from the patois term for a pickpocket. Reggae Regular and Misty in Roots emerged from South and West London respectively. Steel Pulse, Gladwyn Wright, and Tabby Cat Kelly took the top three places at a talent contest on Birmingham's Soho Road; first prize was a single's worth of studio time with Dennis Bovell, utilized by the victorious Steel Pulse to cut the classic "Nyah Love."

And poet Linton Kwesi Johnson burst through with a succession of commentaries that were ultimately destined to rewrite the cultural and political map but, for now, were simply guaranteed to agitate an already volatile ferment.

The first journalist to commit the local London-Jamaican patois to print, Johnson was long accustomed to giving readings at parties, meetings, and rallies. Beginning in late 1976, he moved onto a wider stage, assembling a backing band and performing his poetry to music.

The top end of Portobello Road was the best place to go to hear all of these emergent sounds. Market stall after stall creaked beneath the weight of so much vinyl, and rattled to the incessant boom of the music.

On any given day, you might spot Paul Simenon of the Heart-drops—or the Clash, as they'd just been renamed—thumbing through the racks for something else to play his bandmates, as he worked to convert them to the music he loved. Johnny Rotten was a pussycat when the conversation turned to his favorite dub albums. Bassist Tony James and a former male model named Gene October, as they pieced together a new band called Chelsea, were usually around. Arianna Foster, fourteen years old, but already planning to rope three of her friends into an all-girl quartet called the Slits. TV Smith. All listened and learned from the reggae on the street, all comprehended how it allied with their own musical ambitions.

For each of them, and for many others as well, *Two Sevens Clash* was not a warning. It was a manifesto. And it was to be given its first public reading on the opening night of the annual Reading Rock Festival.

Headlining the evening were performances by Gong, Anglo-French psychedelic jazzers who'd cornered the market in whacked-out eccentricity by presenting three successive concept albums peopled by flying teapots and pothead pixies, and Mallard, an introspective jam conglomerate that effectively presented Captain Beefheart's Magic Band shorn of Captain Beefheart. There was also room for Supercharge, a permanent fixture on the pub circuit for the last year or so, who combined tedious funk with an almost Pythonesque grasp of musical humor. Their showstopper, the doo-wop drama of "She Moved the Dishes First," discussed the niceties of pissing in the kitchen sink (among other things), and it was worth sitting through any number of their other songs just to revel in the delights of their comedy routines.

But the meat of the evening would be appearances by three visiting Jamaican superstars: Sly and Robbie's band, the Revolutionaries; toaster U-Roy; and the harmonic Mighty Diamonds, all merging with the English heat to bring a little taste of Kingston to the outskirts of suburbia.

No matter how many white kids actively enjoyed it, reggae was very much a minority interest among rock audiences at that time, and white rockers were what Reading was all about. I'd only ever owned a dozen or so reggae albums my whole life, and already I'd lost count of the number of times a friend had dropped by and flicked through my record collection, paused at my stash of Prince Buster, Peter Tosh, and the *Tighten Up* collections, and asked what the fuck I was doing listening to that shit?

There was one guy I knew who shared in my secret, a weasel-like fellow named Jake, who had a table selling bootleg cassette tapes at Camden Market. I started out as a customer, but we quickly hit it off—it was Jake who taped Patti's Paris show for me—and, although our musical tastes didn't dovetail too frequently, his knowledge and love of reggae was something I could always bank on. Plus, he had transport, a battered old Ford Zephyr, so when he asked whether I needed a lift to the festival, I said yes even before I bought a first-day ticket.

And I forgot my Wellington boots.

There was mud everywhere, mud as far as the eye could see, and I couldn't even imagine where it all came from. Everywhere else, the country continued parched beneath the hottest summer and longest drought on record. Kew Gardens was dying, for fuck's sake, for the lack of a few drops of water.

Yet, somehow, from somewhere, someone had not only obtained enough precious water to hydrate a small city's worth of festival goers, they'd then had enough left over to slosh it across every square inch of ground, to transform a baking field into a virtual swamp. It was called "rain," and people were so pleased to see it that they stripped off their clothes and rolled in the consequences.

For the third time in ten minutes, I bent to retrieve a shoe from the stinking, sucking goo, then stood and looked again down the row of tents that I was certain was the right one, but which plainly wasn't. Great. I'd been at the festival site for exactly fifty minutes, and I'd already lost sight of every single person I came with.

Jake rarely went anywhere alone, and Reading was his excuse to take a serious party out of town. Half a dozen of us were crammed into that old car, and another van-load followed us down. And I'd gone and lost the lot. I retraced my footsteps toward the Portaloo, then set out again. Past the bikers with their little group of tents encircled by a dozen gleaming motorcycles, and a fat woman already topless and drunk in the arms of three of them; past the first of so many makeshift hippie communes, half invisible behind a thick fug of smoke and patchouli; a detour around the Krishna kids, chanting and rattling their way between the tents, their bright robes already spattered with the mud that oozed everywhere.

A girl bumped into me. "Do you know who's playing?" A nondescript noise was pounding through the PA as the first of the afternoon's acts ran through their paces. She inclined her head toward the stage. I didn't, and she lurched away, then wheeled back around. "Well, do you want to come and find out?"

"Sorry, I can't. I'm looking for some friends." *I can't believe I just said that.*

"Do you know where they are?" With her head tilted to one side, she reminded me of a very curious kitten. A very cute curious kitten.

"No."

"Then you might as well come with me. You've as much chance of finding them in one direction as you have in any other."

I thought about that. "OK, but you've got to help me look for them." A blue tent, a tall, dark-haired guy in jeans and a Rory Gallagher T-shirt . . . shit. Talk about a needle in a haystack.

"Don't worry. At least *you'll* know them when you see them." She stuck out a hand. "My name's Cassie, by the way. But you can call me Cassandra." She laughed. "I knew that would throw you. It throws everyone."

I smiled and took her hand. "Dave." Then, as we seemed to be behaving so formally, "Pleased to meet you."

We walked, she talked, I half-listened. Somewhere down the line, I learned she lived in a squat in Notting Hill, overlooking the same streets that exploded in flames every year, as the police swept down to clear out the annual carnival—as though the carnival only happened one weekend a year. "Those West Indians, man, I tell you, they know how to party. Every night. Do you listen to much reggae?"

At last, I was on firm ground. "That's the only reason I'm here."

"Great. I was worried you might be one of the idiots." The first band had finished now, and she nodded toward the stage, where a knot of brawny-looking teenagers had gathered to sling insults toward the handful of Rastas who were moving around the equipment. "Anyway, if you want to stick with me, that'd be great, although I'm only here for tonight. I'll be heading home after the Diamonds."

I thought for a moment. Assuming she was suggesting that I could ride back to London with her, it would mean missing Gong. But if I didn't find Jake, then I'd be stuck here forever. "That's fine. So am I."

"Great. I even can give you a lift if you like."

"Thanks." I'd lost my jacket and a couple packets of cigarettes, the program I bought at the entrance, and a Bowie cassette that Jake had made me. But I'd found a pretty brunette clad in combat fatigues, with a personal stash of grass and excellent taste in music. It sounded like a very fair trade.

The mud got everywhere, even into the equipment. The following week the papers would tell how Van Der Graaf Generator took the stage, prepared to kick into "La Rossa," then halted. Several minutes of voiceless pounding later, compere John Peel's tones came drifting over the PA, packing Van Der Graaf back to their dressing room, while the roadies tried to dry out the gear.

Right now, the slime seemed content to cling to people's shoes and start inching up their legs, with the first beaten paths across the festival site already taking on the constituency of quicksand. We staked out a dry patch to the left of the stage, away from the idiots we'd spotted before, and chattered through the next performer, folkie Roy St. John. Then the Revolutionaries took the stage.

The trouble kicked off within moments of their appearance, and it expanded from there. Drummer Sly Dunbar, all the way at the back of the stage, only narrowly avoided being hit by a full can of beer, a weighty projectile after twenty feet of flight. Empty containers clattered across the stage while the silence between the actual songs would have been deafening were it not for the percussive ting of another Colt 45 bouncing off the boards.

Then the Diamonds appeared, and it grew scary. Insults and complaints that were sporadic through the Revolutionaries and U-Roy performances, and died away completely for Supercharge, began picking up again. Except they weren't the random bellowings of a few disgruntled drunks. They were organized, concerted, and determined, slogans and chants lifted wholesale from the right-wing racist handbook, and tactics that would not have been out of place at a Nazi Party rally. Except they weren't called the Nazis anymore, they were called the National Front, and if any political party came to represent the sheer ignorance and evil that permeated British society in the mid-1970s, they were it.

The Front had been around since the late 1960s, but it was only over the last couple of years that they had become a force to be reckoned with, first shocking local libertarians with ever more impressive scores in the local elections, and then by launching a recruitment drive that brought new meaning to the term "lowest common denominator."

Throughout the summer of 1976, the party moved purposefully into the inner cities, leafleting and fly-postering, and pitching itself unerringly toward those elements that, to put it bluntly, "respectable" society would have no problem in identifying on the street: football hooligans, skinheads, "yobbos," and "bovver boys." The disenfranchised youth of the day.

Racism was not rampant, it was endemic. Among Johnny Rotten's most poisonous memories of growing up in the London of the early 1960s were the signs that once hung in almost every boarding-house window declaring "no Irish, no blacks, no dogs." Except they weren't only on display in the boardinghouses. Shops, jobs, pubs, cafes, anywhere that people might be brought together, broadcast the same prohibition, some overtly, others more subtly, but all with the same unswerving vehemence.

Those attitudes had only slowly modified. The prohibition on dogs was lifted first, given the English people's much-publicized love for their furry friends. The Irish followed, because who knew when you might need to have the road outside fixed? Blacks (which, naturally, could be expanded to take in every other conceivable color that was not Anglo-Saxon white), however, remained at the bottom of the heap, and it looked as though they were going to stay there. The British People needed somebody to blame. They started with what they saw as the non-British People. They started with the blacks.

With grotesque choreography, one section of the Reading crowd began flashing Nazi salutes and chanting "Sieg Heil." Another knot waited until the Diamonds paused between numbers and struck up a chorus of "Deutschland Über Alles," and the fact that they only knew the opening lines did not negate the menace of the moment. "This is not straightforward disapproval," the *New Musical Express*'s stunned commentary on the show declared the following week, "but a malevolent, downright sinister display."

The Mighty Diamonds were clearly rattled. Just a few days earlier, they had made their UK concert debut at the London Lyceum, the same venue where, a year before, Bob Marley had been transformed into a media superstar. There, they were received with unforgettable fervor. But they were playing to their own audience there, the Jamaicans who poured out of their enclaves around town, the white kids who'd been listening to reggae since their elder brothers first brought home a copy of Prince Buster's *Fab Hits* LP.

Reading was different. Reading was rock. Reading was ugly and, as the Diamonds responded to the violence by upping the tempo of their music, so the crowd reacted with equal vehemence. The little cans of beer were replaced by larger, deadlier projectiles. "Party Fours," hefty quart cans of beer, were being turfed into the air. One journalist witnessed an onlooker catching a can full in the face. "His nose and mouth jet blood everywhere." And when someone else, a Jamaican, leaped out of the press pen to try to prevent another from

being hurled, he was ambushed by a crowd of longhairs who proceeded to stomp him into the mud.

Then the Diamonds left the stage, and it was as though a switch
had been flung, a big switch with "racist scum" printed above it, and
the crowd was all happy hippies again, prepared to bliss out to the
mellow quacks of Mallard. From race war to Woodstock in under a
minute, and that was frightening as well, in the same way as the Two
Minute Hate in *1984*.

Later, a few people were overheard defending their reactions,
and their logic doubled back upon the festival's own traditions. It
was for rock, not reggae. The crowd was simply repelling boarders.
How noble of them. But what would happen if the boot was on the
other foot?

While Reading rocked, Notting Hill partied. That same end-of-
August weekend saw the capital's West Indian community descend as
one upon the West London neighborhood, there to celebrate an
annual carnival that had been a part of the calendar for as long as
many of the families had lived there. That was why Cassie was so
keen to get back home. "Once the carnival gets going, it'll make
this"—she gestured around the festival site—"look like a funeral
service."

It was back in the mid-1950s that sundry British governmental
schemes started offering new jobs, new homes, a whole new start, to
the people of the Caribbean, to precipitate one of the largest cultural
exoduses in modern history. From across the region they flooded,
entire families and, with them, an entire way of life pouring across
the ocean to find a brand-new start in the heart of the Motherland.

Few of them truly discovered the Promised Land they were
expecting. Dumped into dank, damp flats converted from the decaying relics of London's Victorian splendor, ruled by penny-pinching
landlords, beset and abused by gangs of whites, and governed by
laws that seemed single-mindedly set to keep them down, the new
arrivals took the worst jobs in the worst parts of town because that

was all they were offered. The lucky ones among them were still doing the same jobs today.

The people felt cheated. They had been promised the earth when they first came to England; instead, they were treated like dirt, third-class citizens in a second-class country. Families were still living in the same rundown tenements that they'd been thrown into when they first arrived in the country, with the assurance that it was mere temporary housing. Yes, there was an unemployment crisis that affected everyone, whatever his color. But did the government even attempt to explain why jobless rates among young blacks were to soar by 350 percent between 1974 and 1977, almost three times the rate among whites? Or why the national unemployment rate of 8.1 percent among whites was doubled among West Indians?

But they flourished regardless, some of them prospered, and now, entire inner-city districts were little slices of Jamaica, Trinidad, Tobago, and Barbados, each one exploding with the comforts of home. New foodstuffs, new slang, new fashions, new music, and, beginning in 1965, a new carnival.

The Notting Hill Carnival started small but quickly developed. For one day at the end of each August, it transformed drab West London into a kaleidoscope of color, noise, and music. Steel bands vied with reggae groups, brightly painted floats clashed with extravagantly hued costumes. It was mayhem—beautifully, brightly, brilliantly colored mayhem. When the organizers were asked how many people they expected to attend this year, they were proud to project around 150,000.

The police's greatest fear was that they might be correct.

10

A Riot of My Own

LATE AUGUST 1976

We woke late, breakfasted for lunch, and I got my first look around the squat where Cassie had spent the last eight months living, a decaying four-story terrace that she shared with her best friends, Margarita and Phyllis, Margarita's boyfriend, Winston, and an ever-changing coterie of friendly Rastas and their women. Electricity was piped in from a defiantly illegal and potentially fatal splice out on the street somewhere, water was pirated from the main supply, and there was more cardboard than glass on the windows. But it was home and, after what we'd witnessed at Reading, it was an oasis of sanity as well.

At least for the time being.

She showed me around, even pointing out the locks on every room. "There's no key, so it's only useful if you're already in here, but at least no one can creep up on you when you're sleeping."

My alarm must have showed on my face, because she hastened to reassure me. "Not that anyone here would do something like that. Winston would make sure of that, no matter who you are. But you know what this area's like. Especially with the carnival happening just down the street. Kids coming in from the suburbs, looking for some trouble . . . the same sort of idiots that were at Reading yesterday."

"I didn't realize."

"What, that there's trouble at the carnival? Or that there's trouble here all the time? You stick around for the next few nights, you'll realize all right. But don't worry; you're in a house with a dozen Rastas to protect you. The only way anyone will get to you is by burning the place down." She stopped, presumably as the color drained from my face. "Sorry, sorry. Even the Front haven't stooped that low yet. Not around here, anyway. And hopefully they never will. Anyway, do you want to come down to the carnival? It doesn't officially happen until Monday, but there's a few bands playing around this evening, a lot of great food and dancing. . . . It's not all trouble here, despite what tomorrow's papers will say."

I looked around the room. "Are we going on our own?"

"No, safety in numbers, I think."

"But—"

She laughed. "You were going to say 'but we're white,' right? If things do kick off, that won't make a blind bit of difference, because if the Front don't hang us as nigger-lovers, then the Rastas will get us because they'll be hitting out at anyone who's not from the islands. And the pigs will just wade in to everyone. Believe me, I've seen it before. But we'll be OK in a crowd, especially if some of the others from the street tag along as well."

I was horrified. Just how insular had boarding school made me, and just how unaware of the world beyond my doorstep? I couldn't imagine what it was like living someplace where you had to find a crowd before you could even walk around your own streets. Tottenham wasn't exactly the safest part of London, but you learned to live with that and, besides, that violence made sense in a strange kind of way, hooligan hunting hooligan, and the only innocent bystanders who ever got hurt were those who weren't quick enough to get out of the way.

This was different, though. It seemed so totally indiscriminate . . . it *was* indiscriminate, and not simply on a racial, black-skin-versus-white-skin level. Because that wasn't what the issue was. It went deeper than that and, at the same time, it was more superficial. It was violence for the sake of violence, different hunting different. We were barely out of the front door and I was already hoping the others got here before the firebombers arrived.

Later that evening, sitting around the basement that had been opened up as a free-for-all shebeen, I was wondering what all the fuss was about. Cassie was right, the music had been wonderful, the food ecstatic, and when Sunday morning broke, a band was still playing. A few people had drifted home in the night, but others came in to replace them—the entire Hill, it seemed, was jumping tonight, with a shebeen in every basement, and even All Souls Church pounding with the beat.

Cassie was asleep, her face cradled in her arms on the hard Formica table, and her nose just inches from a congealed plate of fiery pork jerk and foo foo. I wondered what the smell was doing to her dreams. Winston drifted over, with Margarita on his arm, and we chatted for a while. Then it was back to the squat to sleep the rest of the day away, an evening spent bouncing from party to party, and the carnival still hadn't officially kicked off.

Neither had anything else.

Sirens were sounding all night long, but they tended to be isolated blasts that soon faded into the distance. By late afternoon on Monday, however, they were incessant, undulating in and around a host of other, less familiar sounds. Raised voices, breaking glass, chanting anger.

"There's something going on."

Cassie sat up, startled, looking around the room.

"Outside," I said. "Maybe a couple of streets away." And then, "It sounds like a riot! Let's go."

We took the stairs two or three at a time, burst out of the front door onto the street. It was deserted, but the noise was louder now, and the air was ripe with the onion sting of gas. We ran to the end of the street, turned the corner and then rounded another, straight into a mob of white kids, advancing in the general direction of Ladbroke Grove, chanting slogans that had sporadically echoed through these streets since the race riots of the late 1950s. "Blacks out," "England for the English," and that old, faithful standby, "Sieg Heil." It was the Reading Festival all over again, only this time with added chaos.

The National Front had a long history of marching through, or at least infiltrating, predominantly black areas, usually timing their activities for maximum exposure and impact. The carnival was one of the Front's informal gatherings, the word spreading along a grapevine that took in East End pubs and football grounds, private phone calls, and public meetings, but never appearing to be delivered from the party's own headquarters. The lack of formal organization did not appear to hinder the marchers, though. In every aspect except for banners and uniforms, there was no mistaking the army's allegiance. Or its intentions.

A crowd of obvious soccer fans merged with the mob. The sport's new season was less than two weeks old, and already sufficient trouble had kicked off at matches around the capital for today's *Daily Mirror* to headline its coverage with an unequivocal call to "Birch 'Em." A few months ago, the same paper's solution to the hooliganism problem was merely to "cage the animals." That showed how far the problems had escalated, and how fearless the thugs had become. They marched in full club colors, the blue of Chelsea, the red and white of Arsenal, the claret and blue of West Ham. But their personal allegiances were put aside for now. They had other colors in mind today. Or one other color, anyway. Reports that the Front's membership drive had been actively targeting football grounds were clearly not exaggerated.

We darted in to the back of the crowd, shoved our way to the edge, and then squeezed toward the front, the walls of the houses rough against our backs. Ahead of us, a thin line of cops formed a none-too-steady barricade; behind them, a handful of blacks was making its own way toward the invaders, passing seemingly unscathed through the clouds of gas that had clearly been fired into their midst, but had yet to be used against the whites.

The white marchers were vastly outnumbered, which just added to the hateful arrogance of their presence here. I didn't know precisely how many people lived around the Hill, but I guess there were several thousand, and most of them were black. The hundred or so whites who looked so confident now, and the two dozen pigs being swept along before them, wouldn't know what hit them if the neighborhood really turned out. But past experience had taught them that it probably wouldn't.

Or would it? Black faces were appearing at windows all along the road, first to hurl insults, and then follow up with missiles. I saw the contents of what looked like a chamber pot emptied over one knot of thugs, and another group only just step aside as a broken television hurtled down from a balcony. But they were still caught in the explosion, flying glass scythed through the air, and, though the cuts were superficial, you knew the blood would be worn as a badge of honor when they got home this evening.

"Let's go back around," I shouted. "Get back on the right side of the lines." Although it was difficult right now to figure out which side was the "right" side. The way things were going, any white face must have looked like a target, and I couldn't imagine anybody checking our political convictions first before weighing in with the fists and bricks. But then I remembered something I'd read somewhere, splashed across one of those militant fly-posters that occasionally appeared on local lampposts. *Neither side cares what colour skin you have. It's who you want to bleed for that counts*—and, as if to hammer that home even harder, the next face I saw was a black one, running alongside three white guys, in a denim jacket bleached white around the deep blue letters "NF." If and when the shit came down, there'd be no mistaking which side he was taking.

We were caught in a predominantly black crowd sprinting wildly down Westbourne Park Road. Everyone had a weapon of some kind, some were foraged from the trees and gardens they passed, branches and sticks and the occasional iron railing; others were being distributed through the crowd as it marched. One moment, I was clutching Cassie's hand in mine; the next, I was watching her wielding a two-by-four plank and swinging it, with a whoop of delight, against the windscreen of the first car she came across.

A tall kid laughed and grabbed her wrist. "You'll never break it if you do it like that. Let me show you." His hands still on hers, he drew her arms back as far as he could, then pantomimed another blow, twisting the plank edge-on against the glass. "Now try." She paused and positioned herself as he'd shown her, and then whooped even louder as two other guys came running and hoisted a huge piece of concrete through her target.

Glass was shattering everywhere. A newspaper store had been taken, stripped of everything portable, and a bunch of Rastas ran through the crowd, passing out the largesse of the raid: handfuls of magazines, cigarettes and cans of pop, sweets. A little black boy, not more than seven or eight, appeared at the gates of one of the houses that overlooked the carnage. His mother rushed out to retrieve him, and was promptly laden down with more boxes of chocolate than she'd probably seen all her life.

I saw the newsagent, a swarthy Sikh, appear in his shattered doorway and felt a momentary pang of guilt. But then I noticed the copies of *Britain First* that were being scattered across the ground. If he cared so little that he happily stocked the National Front's own hate-filled newspaper, then why should I care if he lost the rest of his livelihood?

I looked around for Cassie, thought I saw her disappearing through the shattered doorway into a chemist's shop, but the melee swept me on before I could pick her out among the crowd being chased out again by a pair of snarling Dobermans. Behind them, their owner was howling a stream of brutal invective, and waving what looked a lot like a shotgun. No wonder everyone piled out of there so quickly.

A wave of heat sent me staggering backward, searing and angry. With one arm protecting my face, I looked toward its source and, for a moment, could see only thick black smoke, shrouding the livid orange of the flames. "Burn the piggies!" someone was shouting, and I realized with iced-water shock that it was a police van that lay on its side, the flames transforming it into so much twisted metal and melted rubber.

Scrambling backward, a few feet behind it, the van's erstwhile occupants, the driver and his partner, were watching the conflagration with the same sense of disbelief that I was feeling—and, looking around, a lot of the crowd as well. Up to now, it had simply been a riot, with all the manic unreality that that implies. But the moment the flames hit the police van's petrol tank, it wasn't just the vehicle that exploded. It was the entire world. The battle lines had been drawn. Cops were converging on the heart of the action. I wondered where the much-vaunted riot squad was, with their plastic shields and rubber bullets? These guys were just the regular beat cops, the ones you'd go up to when you were too young to know better and ask them for the time. But there was nothing regular about their intentions.

Arming themselves with the same inventiveness as their foes, iron bars for batons, dustbin lids for shields, they descended from every direction at once to meet their tormentors in hand-to-hand combat. And I was standing in the thick of it, on the exact point where the two forces must meet, watching my shadow dance in the light of the burning police van and wondering, absurdly, what my parents were doing right now, right this instant?

A cop was heading straight for me, his truncheon raised above his head. That broke the spell. I turned and ran around the van, past the two officers who still sat dazed on the pavement, pushing against the crowd of rioters descending to their brothers' aid. I noticed more white faces among them this time, and thought again of that quotation. *Neither side cares what colour skin you have. It's who you want to bleed for that counts.* But then I dismissed it. This wasn't racial; this wasn't about injustice. This was a free-for-all, and a chance to let off all the steam that the long, hot summer had built up in everyone. And I didn't want any part of it.

Later, back at the squat, slumped exhausted in one of the arm-chairs while voices mumbled death threats at the old man reading the news, I absorbed my first inkling of precisely what I'd been caught up in.

Flashpoints had ignited the whole carnival over, and sporadic flare-ups continued breaking out. Scotland Yard was still trying to work out its stance, still trying to figure out what would win it the most public support. Did its officers react gallantly to a massive and clearly premeditated breakdown in law and order? Or were they caught off guard by the forces of chaos, and barely made it out of the inferno with their lives?

Already, some 150 people were being treated in area hospitals, most of them—close to two-thirds—police. Roads in and out of the area were sealed off, pubs closed, clubs emptied. The last few hours of the Carnival were canceled, and the almost incessant sound of the front door opening and then slamming shut testified to the efficiency of that action. It was barely 10:15 and people were already coming home, filing into the room, and adding their own running commen-taries to the news report.

It was hell out there. But it was also heaven. Babylon was burn-ing, and it was the righteous who set the fires. For years, a line of whites and blue uniforms had treated the Hill as though it was their own private playground, a place to come to crack a few heads, an easy source for suspects when they needed to up their arrest statistics.

Now the Hill had hit back and, within a month, it would have its own soundtrack.

Tappa Zukie, visiting London while "MPLA" continued to tear up the reggae charts, was so horrified by one incident that he quickly penned the vehement "Ten Against One," and dub plates were spinning within a few weeks. "Them started the looting, and them started the rioting . . . ten 'gainst one against the Babylon."

Joe Strummer, Paul Simenon, and the Clash's manager, Bernie Rhodes, were there, too; had, according to Strummer, even made their own contribution to the escalating lawlessness when they tried to torch a parked car, before being mugged by both the police and the thieves. "We got searched by police looking for bricks, and later on we got searched by a Rasta looking for pound notes." The first song Strummer wrote once the adrenalin stopped pumping, the foreboding declamation of "1977," would be in the Clash's live set inside the week. The second was "White Riot."

The next two weeks rocketed past. Everybody was on edge, I think, waiting for the fallout from the Carnival chaos to settle, constantly keeping an eye on the street outside. The police had taken a brutal beating that evening; it was human nature for them to be out for revenge. But, though there were a handful of arrests, blacks *and* whites, I was surprised to hear that there seemed to be fewer cops on the streets than usual.

"That's not necessarily a good thing," Cassie mumbled when I mentioned it to her. "It could mean they're waiting for someone else to do their dirty business for them," and now I knew exactly what she meant. Without anything actually *happening*, the Front seemed to be picking up speed all the time. They'd already moved into local politics, racking up votes in Leicester, in Blackburn, in Thurrock— where in God's name is *Thurrock*? They were on the frontlines at Grunwick, as angry strikers fought pitched battles with the police over their right to earn a living wage. They were everywhere.

Deaths—murders—were being laid if not at their door, at least at those of their supporters. And people were scared. The squat was not the only house in the area where a corner of one room now looked more like an arsenal than a domicile, as weapons were gathered wherever they could be found to be stockpiled against the inevitable. Someone had even thoughtfully propped a cricket bat up in one corner of Cassie's room, just in case she ever needed it; and one of the other guys spent an afternoon chipping away the old paint that sealed her bedroom window shut, so she could escape onto the balcony—again, *just in case*.

One evening, we arrived back to find a brand-new fire extinguisher by the front door, and a bucket of sand beneath the living room window. If I hadn't known any better, I'd have said they were bunkering in for a siege.

11

The Land of the Faint at Heart

SEPTEMBER 1976

SOUNDTRACK

"A You Me Love" — Dillinger (Stars And Stripes)

"African Roots" — Johnny Clarke (Ja Man)

"Back to Africa" — Aswad (Island)

"Bosrah" — Ras Allah (Kiss)

"Babylon Bawling" — Lambert Douglas (Rosso)

"Cincinnati Fatback" — Roogalator (Stiff)

"Crazy Baldhead" — Johnny Clarke (Justice)

"Danger Zone" — Jah Stitch (Locks)

"Fight I Down" — Lizzard (Belmont)

"Heavy Manners" — Prince Far I (Heavy Duty)

"Police and Thieves" — Junior Murvin (Island)

"Riot in Cell Block #9" — Dr. Feelgood (UA)

"Roadrunner" — Modern Lovers (Beserkley)

"State of Emergency" — Joe Gibbs and the Professionals (Joe Gibbs)

"Styrofoam" — Tyla Gang (Stiff)

"What a Way to End It All" — Deaf School (WB)

"You're Driving Me Insane" — Velour Souterain (Skydog)

Eddie and the Hot Rods, the Sex Pistols, the Damned, the Clash,
the Count Bishops, the Gorillas, Roogalator, Sister Ray, Stranglers,
the Jam, Buzzcocks, Slaughter and the Dogs . . . get along and see all
the Punk Rock you can. —Sniffin' Glue *issue 3*

How could you keep up with all the bands now flying around?
The month was a blur but, all of a sudden, everybody you met
seemed to be raving about a different new group . . . or not so new,
in some cases.

Unlike Sister Ray, who I never did hear mentioned anywhere
else, the Vibrators were one of those names that had been appearing
in the gig guide every week for an eternity, grinding around the same
old circuit of Rochester Castles, White Harts, and Nag's Heads, and
it was word of mouth, more than force of personality, that was inching them into punky contention—that and their peculiar habit of
unleashing a wall of buzzsaw noise upon their audiences and chanting "Fuck off! Fuck off!" at the tops of their lungs. But they might
also have profited from the same nomenclatural misunderstanding
that afflicted the promoter of a certain North London pub, who
swore up and down that he'd turned down the opportunity to show-
case the Buzzcocks, months before the band even played its first gig.

I didn't believe a word of it. "You can't have."

"Well, I'm telling you I did. Back in the spring. I've even got the
tape they gave me."

My eyes lit up. It's difficult being a record collector when none
of the bands have released any records, when the hottest property of
the week is a live EP by Eddie and the Hot Rods, and the promise of
whatever Chiswick and the newly launched Stiff labels might have
up their sleeves. "A tape? Could you make me a copy?"

"You can have it, it's crap. I'll bring it in next week."

He was true to his word, he did. Except it wasn't the Buzzcocks,
it was the Vibrators. And he didn't even bat an eyelid as he shrugged
the error away. "Buzzcock, Vibrator, what's the difference?"

Hmmm, maybe you had to be there.

Right now, the Vibrators were cruising on their friendship with guitarist Chris Spedding, who adopted them as the backup on his latest single, "Pogo Dancing." That, in turn, brought them a deal with pop entrepreneur Mickie Most's RAK label, and when word first started spreading of an upcoming Punk Rock Festival, the Vibrators were one of the first names to be penciled in. Alongside the Buzzcocks.

The festival was the brainchild, naturally, of Malcolm McLaren, as he aimed to prove to the watching world that punk now had its own marketable audience, and Ron Watts, promoter at the 100 Club and one of the few people in town who was regularly staging "punk" concerts. Other venues, while not issuing outright bans on bands, were at least cautious about whom they would book. Even the Stranglers were finding it hard to land gigs, and they'd played most every place in town at least once. Yet there were more new groups chasing stage space every week and while not all of them were deliberately climbing aboard the good ship Punk Rock, it was sometimes difficult to tell them apart.

The rush, if you can call it that, to either accept punk or reject it was wholly the work of the music press. Like the audiences whom they preached to, journalists were already lining up on one side of the divide or the other; either punk was the most refreshing change to sweep through a stale and stagnant music scene in years, *or* it was a talentless yowling perpetrated by a gaggle of untalented yobbos.

Musicians, strangely, were less prone to take sides quite so unequivocally; for every interviewee who murmured querulously around the punks' so-called lack of talent, there was another who at least remembered what his first band sounded like, back when he was seventeen or eighteen. But a dividing line was yawning, and it was centered on age, either perceived or actual. "If we had formed a few years later," Heavy Metal Kid Keith Boyce once told me, "we would have been up there with those bands. We felt like we had helped start the punk thing in the UK, and a lot of those guys became our friends. What's weird is, we were the same age as most of those guys, because they were all late starters! Instead we were stuck in an uncomfortable place between the old guard and the new."

The event that best illustrated this rift, although it took place so far from the spotlight that many people weren't even aware of it, was that which inspired the 100 Club event in the first place. Six weeks earlier, in the Franco-Spanish border town of Mont-de-Marsan, French record-label head Marc Zermati staged his own punk festival and, if hindsight insists that his own wish list of potential players was almost completely unsuited to his intentions, then hindsight has no understanding of just how fluid the punk label was at the time.

In later days, critics would look back on Zermati's use of the punk label as misleading, if not a total misnomer. Yet, the music papers of the day were no more certain as to what it represented than anybody else. In the United States, "punk" was still a disreputable term, best associated with street toughs and hoodlums, and it was less than a year since the likes of Bruce Springsteen and Nils Lofgren were rejoicing beneath that very imagery, reflecting back the lineage that they appeared to share with the Dead End Kids of 1930s Hollywood, and the James Cagney gangster culture that first thrust the word into the popular lexicon.

In France, it had another meaning, courtesy of that peculiarly Gallic strain of adolescent antiestablishmentarianism that stretched from Jean Genet to Alain Delon and on to Serge Gainsbourg, and was now manifest in the strivings of the handful of French acts, familiar from Zermati's Skydog label, who were first on the festival bill.

And, in the UK, it was still so broad that the Sex Pistols, Eddie and the Hot Rods, the Hammersmith Gorillas, Graham Parker and the Rumour, the Clash, the Pink Fairies, Roogalator, the Tyla Gang, Nick Lowe, and the Damned were all issued with invites, and nobody thought anything of it. Nobody, that is, aside from journalist Caroline Coon, traveling to the festival on the same hired bus as the bands, and devoting great swathes of her final report to dismissing the claims of almost all of the passengers.

A Skydog classic, former Ducks Deluxe frontman Sean Tyla's "Suicide Jockey" 45. *Author's collection*

Parker dropped out early on in the planning, and the Pistols and Clash followed at McLaren's insistence. Coon was not impressed by what remained. The Tyla Gang, she deduced, were broadbellied enough to be West Country cider drinkers; novelty farmhand sing-along act the Wurzels were enjoying a few minutes of chart fame at the time and Coon's inference was obvious. The Gorillas had quiffs and sideburns to swing from; Danny Adler was a "studiously pseudo-academic, jazz-rock virtuos[o]." The Pink Fairies were too old; the Hot Rods were too treacherous; and Nick Lowe was Nick Lowe, a singer-songwriter who had been at it for almost a decade already, with Kippington Lodge and Brinsley Schwarz.

That left the Damned. Now they *were* punk, weren't they?

They didn't think so. In another conversation, on another occasion, Brian James shook his head and proffered his passport photograph. It made him look like a member of Black Sabbath. Rat Scabies, too, was in denial. "You can call it punk rock but I don't think I like that definition. It's just a slag down, I can see how the tag came about, but I don't see how it applies to me."

And why not? "I didn't like it because I wanted everyone to take me seriously as a musician, and I knew that they wouldn't if I was a 'punk rocker.' It wasn't the word so much as being pigeonholed, because that wasn't what it was about. What it was about was making the music that we wanted to make, that had nothing to do with anybody."

Sniffin' Glue issue 3, featuring a superb shot of the Damned's Brian James. *Author's collection*

But Coon was not to be dissuaded. Punk was the music of youth; short-haired, clean-shaven, undernourished, unrehearsed youth. "As far as punk rock goes, there was no contest. The Damned wiped up."

I read her review in the next week's *Melody Maker* and shrugged it off as bellicose posturing. Punk already had enough faultlines of its own—what was the point in drawing any more? Maybe the best of the festival bands were a generation apart, but that's just chronology speaking. In terms of energy, intent, and intensity, and on the evidence of all the nights I'd spent watching them play in the pubs, you could have pointed at almost any one of them and said, "And the future will sound like this." And, right there, right then, you'd have been spot on.

But, though I thought Coon was wrong, she was correct all the same. With the exception of the decidedly veteran Vibrators (frontman Knox was a decrepit thirty-one, two years older than either David Bowie or Iggy Pop, and only two years younger than Mick Jagger!), the lineup for the two-night 100 Club Punk Festival was drawn almost precisely from the formula that her article laid out. Joe Strummer was twenty-four, the remainder of the Clash were twenty-one, the same age as Captain Sensible, the Buzzcocks' Pete Shelley, and the Pistols' Steve Jones. The rest of that band were twenty. Siouxsie Sioux was nineteen, Subway Sect's Vic Goddard was seventeen. There wasn't a beard or a beergut in sight.

The bulk of the queue outside the first night's show was just as youthful, but what exactly were the assembled ranks of converts and the curious really letting themselves in for? So far as they were concerned, the first night of the festival was the one to go to, by virtue of the headlining Pistols. They were a lean, mean gigging machine by now and knew precisely which buttons to push in their audience. "How sad," Cassie murmured as they finished their performance. "They've become their own cliché and they don't even have a record out."

The Clash, on the other hand, were foundering. Keith Levine, whose studied lead guitar had allowed Mick Jones to coast in his wake for so long, walked out of the lineup just days after their previous show, supporting the Kursaal Flyers at the Roundhouse. Being taught "White Riot" by a cocksure Strummer was the final straw. The Clash, he believed, was a rock 'n' roll band, not a political platform. At the 100 Club Festival, they really weren't either one, just a buzz of noise and energy that might one day resolve itself into something, but which right now was still trying to regain its balance.

Subway Sect were another of the acts lurking under the wings of McLaren and Bernie Rhodes, and were so untogether that even management doubted whether they'd be able to pull off a show, while Suzie and the Banshees (as they were titled on the ads) struck most people as an even more dubious proposition.

The idea for the Banshees was less than a month old, conceived at a Sex Pistols gig by the Bromley Contingent—Siouxsie, Steve Spunker, and blonde bombshell Billy Idol—after McLaren mentioned the festival was coming up fast.

"Why don't we do something?" Idol suggested and then absented himself from the proceedings when he was invited to join the still gestating Chelsea. But McLaren suggested Sid Vicious as drummer, and an afternoon sunning themselves in Hyde Park, two days before the festival, introduced the "band" to guitarist Marco Pirroni. The day before the show, the Banshees rolled up at Rehearsal Rehearsals to perform before an invited audience of two, Clash manager Bernie Rhodes and bassist Paul Simenon, who spent the entire performances pulling faces, so awful did it all sound. But the posters were printed; the running order was confirmed. The Banshees would be playing.

Or not. They arrived at the 100 Club in all the finery they could manage—Vicious resplendent in a yellow T-shirt adorned with the legend "Belsen Babies," Spunker in a white shirt that he'd spattered with paint, Pirroni in a T-shirt emblazoned with a swastika and Luftwaffe insignia, and Siouxsie in leather with her own swastika armband. The gear had already caused them to be thrown out of the nearby Ship pub, the jobbing musicians' watering hole of choice, and now Rhodes was to make similar noises at the 100 Club. The original idea was for the Banshees to borrow the Clash's equipment. That offer was now rescinded.

It didn't matter how apolitical the Banshees' badges of choice may have been intended, nor that they wore them for no purpose other than to shock the tiresome old men who lurked in pub corners, complaining about how they'd fought a war to guarantee our freedom to say, do, and—oh, what was that? *wear?*—what we wanted. Rhodes was not going to have his babies associated with the Nazi emblem, and he didn't care how many times a disgruntled Vicious called him an "old Jew." Rhodes would not budge.

Siouxsie turned on the charm and approached the Subway Sect. Could she borrow their gear? Of course. And the stage was set for the most radical performance of the evening. "All the other bands were talking about not being able to really play and being unrehearsed and into chaos," Siouxsie told the *New Musical Express* a few months later. "We [decided] to take the whole thing to its logical extreme."

Which was . . . "We entered into the pure spirit of it, on the spur of the moment," Siouxsie told me. "Forming a band to fill this slot, then disbanding after it, one night only, taking the Andy Warhol idea to its extreme, and also the idea that now is now, and it's important, no future, no

An ad for the 100 Club, again before the running order was extended over a second night. *Author's collection*

past." Then they kicked into an endless, atonal version of "The Lord's Prayer," drifting through a murderous medley with "Knockin' on Heaven's Door" and "Twist and Shout," storming and hypnotic, and wholly improvised by musicians who'd never improvised before. "It seemed like some horrible sixth form windup arty band," a watching TV Smith shuddered. "I know they were doing it with the intention of sounding terrible, but they really *were* terrible."

*　　*　　*

Cassie had landed us a paying job, and we had her grandmother to thank for it.

Granny was one of the original suffragettes, and she still carried the banner today, tottering out of her little house in Battersea on her way to the post office, and always pausing for a moment at one particular spot, to shed a tear for a little brown dog.

In 1903, two students at University College published one of the most shocking books ever issued in the UK. *The Shambles of Science*, by Liese Scartau and Louise Lind-af-Hageby, exposed the cruelty of vivisection for the first time, drawing upon the two medical students' own diaries to document the horrific life and death of one particular subject, a little brown dog.

The public outcry was deafening, but it was also impotent. Science was too slippery to allow legislated torture to fall from its purview; animals *needed* to be sliced and diced, the wise men patiently explained, so that we might better understand human frailties, and besides, it's not as if they felt any pain. Different nervous systems, you know. William Bayliss, the doctor at the center of the controversy, even took the book to court and won £2,000 in damages. But he also won himself some powerful enemies far beyond his traditional foes at the Church Anti-Vivisection League and the National Anti-Vivisection Society. The women's suffrage movement became involved, recognizing more analogies in the animals' struggle for humane treatment than perhaps even they were comfortable with.

In September 1906, members of the radical Women's Social and Political Union were among the most outspoken of the donors who presented Battersea Council with a public drinking fountain dedicated to, and surmounted by a statue of, the little brown dog.

The fountain became a symbol of both causes, women's rights and animal rights, as opponents of both descended upon Battersea to try to destroy it, and supporters gathered to repel the vandals. But with the police constantly complaining at the cost of protecting it from nightly raids, and the local council tired of the incessant rioting, the fountain was doomed. It was finally dismantled in March 1910, under the watchful protection of 120 policemen, and the so-called Brown Dog Riots passed into history.

But they also passed into folklore, and in early September, Cassie recalled Granny's memories when a couple of her friends announced they were launching a militant animal rights fanzine.

The first issue of *The Brown Dog Fountain* came off the presses two weeks later, and Cassie volunteered our services to help sell it. We could take 5p from the cover price of every one we shifted as we walked the line outside the 100 Club. Then, once we'd sold as many as we could, we'd stash the remainder behind a bin somewhere (there was a convenient alleyway running behind the club), and use the proceeds to get into the show.

The first night of the festival went reasonably well. True, Cassie probably spent longer trying to explain to people what the fanzine's title meant than she did collecting their money, but we sold through one satchel of *The Brown Dog Fountain*, and dented another, paid our money at the door, and could even afford a drink apiece.

Tuesday, though, was slow. Maybe everyone had bought a copy the previous evening. Maybe feminist antivivisectionists didn't like the Damned. By the time we'd finally raised enough cash to get in, we'd already missed the visiting French band Stinky Toys, and the Vibrators' show was almost over too. But we caught Chris Spedding joining them for a motorvating "Motorbiking," and Captain

Sensible was up onstage, too, reveling in the moment even as some overofficious bouncer tried to wrestle him off the stage.

Next up were the Buzzcocks, humming angrily around whatever twist of fate it was that decreed Pete Shelley spend the night wrestling with a broken, cheapo Woolworth's guitar on which he could do little more than pick out two-note guitar solos. It was mad and, in hindsight, it was magnificent, but it was scarcely anything you'd really want to listen to. And finally, there was the Damned, damned indeed to spend most of their performance either arguing with the audience or standing around as Brian James took an ice age to replace a string on his guitar—five minutes, ten minutes, fifteen— while Dave Vanian entertained himself by throwing beer over the crowd. Who responded in kind.

"It kind of sucked," Rat Scabies sighed. "There's nothing worse than being a sitting target, which you are onstage. That's why we always jumped around so much, we were avoiding missiles. That's why we were the most visual band in the world, because we were good at ducking!"

Such antics usually passed off harmlessly enough. But tonight, someone got hurt. On the other side of the room from us, a flying glass shattered on a pillar. A girl standing nearby went down clutching her eye, as the music fizzled out and a bouncer took the stage. "There's three people waiting outside for an ambulance. If there's any more glasses thrown we'll stop the show and have you all out."

The Damned only became aware of the seriousness of the situation later—just a few hours, in fact, before the horrified tabloids informed the rest of the country that the girl had lost an eye. "It's kind of a can of worms story now, because it was Sid Vicious that threw the glass," Scabies continued. "My publisher watched him do it. He was arrested that night."

Horrified, the Damned immediately tried to organize a benefit for the stricken girl. But their venue of choice, the Nashville, was having none of it. "We went down there, but they wouldn't let us play." (Eddie and the Hot Rods replaced them.) The official reasoning revolved around a fracas or two that took place when the Damned played the pub during the summer. But it was also apparent that the media coverage surrounding the 100 Club Festival had played its own part. If the papers predicted problems, they would inevitably arise; it only required half a dozen knuckleheads to read that such-and-such bands enjoy fighting for every gig to be transformed into the Battle of the Somme.

"What happens," Scabies explained, "is a couple of incidents will [take place] and then it gets all over the papers, violence, violence, violence." When the Jam came up from Woking to pump retro-1960s mod and Motown through the tiny Upstairs at Ronnie Scott's venue, a passing hardnut started swinging out at punks, simply because they were there. Scabies wasn't the only onlooker who lost count of the number of occasions upon which "you'd be in the dressing room, and somebody would come in, and there's blood everywhere, and they just been beaten up outside."

Trouble wasn't confined to the Festival, either. That same evening on the underground, a bunch of self-styled bovver boys spent their journey steaming their way down the Central Line, snatching anything and everything they could lay their hands on. Including Cassie's friends' entire stock of *The Brown Dog Fountain* issue one, as they carried it from the printers to the flat they shared in Camden. With the exception of the satchel-full that we'd shifted, three weeks' work and six weeks' savings were gone in an instant. There would be no issue two.

There would be no more festivals, either; not on the scale of the 100 Club, anyway.

The press backlash was immediate; maybe it would seem muted when compared with the headlines that were still to come, but still it was apparent that the mainstream media had already determined that this punk junk had the potential to fuel a lot more shock-horror-outrage-style scandals than your average musical movement.

Is this what society had come to? they asked. The Sex Pistols
with their avowedly antisocial stance and penchant for abusing their
audience, Siouxsie with her apparent fascination for Hitlerite regalia
(although it was the Vibrators who insistently sang "I Wanna Be
Your Nazi, Baby"), Sid with his manic style of dancing, McLaren
and Westwood with their shop filled with perversions, catering to
the self-mutilating misfits who tattooed their flesh with razor blades
and put safety pins through their faces, cropped their hair and dyed
it green, then spit and vomited their way down the road?

*Ten tell-tale ways to spot if your teenaged child is a Punk
Rocker!*

What to do if your kid is a Punk!

Exposed! The violent sect that believes disfigurement is fun!

And so on, until the fashion fancies of a genuine minority had
become so distorted through the mirrors of the media that even an
inadvertent tear in a well-worn T-shirt could draw the eyes of a bus-
load of commuters suspiciously over to your direction, all of them
watching and waiting to see whether you might not start cutting
your leg off for fun.

Weeks before I brought home my first *bona fide* "punk record,"
which means weeks before there was even one to buy, my stepmother warned me in no uncertain terms that she would not tolerate
such garbage coming into the house, while Cassie was getting hit
from both directions. It was bad enough, a letter from her parents
complained, that she was living in a house filled with black men, but
now she was going out with a punk rocker as well. The one time
they saw me, incidentally, I had hair down to my shoulders and was
wearing a Roger Dean T-shirt.

Still, it could have been worse. She could have been planning to
color her hair and add a few extra holes to her earlobes.

Oops.

12

Nightclubbing, We're Nightclubbing

OCTOBER–NOVEMBER 1976

SOUNDTRACK

"Ask the Angels" — Patti Smith Group (Arista)

"Black A Kill Black" — Gregory Isaacs (African Museum)

"Boogie on the Streets" — Lew Lewis (Stiff)

"Cherry Bomb" — The Runaways (Mercury)

"Drip Drop" — Rocky Sharpe and the Razors (Chiswick)

"Jah Will Guide" — Silver Shadows (Well Charge)

"Lady Doubonette" — Bizarros (Gorilla)

"New Rose" — The Damned (Stiff)

"Rasta Business" — Gregory Isaacs (Olympic)

"Roxette (live)" — Dr. Feelgood (UA)

"Step on the Dragon" — I Roy (Observer)

"Stop the War in Babylon" — James Brown (Mango)

"Teenage Depression" — Eddie and the Hot Rods (Island)

"Under Heavy Manners" — Derrick Morgan (Justice)

"Universal Natty" — I Roy (Well Charge)

"Weeping" — Junior Byles (Thing)

"Zion Call" — Prince Far I (Cry Tuff)

In 1974, the RAK label had launched the latest in a long line of clean-cut UK pop sensations, Arrows, with a storming hit single, "A Touch Too Much," and a three-piece mugshot to die for. Two New Yorkers, Alan Merrill and Jake Hooker, and an English drummer, Paul Varley, glowered so seductively out of their photographs that it was a wonder they could even stand to be in the same room with one another. Misery loves company, but beauty demands isolation.

Two years later, they were facing imminent execution.

"A Touch Too Much" was massive, its follow up, "My Last Night with You," slightly less so, and although label politics ultimately conspired to keep the Arrows at arms' length from any further chart success, television producer Muriel Young had no reservations. In March 1976, over a year since the last hit single, she gave Arrows their own teatime television program, thirty minutes a week for fourteen weeks that they stuffed with so much fine music and guests that when the series ended, she promptly offered them another to kick off in September. RAK had not released a single new Arrows record since their telefame began. But the television ratings didn't lie. Arrows were hot.

Malcolm McLaren certainly thought so, especially after he discovered that Alan Merrill lived in the flat directly below one of his own employees, Sex shop worker Cheryl Newton.

Merrill recalled the entrepreneur's first advances, early in 1976. "Malcolm wanted Cheryl to bring me around to the shop. He knew about Arrows. He knew that we had some hits and a media profile. He wanted to pick my brains, to know about how to put a pop group together."

Merrill resisted McLaren's maneuverings. London life was far too much fun to waste time dispensing advice to the shitty end of the rock 'n' roll stick. But he did eventually surrender to Cheryl's urging that he attend the Sex Pistols' next show, at the El Paradise strip club in Soho in April 1976.

Accompanied by his two bandmates, Merrill made his way into the venue, paused while photographer Kate Simon fired off a handful of shots, and then relaxed at the bar with McLaren buzzing around him, watching Johnny Rotten berate the crowd for "being stupid enough to stay through this shit," for being "ugly stupid fuckers," and hissing insult after insult at the tiny audience.

It was, Merrill mused to himself, "a negative masochist bizarre cabaret. I didn't think it a serious project, just a dark joke. You know the concept, bad is good. Garbage is valuable. An antiworld. Just like in the *Superman* comics that I read as a child, where it was called the Bizarro World."

Once the Pistols finally filed off the tiny stage, McLaren asked, "What did you think? Did you like it?"

"Are you serious?" replied the pop star. "Your singer can't sing and he demeans the audience like it's a joke. Your bass player is too busy, he plays too many notes." So far as Merrill was concerned, these Sex Pistols had two things going for them, a drummer who played like the Kinks' Mick Avory, and a guitarist who obviously watched a lot of Pete Townshend.

But McLaren didn't bat an eyelid. "You're wrong. What you've just seen is the destruction of your lot." He ran through a litany of the day's most spangled pop sensations: "Arrows, Mud, Sweet, Bolan, all of you. By this time next year, the entire face of the music scene will have changed." Then he grinned such a mad grin that Merrill swore he would never forget it. "It was like the Joker in the *Batman* comics. Or Dr. Sardonicus." Because, when he recalled that conversation less than six months later, he knew that McLaren was correct.

You could forget the hits, forget the television show. You could even forget the fact that Patti Smith was a fan of the Arrows' debut album, laughing and dancing delightedly when Merrill and Newton dropped by the Portobello Hotel to say hello and play her a copy. "Arrows were dealt a death blow that night, and I smiled right through it smugly, not knowing my band was being executed right then and there."

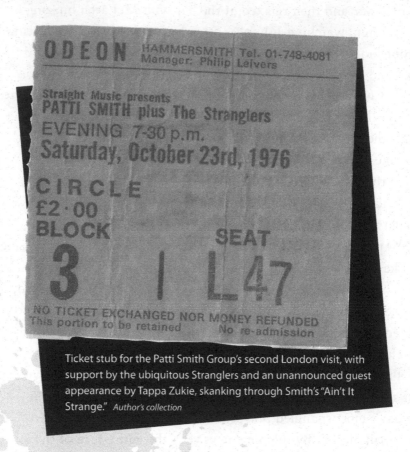

ODEON HAMMERSMITH Tel. 01-748-4081
Manager: Philip Leivers

Straight Music presents
PATTI SMITH plus The Stranglers
EVENING 7-30 p.m.
Saturday, October 23rd, 1976
CIRCLE
£2·00
BLOCK
3 | L47
SEAT
NO TICKET EXCHANGED NOR MONEY REFUNDED
This portion to be retained   No re-admission

Ticket stub for the Patti Smith Group's second London visit, with support by the ubiquitous Stranglers and an unannounced guest appearance by Tappa Zukie, skanking through Smith's "Ain't It Strange." *Author's collection*

They were not the only casualties. It is usually only with lashings of hindsight that you can isolate the precise moment when the practiced rhetoric of one generation is displaced by the unschooled yowling of the next. This time, however, it was easy. The Heavy Metal Kids and the Kilburns had already perished. Next up were the Doctors of Madness. In reality, they would soldier on until late 1978, but Kid Strange knew, deep down, that the game was up more than two years before that.

May 21, 1976. The Sex Pistols were opening for the Doctors of Madness in the northern city of Middlesborough, and Strange is adamant. "The Doctors of Madness weren't a mega stadium band but we were doing OK . . . we were doing well, we were able to attract a thousand people a night to watch us. And I knew, as soon as I heard the Pistols, that we were finished. We were suddenly too old and we couldn't do anything about it. I was twenty-five—and too old for rock! Everything we were trying to do was blown away that night."

What was it about the Sex Pistols that so disheartened these old farts? What did people see in a band that, by any conventional musical wisdom, was so bad, so undisciplined, so chaotic, that they would have been booed off a high school's talent contest stage?

The answer is simple. They were direct, they had energy, they had aggression. There was no need for dressing up to get a musical point across, no demand for drama or makeup or solid production values. It was rock 'n' roll at its most primal, and played with a passion that completely belies the standard muso's retort that "they can't even play their instruments properly," because they didn't need to. They played them well enough to get their point across, and then made up the deficit with pure self-belief. Most bands of the day, the classically trained prog rock superstars and well-schooled glam rock darlings, probably played to one-half of their actual ability because that's all they needed to do. Punk bands not only pushed themselves to the limit of their abilities, they then also worked to exceed them. That's what made the difference, that's what caused such an impact.

"Our attitude to punk was, we were kind of jolted," Graham Parker growled. "We were in a field of one, we were the happening kids, we were outrageous, doing things like 'Can't Hurry Love' really aggressively; doing reggae with this angry attitude; we had it all together, and suddenly we were not the only ballgame. There was this thing called [punk rock], and it was 'oh my God, what's going on?'"

He wasn't impressed at first. "When I heard [the punk bands], I didn't think much of it, because singing in an English accent is something I don't quite get. I find it a little arch, not to my tastes. But it was all very shocking that these bands suddenly came along, and it was a bit scary for us. So we thought we'd better crank it up another level and came back really nasty."

In musical terms, the Rumour were never that far removed from the energies of punk; indeed, their audience was visibly increasing as the year wore on. "Until punk, we were not reaching a mass audience, we weren't really solidifying what we had, we were still a press act in a way. But when punk happened, we increased our audience. We'd play some gigs where the whole front rows were swarming with kids who read somewhere that I was the godfather of punk, or the grandfather of punk, and so we did start to attract a wider audience. So I had to keep up by being even more angry." It was only at the back of his mind that Parker began to face up to the fact that the Rumour, like the Kilburns, the Doctors, and the Heavy Metal Kids, might just be about to get passed over.

"At the time, I thought it was good I was before everyone else, because I thought everyone would remember that. I thought the attitude of the music I was doing would be reflected in what was going on, because it wasn't just punk, remember, it was all these other people with a songwriting background, who were not that far away from the hippie-dippy thing, or who were sardonic, satirical, intelligent, sometimes with anger, pretty much what I was doing. So I thought, because I was first, that was great, I started it. I didn't have that self-aggrandizing 'this is mine' attitude, but when you're there and you're doing it, it felt like that."

Parker had wanted musical change, and he did his bit to forge it. But be careful what you wish for, it might just come true. Punk might have breathed a new breath of fresh air into the music scene, the same liberating breath that would allow Parker to remain true to his convictions long after "fame and fortune" had passed along. But it also derailed Parker's love affair with the media and might even have helped prevent him from attaining the peaks he deserved. And the first band to open fire on him was the Damned, on October 22, 1976. Because that was the day that Stiff Records released their debut single, "New Rose"—chronologically, historically, and spiritually, the first-ever British punk rock record.

Chiswick was the first label to show any interest in the band. The Damned were opening for the R&B of SALT at the Nashville on July 15, plowing through a set that really wasn't going anyplace, and wrapping up with Scabies demolishing his drum kit out of sheer frustration. They came offstage to be greeted by label manager Roger Armstrong, who asked whether the band wanted to make a record. Days later, however, Stiff stepped in and that was it.

Malcolm McLaren was furious. His entire master plan was predicated around the Pistols getting onto vinyl before any of the other so-called punks. They certainly landed the first major-label deal, when EMI picked them up after the 100 Club Festival. But signing with a massive conglomerate and needing to take your place in a schedule that is already brimming over with sure-fire hits—the Wurzels, Manuel and His Music from the Mountains, Paul McCartney and Wings—is different from simply walking into Pathway Studio, where producer Nick Lowe is already waiting, bashing out two songs in little longer than it took to play them, and then sitting back while Stiff gets the record into the shops.

Besides, it was good that the Damned beat the Pistols to the punch, partly because it proved that there was life outside of the Sex shop, but also because the Damned had made a damned good record, and deserved a few plaudits of their own, even if a lot of them did revolve around passers-by coming up with ever more damning epithets for the record itself.

"New Rose" was tremendous, an inchoate barrage of noise and energy, and was over before most reviewers could even sharpen their poison pen. But flip it over and the Beatles' "Help" was trampled with even less respect than Patti Smith reserved for "Hey Joe."

National Rock Star, a short-lived music paper that launched the previous month with a blatant headline lie about Elvis Presley coming to gig in London, proclaimed it the worst record ever made, and a lot of other people agreed. But quite a few didn't, and while Stiff's home-spun distribution network would never allow the label to threaten the UK chart, still "New Rose" was selling as fast as Stiff could press it. And I know I wasn't the only purchaser who smiled secretly to himself as he brought it into the house, secure in the knowledge that the great thing about parents is that they're deaf. Especially where pop music is concerned. I had already played it three times before I was even told to turn it down, but that was all that was said. Nothing about it being punk rock, nothing about it being thrown out of the house. It was, so far as they were concerned, just another few minutes of tuneless noise, no better or worse than all the other tuneless noise that rattled out of my bedroom on a daily basis.

The sudden shock of punk rock, personified by "New Rose," continued to ripple through the musical old guard. In terms of press coverage, certainly, teetering-on-the-brink-of-the-big-time acts like Deaf School and Supercharge seemed to disappear overnight. But others just kept pounding on, not because they couldn't think of anything else to do, but because they knew they still had a part to play in the unfolding drama. So, while the Damned grabbed all the headlines, Roogalator simply got on with their job.

Another lineup shift had seen Adler and Plytas rebuild the group around yet another new rhythm section, but they didn't miss a beat while the new boys settled in.

True, they'd had their share of bad luck. The Stiff single was unceremoniously withdrawn from sale after EMI objected to a spot of minor copyright infringement on the picture sleeve—designer Barney Bubbles styled it after the Beatles' *With the Beatles* LP, all the way down to an ad for the Emitex record-cleaning product on the back cover. EMI's lawyers swooped and Stiff, for whom all publicity was good publicity, loudly deleted the offending item, picture sleeve, vinyl, and all.

Worse was to follow. Arriving at the Mont-de-Marsan festival back in August, Roogalator discovered that the promoter's promise to locate a piano turned out to have been harder to fulfill than he thought.

Adler was furious. "What was going on onstage was such crap and I just wanted to get up there and show them how it should be done. I spent most of the day running around the town trying to get keyboards, I was so amped up. But when it became clear that there were no keyboards to be had, we had to decide whether we were going to do it or not. I was torn, I just wanted to get out there and play. I saw what was going on, saw the other bands, and I thought we could get up there and be the future. We had so much total energy and style and originality, we could just get up there and wipe them all out. But Nick [Plytas] was so sad, and in solidarity for him, I said no. I still wonder what might have happened if we had played."

So did I. They were a phenomenal live act, still one of the best live bands I'd seen all year. Adler had taken to wearing a boiler suit onstage, topped off by a pair of big, harsh-framed glasses; caught in the right light, he looked like a locomotive bearing down on the first few rows of the audience. His bandmates, boiler-suited, too, seethed around him: "We went on stage," Adler shrugged, "and we blasted everybody away. We were on the road, doing 1,500 miles a week in a Ford Transit, we'd play the all-nighter in Wigan where they hated anything rock, and they loved us. We killed every town we went in. I had learned my lesson at Hammersmith Odeon. We had segues, we were playing things way up-tempo. I had whipped these guys into the shape that I wanted, and we killed. A boiler-suited killing machine."

The killing machine was in Fulham tonight, headlining a show at the local town hall, with two more red-hot bands on the bill.

The Vibrators were opening, still buzzing from hearing themselves on John Peel the previous evening, a four-song session that really hadn't developed far from the fare they were dragging round the pubs in the spring. But it was amazing what a new attitude could do. "We Vibrate," their upcoming debut single, had a genuine punky slash to it, even if the chorus did sound like the Bay City Rollers (*quick, where's my scarf?*), and "I'm Gonna Be Your Nazi, Baby" had at least as much nastiness as its title demanded. If they just maintained that standard, we'd be in for a good gig tonight.

Second on the bill, the Clash were equally fascinating. Realigned as a quartet with the 100 Club teething troubles firmly behind them, they were certainly on the move now, riding a wave of press support that put Adler in mind of his own recent past, a year before when he was constantly beset by would-be business managers, all looking to catch a ride on his star. Sometimes he wondered what might have happened if he had not so stubbornly resisted their overtures. But now was not the time to worry about that. Roogalator did have a manager now, Robin Scott, and he was confidently predicting a record deal for the new year. All Roogalator had to do to earn it was keep on destroying every stage they came in contact with, and that they could do as naturally as breathe.

"So we went onstage and we kicked ass." The Vibrators were fun, and the Clash were phenomenal; it was probably the best show I'd ever seen them play, tight, riff-laden rockers barked out with stentorian precision. But Roogalator wiped the floor with them regardless.

"We were really at our peak, we were like a well drilled army, two months solid on the road, two hours of blinding, brilliant music. I really felt, by that point, that everything I had designed and engineered to put into Roogalator came to fruition in that band."

The Clash were still in the building, watching as Roogalator played, and marveling as well, because something they'd been talking about trying to do with their own music—and "trying to" was the operative phrase, because they hadn't figured out how it could be done—was suddenly unfolding before their disbelieving eyes.

It wasn't only Roogalator who were well drilled. Their sound crew was, too. "We were the only white band at that time to play

A boiler-suited killing machine. Danny Adler and Roogalator.
Courtesy of Danny Adler

live dub reggae," Adler boasted. As the quartet began the seamless segue from "Tasty Two" into "Humanitation," the PA suddenly came into life with backward, surreal grooves, lashings of echo and buckets of panning, while Adler, abandoning singing for some unrestrained toasting, let rip on the guitar effects. It was astonishing, one of the most amazing sounds you ever heard from a stage; and if the rest of the audience was spellbound, the watching Clash were surely taking copious notes. Not quite overnight, but certainly while the Roogalator gig was still fresh in the memory, they began working to pull off the same effects themselves.

Backstage, meanwhile, Sex Pistol Glen Matlock was hanging out with the Clash. Adler congratulated him for having landed a record deal.

Matlock smiled. "It's going to be daunting."

* * *

I was working now, five days a week (including Saturdays) at a travel agency whose manager was so impressed by my geography O-Level that I didn't even think to ask how a working knowledge of the forces that created the Norwegian fjords was possibly going to assist me in selling weeklong trips to the seaside—the English seaside, because foreign travel really hadn't taken off at that time. Besides, I was still reeling from the astonishment of learning my weekly wage. Eight pounds was a princely two pounds more than I'd been receiving from unemployment and, once the taxes had been taken out, it would be a lot less than that. Indeed, if my stepmother followed through on her threat to up my "rent" by another 50p, I'd end up a few pence worse off working than I had been on the dole.

I thought of turning the job down, but that probably wasn't wise. Amid all the red tape with which the unemployment office bound itself up was the follow-up phone call to prospective employers to ask how such-and-such a job hunter got on. It prevented the clumsier aspects of benefit fraud, but it also stopped greedy little toerags like me from turning down the opportunity to do an honest week's work, simply because it didn't pay enough. I was still biting my lip when I turned up for my first day of gainful employment the following Monday.

There were a few perks to my newfound career, though: discounted bus and train tickets, daily luncheon vouchers, and, just a few doors away, a record shop whose owner came to know me so swiftly that he was offering me a job before the year was out. It was November 19, and I walked in during my lunchbreak to pick up a copy of "Anarchy in the UK," the Sex Pistols' first record. I walked out with a new career (at almost double the pay), to commence the moment I'd worked out my one week's notice to the travel agency. I'd been there a month, and still that day could not arrive soon enough.

Across the country, but especially in London, "Anarchy in the UK" sold fast, even if it wasn't in huge quantities. The shops that ordered copies were gratified to see them fly out of the door. But few of them had asked for more than a handful, and many more stores just ignored it altogether. Every week of the year saw another few hundred 45s hit the marketplace, no single store could be expected to order them all and, for all the impact punk was having in the pages of the music press, in terms of national importance, it was barely a fart in a hurricane. For far more people than history would ever confess to, "Anarchy in the UK" was just this year's version of whoever last year's forgotten heroes might have been.

Neither were the Pistols' peers unanimously overwhelmed by the record. His voice raised above even the sea of reviews that remarked upon its primitive sheen, Captain Sensible recalled hearing "Anarchy in the UK" for the first time, while sitting around the Stiff offices with the rest of the Damned. "We sat around laughing. It was like old man Steptoe [a then-popular television character] singing over a really bad Bad Company b-side. It was like slow metal."

For others who heard it, however, it was a revelation, kicking in on a guitar that still sounds triumphant, ranting on a lyric that still promises revolution, and then fading out on a stream of consciousness that sounded increasingly pertinent the more incoherent it became.

A decade later, rock journalist Sandy Robertson, a favorite of mine when he wrote for *Sounds* in the late 1970s and now a coworker in the world of men's magazines, played me an American metal band's cover of the Sex Pistols' finest hour. Oh, how we laughed when they replaced, or more likely misheard, the line "council tenancy" with the far more abrasive "cuntish tendency." I can still hear Sandy's closing guffaw. "I wonder if they got the words out of *The Sun*?" The tabloid newspaper would become renowned for misconstruing the lyrics to sundry "offensive" punk songs. This one would have been right up their street.

The first and only issue of Malcolm McLaren's *Anarchy in the UK*
newspaper, a morass of photographs and missives produced for sale
during the Pistols' ill-fated Anarchy tour. *Author's collection*

So "Anarchy in the UK" didn't change the world. But it certainly altered many people's lives. The last time I'd seen Bernie Tormé, for example, he was playing through the final days of the band he'd formed back in the summer, the lurching metallic leviathan Scrapyard. A new bassist, John McCoy, was on board now and, although the band's set list scarcely screamed originality, when Scrapyard nailed an audience, they stayed nailed.

Playing two sets a night, blistering originals would be punctuated by seething takes on Eddie Cochran's "Something Else," ZZ Top's "Nasty Dogs and Funk Kings," Free's "I'm a Mover," Bob Seger's "Rosalie." Scrapyard dressed the part, too, even if Tormé would soon be looking back on his wardrobe with a justified wince. "Oh dear. A little flowery bolero jacket over a faggy eighteenth-century-type shirt, tight velvet slightly flared strides, and, wait for it, fucking cream platform shoes like Elton John." Not boots, because he couldn't afford them. Just the shoes. "And I can remember playing the Greyhound in those clothes, with some mad smacked-up hippie bint trying to stick a syringe into my leg while I was singing, till she fell over in the pissy liquid that was oozing from the blocked gents toilets by the stage."

But there was a power struggle going on behind the Scrapyard scenes, as John McCoy pushed for a bigger say in the action . . . bigger, as in changing the name of the band to McCoy. He could argue convincingly for it as well; so much so that, when Tormé walked into rehearsal one day, his rhythm section was waiting with an ultimatum. "Either the name goes, or you go. In fact, we've already decided—you both go." The first generation of McCoy, fearless purveyors of molten heavy metal, was born there. And Tormé, sacked by his own group ("the bastards"), was back to square one.

Or maybe not. Early on in Scrapyard's genesis, a friend named Pete agreed to act as their manager. He pumped some money into the group, but then lost interest somewhere deep within the bassist merry-go-round. Now he was back, but he didn't come empty-handed. He had with him a copy of a single that Bernie ought to listen to.

Tormé barely glanced at it. One of his guitar pupils, Burt Salvaray, had put him in touch with a couple of North London jazz-rockers, drummer Mark Harrison and bassist Phil Spalding, who were looking for a guitarist to form a band with. It wasn't anything like Tormé had ever dreamed he'd be playing. There were nights when he hated it even more than the Irish country and western. But not only was it a group, it was *his* group. No matter that the music was "fucking awful . . . I called the band the Bernie Tormé Band on the principle that it would be difficult for them to conspire against me and sack me."

He placed Pete's proffered single to one side. It was bad enough, he reasoned, that he was stuck playing jazz-rock in his own group. He wasn't going to listen to some other horrid rock in his own home. Especially when he looked at the label and saw who it was.

"I'd not heard the Sex Pistols. I'd not seen them, I'd not read the reviews. The first thing I knew was people talking about them. Then Pete reappeared and he was besotted with the Sex Pistols in particular and punk in general. I knew nothing about it, and what people said about it appeared pretty silly. Obviously, they were just trying to attract attention. I had heard 'New Rose,' and I hadn't really liked it all that much."

He wasn't keen on the clothing that was creeping into view, either. Making his way to rehearsal one day, "I saw this guy in tight PVC trousers and pointy, Cuban-heel-Chelsea boots. He looked like a feckin' alien in the context of flares, desert boots, and Elton John shoes."

But Tormé finally succumbed to Pete the manager's entreaties, placed the Sex Pistols single on the turntable, "and it blew me away."

So, a few nights later, did the sight that greeted him on the way to a gig. "We were in the van up past where Tottenham Court Road and Oxford Street cross at Centrepoint, at about 5P.M. There was loads of traffic, and hey ho, the Sex Pistols were walking across the crossing with guitar cases, and Johnny Rotten was raising two fingers to all and sundry. All the taxicab drivers were going mad, beeping and doing their Alf Garnett impressions. It was an iconic polarizing moment. I was sold, instantly. That was where I wanted to be. Who cares about music, fuck the Mahavishnu Orchestra, let's cause some chaos and make some noise!"

The Bernie Tormé Band played their regular show that night, then went home. The next time I saw Tormé, he had chopped off his waist-length hair and pegged his trousers tightly in. Visually, the transition was brutal; musically, it was abrupt. But even as the repertoire shifted to reflect his new appearance, Tormé was simply being true to his own deepest musical instincts.

"I was a rocker. I liked the raw stuff. I hated that whole serious musician thing, for me it was just play your ass off and have some fun, and please don't take it too seriously because it's really not going to cure cancer. I liked the rebel stuff, not the stuff people tell me is really well played. More testicle and heart and less clever, please waiter, and I don't care if it's out of tune as long as it conveys something."

Tormé was smart; he was willing to adapt, and he was still young enough to do so. So many others, however, weren't so lucky.

13

I Was Saying, "Get Me Out of Here . . ."

NOVEMBER 1976

SOUNDTRACK

"Anarchy in the UK"	Sex Pistols (EMI)
"Ballistic Affair"	Leroy Smart (Well Charge)
Blank Generation EP	Richard Hell (Stiff)
"Chase the Devil"	Max Romeo (Island)
"Disgraceful Woman"	Johnny Clarke (Attack)
"Gimme Gimme That Punk Junk"	The Water Pistols (State)
"Hang on Sloopy"	Trinity (Well Charge)
"Jah Jah Go Beat Them"	Cornell Campbell (Jackpot)
"Pogo Dancing"	Chris Spedding and the Vibrators (RAK)
"Silver Shirt"	Plummet Airlines (Stiff)
"Ten Against One"	Tappa Zukie (Klik)
"Tradition"	Trinity (Prophets)
"We Should Be in Angola"	Pablo Moses (Klik)
"We Vibrate"	Vibrators (RAK)

A quarter of a century later, reading Nick Hornby's *High Fidelity*, about life in a small, independent record store, I had to wonder whether we had even been in the same trade. Yes, of course. But not in the same time.

There was no quote/unquote alternative scene in those days, and no vibrant underground of independent labels and bands to ensure that every day brought a fresh new surprise. There were half a dozen major labels with a few dozen more subsidiaries, and they didn't simply control the record business, they *were* the record business. The handful of independents that were around, in the UK and abroad, did so on shoestrings so tight that a lot of stores didn't know they even existed, and wouldn't have worried about them if they had.

There was no network of fanzines and small-press magazines, just the big weekly papers to tell you what was hot, what was not, and which record you needed to be buying this week to ensure you could still hold your head up in mixed company. So my time at the record shop was not, as I had spent the last sixteen years imagining, devoted to locking myself in the listening booth, playing through the world of unimagined sounds that awaited me—because there wasn't one. It was spent sorting through and selling multiple copies of precisely the same Top Thirty singles that I heard every day on Radio One. I'd often wondered what kinds of people were responsible for sending the soft pap pop of the Brotherhood of Man to the top of the charts. Now I was meeting them every day.

Except on Fridays. That was the day when Will, the owner, and I would sit down with the new release notifications, and plan out what we'd be ordering into stock for the next week. I'd always known that far more records hit the market every Tuesday than I could ever have been aware of from the music papers and my own browsings, but this was ridiculous. Anything up to and sometimes beyond four hundred new singles were pumped out every seven days, everything from reissues and occasional repressings through to hot new releases, and on to a veritable jungle of tiny labels (more major label subsidiaries, of course) I'd never heard of, with bands that nobody else knew either.

Now I was excited. Now I wanted to hear them all.

Will quickly disavowed me of that ambition by sending me into the back storeroom one day with instructions to wade through shelf upon shelf of unsold oldies, to see if there was anything worthwhile. In fact there was; by the time I'd finished my explorations, I must have emerged with around forty singles that I wanted to take home with me. Which sounds great, until you consider there were maybe ten thousand that I rejected.

Failed follow-ups by once-fashionable one-hit-wonders; we all remember the Starland Vocal Band scoring big with "Afternoon Delight." But who recalls the stone-cold failure that succeeded it? I don't, and I must have counted fifty copies of it on the shelf. Next Big Things who were dropped like hot potatoes the moment it became clear that only the record company knew who they were; any bids for "Seagull" by Rainbow Cottage? Or, whoops-a-daisy, "She's No Angel" by the Heavy Metal Kids? And so on and so forth, until I was convinced that no one had been into that room in five years, except to add more shit to the shelves.

Our job was to ensure that the shelves grew no heavier; to order in the new singles according to what we *knew* would sell, as opposed to what we thought might move, or hoped would go. In other words, what we liked was irrelevant. It was what the girl in the baker's store over the road might like that mattered. Namely, the Brotherhood of Man.

Yeah, but I was working in a record shop! I'd stayed in touch with a few of the kids I was at school with. One had joined the army, another was in the mail room at some big electronics company, a couple had gone on to college, and the rest were either on the dole or doing jobs so trivial that they might as well be. But I'd landed on my feet, surrounded by music from dawn to dusk and, as

my feet slipped further under the table and Will started trusting my
more left-field instincts, beginning to carve out a customer base that
he never knew existed.

Among our most regular customers were the denizens of the
local high school, filing in during lunch break or on their way home
after classes, and mostly what they wanted was whatever they'd just
seen on *Top of the Pops*. Mostly. But a few of them had more esoteric tastes, a few of them might even have shared my own.

I ordered in a couple of copies of Patti Smith's "Ask the Angels"
single, from the just-issued *Radio Ethiopia* LP. Unreleased in the UK,
I'd found a company that was importing copies of the French
release. It was expensive, 75p, I think, compared to the 60p we normally charged, but both copies went the day they came in. I ordered
the Ramones' now five-month-old "Blitzkrieg Bop" debut, and
"Cherry Bomb" by the Runaways, five California schoolgirls straight
out of an X-rated Beach Boys single. I'd seen them play the Roundhouse back in October and been as surprised as everybody else that
their most obvious charms ran in second to the excitement of the
show. The record came in one door and went out through the other.

Over the next few months, I found a source for all those fabled
45s that documented the first baby steps of the New York scene,
original U.S. pressings of Television and Richard Hell, and then traveled further afield, to the output of Marc Zermati's Skydog and the
Belgian label Dynamite, home to some of the best yet still overlooked 45s of the entire era.

I knew better than to stuff the shelves with reggae 45s, despite
one of Cassie's housemates offering us an unbeatable deal on anything we wanted (no questions asked or, presumably, answered), but
I did discover the Saints, an Australian band that looked like a
bunch of motorcycle mechanics and left even the Sex Pistols in the
dust when it came to high-octane rock 'n' roll. "I'm Stranded" was
self-released on their own Fatal label and it was still a month or so
away from a UK issue. But *Sounds* had made it their Single of the

Week, John Peel would soon be spinning it on his show, and everybody who heard it stepped back in amazement, at home and abroad.

"The Saints were a massive influence in their attitude towards things." Nick Cave was still a teenager when he first clapped eyes on the Saints, but he would never forget them. "They would come down to Melbourne and play these concerts which were the most alarming things you've ever seen, just such antirock kind of shows, where the singer [Chris Bailey] wouldn't come on stage, and when he did, he was this fat alcoholic. It was so misanthropic, it was unbelievable, and the whole band were like that. They were so loud!"

Singles were my specialty, but I was growing cockier, and sometimes I miscalculated. I made sure we never sold out of Iggy and the Stooges' *Metallic KO* LP, a live album's worth of tapes documenting the last gigs the band ever played, before they were beaten into submission on a Detroit stage, while a gang of Hell's Angels hurled death in their direction.

But I was also responsible for a shocking back stock of *Live at CBGBs*, a major-label mishmash that took the most sacred name on the New York club scene, then applied it to a double album's worth of tracks by bands that would never rise as far as those who played there in the past. No Television, no Ramones, no Patti, no Blondie. Instead, the Tuff Darts and the Fast were probably the best bands on board and, when John Peel aired a two-hour-long punk rock special in mid-December, both groups were in the show. The rest of the crew were nowhere in sight, and neither were the queues of happy customers whom I'd insisted would be lining up for their copies.

Velour Souterain's "You're Driving Me Insane," on the other hand, didn't stop selling, and that despite the fact that there was only rumor, at that point, to confirm that this was a lost Velvet Underground track, a quasi-bootleg (hence the French translation) supplement to the double album compilation's worth of regular tracks that was, at that time, the only readily obtainable Velvets music on the market.

My greatest idea, however, was shot down in flames before I'd even finished the sentence. I had reconnected with my bootleg-dealing friend Jake once the Reading weekend was over, and someone, somewhere among his various tape-trading contacts seemed to have cultivated sufficient friendships around the punk scene that he was now being entrusted with various bands' rehearsal and demo tapes.

In years—or, more accurately, decades—to come, such recordings would begin showing up as bonus tracks on archive CDs, rounding out a classic album with the shambolic chaos of its makers' early vision. No big deal. But think about what it would have meant back then, before most of the bands had a record deal, and before some of them even had a name. Think how excited I was when I thought I was going to get a tape of the Buzzcocks (and how quietly thrilled I was even after it turned out to be the Vibrators).

I visualized striking deals with aspiring musicians, selling their tapes through the record shop, and who knew where that could take us? At the very least, we could branch out to become a record company. Or not. Will didn't even bother giving me a reason why the likes of the Clash, the Jam, the Stranglers, and Chelsea, unsigned one and all, might not leap at the chance of having their dodgiest scrambles sold through a tiny, independent record store on the outskirts of Enfield. He just sent me back to put the kettle on, and told me to make sure we had enough copies of Chris Hill's "Bionic Santa" novelty hit on hand, to see us through the weekend rush.

I shrugged and followed his orders. He was the boss and, besides, I knew he was right. For all my dedication and effort, punk rock remained a mere sideline in the store. The big sellers through my first month working there were the same as they'd always been. Pussycat simpering through the disco "Mississippi." Chicago weeping "If You Leave Me Now." Greek balladeer Demis Roussos, rock 'n' roll revivalists Showaddywaddy, the Electric Light Orchestra, and Abba. Any one of those, and a hundred more besides, generated more revenue in one day than all of my punks put together managed in a week.

Things would change; of course, they would. Even Will admitted that. "But how about if we see if any of the other groups actually have a hit record first," he counseled. "Or even get a record deal." I nodded and picked up the latest edition of *Music Week*, the British industry's weekly bible. "Anarchy in the UK" had still to even sniff the charts.

*   *   *

Of all the bands forming and fermenting around London at that time, the one I was most curious to see step out was the Adverts.

I knew TV Smith and Gaye Advert by sight alone, a self-contained unit who seemed to be at every show I went to and talking with the same musicians that I passed the occasional hello with, but radiating such glamour and beauty that I was halfway convinced that even speaking to them would shatter the illusion of their presence in the room, and send them whirling back to whichever other universe they had deigned to visit us from.

Six months later, Gaye would be the pinup adorning every love-struck young punk boy's wall. *The Sun* described her as "one of the saucy girl singers who've taken over pop," without her even opening her mouth for more than the occasional inaudible backing vocal; while the *Daily Express* assigned to her "the fragile beauty that made the world and Mick Jagger fall in love with Marianne Faithful.

"Gaye is beautiful, she is as dark as Marianne was fair, with black hair and Castillian white skin. She wears black nail varnish to match, and the black make-up encircling her eyes gives Gaye a sort of morose panda look."

Or, as Jane Suck of *Sounds* said, "She carries her clothes better than any Punkette I have ever seen. She could have the impact of five Runaways, Patti Smith's armpit, and Blondie's split ends on Britain's vacant female scene."

Punk's reluctant pin-up queen, Gaye Advert.
Courtesy of Gaye Advert

Certainly she redefined the traditional notions of beauty at a time when Bond Girls and Page Three models were considered the height of perfection; dark and glowering, distant and disinterested, she would be responsible for opening the door through which a host of subsequent home-grown punkettes—Siouxsie, the Slits, Penetration's Pauline Murray, and, most unconventional of them all, X-Ray Spex's Poly Styrene—would subsequently push.

At the time, however, she was simply Gaye, illuminating every room simply by walking into it, and one-half of an inseparable duo whom everybody knew was forming a band, but which still hadn't quite come together. In my heart, I knew the Adverts were destined to become my favorite band of the day. But, as week piled upon week, I did wonder if that day would ever arrive.

So did they, Smith told me once we did meet. It's one of the unwritten laws of the music industry. Advertise for musicians in the music press and you never know what is going to walk through the door, and the more specific your requirements, the less likely you are to find what you want.

Smith's ads were very specific, a nasty guitarist for a brand-new band, with musical influences that more or less began and ended with the Stooges. Then he sat back and waited while player after player came trouping up the stairs to the attic flat, to run through their paces with little regard for a single word they had read, would-be rock gods with Jimmy Page haircuts, queuing up to prove what great solos they could play. Smith, on the other hand, had already decided there'd be no solos in his songs, so anyone who deviated from the simplest chord structure was out the door before their plectrum left the strings.

Then Howard Boak called up to invite Smith round to his flat in nearby Leamore Road. And he was so tight and economical, so willing to be shown what Smith wanted him to do, before turning it around and into something even better, that he was offered the job on the spot. Plus, he lived so close, *plus*, he worked in a music shop in the West End, complete with its own rehearsal center, and *carte blanche* from the owners to go in there himself, whenever there were no paying customers using it.

"So Howard was obviously the right man for the job," Smith laughed. There was just one hint of puzzled regret. The newcomer had already changed his surname to Pickup before he revealed that his given name, "Boak," was a northern English colloquialism meaning "vomit." In a world already inhabited by Vicious, Rotten, and Scabies, he would have fit right in.

Again, assuming the band ever got out of the practice room. Six weeks of rehearsals left the Adverts desperate to complete the package. But few worthwhile responses greeted the next *Melody Maker* ad, this time requesting a drummer, and those who did were frightened off by the Adverts' neighbors in the rehearsal studio.

Led Zeppelin was rehearsing in another part of the building, and made a regular habit of looking in on the Adverts as they staggered through their paces, just to say hello and ask how it was going. At least one prospective percussionist was so overwhelmed by the sight of the superstars standing in the doorway, watching while he set up his kit, that he promptly fled the building.

Another was snapped up by another band, just as he was about to fall into place. One of Pickup's workmates at the music store, John Towe, had certainly shown an interest, only to be invited to join Chelsea instead—the same Chelsea that snatched Billy Idol away from the formative Siouxsie and the Banshees. Cassie and I went to see Chelsea at the ICA, as part of the guerilla art collective Throbbing Gristle's *Prostitution* exhibit, and left halfway through the set. Their repertoire comprised nonstop old Rolling Stones numbers, and they were sharing the stage with a stripper. Doubtless espousing a very early manifestation of the subsequently fashionable mantra of "Fuck art, let's dance," we headed off to a Roogalator show instead.

The Adverts soldiered on. "It was getting to the point," Smith lamented, "where we had a whole set in place, and we were looking to do gigs, but we couldn't get a drummer for love or money." Then Pickup suggested they try out another of his friends; Laurie Muscat had dropped by the occasional rehearsal to watch, and he reckoned that he could play drums. In fact, he'd never even tried, but how difficult could it be?

He begged two days of lessons from a laughing John Towe, then walked into his audition. It was, Smith deadpanned, "interesting. Not what I expected! I expected a normal drummer and he wasn't. He had this rigid but extremely fast style that was very unconventional. I didn't know if I liked it first of all, but there was no denying that his playing was different to anything else going on, and he gave us a very distinctive sound. There was no way you could dance to the Adverts!"

It was difficult to keep up with him as well. Songs that the trio had learned at more or less the pace that Smith intended them were racing by at twice that speed, a steep learning curve for Gaye to handle, but even harder for Smith, who suddenly found entire mouthfuls of lyrics needing to be spat out in the space of one word. Smith renamed the newcomer Laurie Driver. It seemed to fit.

Finally, the concept with which Smith and Advert had set out, of a little punk band called the One Chord Wonders, who couldn't play but were going to do it anyway, had solidified. They started taping rehearsals on a portable cassette, and then taping over them the next day because they couldn't afford a new tape. Each one, though, was a little better, a little sharper, a little more focused than the one it replaced, and each one proved that Smith's vision had indeed found the ideal conspirators.

Gaye's bass pounded through the demo of "One Chord Wonders," Driver drummed like thrashing trashcan lids across the tumultuous "Newboys," and, all the while, Pickup's pent-up guitar would be probing the edges, looking for an escape route, somewhere between the frenzied, quicker-than-quickstep rhythms and Smith's breakneck delivery, protracted streams of syllables that he machine-gunned over the clatter of the music. Even the pogo would flail inadequately in the face of the Adverts' staccato barrage, but there was purity to the presentation that no other band could match.

Six months after moving to London, looking to start a band, the Adverts were ready to start gigging. Assuming anybody would book them. Assuming anybody would book *any* band any longer.

14

You Can't Say "Crap" on the Radio

DECEMBER 1976

SOUNDTRACK

"Can You Feel It" — Junior Byles (Thing)

"East Man Skank" — Dillinger (Well Charge)

"Free Black People" — Burning Spear (Total Sounds)

"His Majesty Is Coming" — In Crowd Band (Evolution)

"I'm Crying" — Little Bob Story (Chiswick)

"Jah Bring I Joy" — Bobby Melody (Trojan)

"Kingston 11" — Royal Rasses (God Sent)

"Let's Get Started" — Tetrack (Rockers)

"Philistines on the Land" — Junior Murvin (Upsetter)

"Punky Xmas" — Matt Black and the Decorators (Punk)

"Ragmanpaiza" — Dillinger (Well Charge)

"Satisfaction" — The Residents (Ralph)

"S'cool Days" — Stanley Frank (Power Exchange)

"Special Request" — Dennis Alcapone (Jackpot)

"Stranded" — The Saints (Power Exchange)

"Unitone Skank" — Dr. Alimantado (Ital)

"Earlier this evening, Thames Television broadcast an interview between Bill Grundy and the Sex Pistols pop group. There was some foul language broadcast which offended many viewers. We very much regret this offensive interview and apologise most sincerely to all our viewers." —Thames television on-air apology

The scene was repeated all over London, with more or less precise symmetry. People left work at 5:30, waited for one bus, changed onto another, and walked into the living room just in time to be told to shut up.

"Sit down, watch this. It's incredible."

Or . . .

"I don't believe what I'm seeing. It's disgusting."

Or . . .

"I'm not having fucking filth like that in my cunting house. Not in front of my children."

Or . . . my stepmother sitting staring in disbelief, too shocked even to shift herself across the room to change the channel to something less unpalatable.

Each of them responding to the same couple of minutes of broadcast television.

"You dirty bastard."

Standing in the doorway, watching the scene unfold, the words didn't register for a moment. For me, anyway. The middle-aged man conducting the television interview knew exactly what was happening.

"Go on," he prompted. "Again."

"You dirty fucker!" What the fuck?

"What a clever boy."

"What a fucking rotter!"

Is that Bill Grundy?

Fuck.

Eyes were aflame. "I don't believe it." Grundy, an amiable television news host who'd been around since the year dot, was facing the camera now, talking his way out of the nightly magazine program

he'd been hosting for years. The credits rolled. There was silence.
Followed swiftly by an eruption.

Parents seething, shocked and silent.

Their offspring staring in stunned amazement.

A truck driver kicking in his television screen to protect his children from the barrage, then telephoning the *Daily Mirror* to brag about what he'd done.

The program, Thames Television's *Today* show, was only broadcast to London and the southeast of England, but that was enough. By mid-evening, the events would be known around the country; by morning, they would be front-page news. And still you just sat there, replaying the dialogue in your mind.

What a fucking rotter.

What a fucking marvelous publicity stunt. The Sex Pistols were invited onto prime-time television, and then sat there and swore their heads off. Which, if we were speaking literally, would have saved the public executioner the bother of cutting them off, but only just. It had been a long time since the English tabloid press truly embarked on an antipop witch-hunt . . . the early Rolling Stones were probably the last true victims, and two of them ultimately wound up in jail. A decade later, jail was not even on the list of possible punishments for the Sex Pistols.

You didn't swear on teatime television in those days. You didn't swear on television, full stop, and the handful of people who had let the odd expletive slip on a live broadcast had paid dearly for their mistake. The fact that both McLaren and the Sex Pistols looked as shocked as everyone else let you know that they were aware of that, too. Landing a slot on the *Today* show was one of the biggest breaks of their career so far. Now there was the distinct possibility that it was the last thing they'd ever do.

I couldn't stay home after watching that, with my stepparents eyeing me suspiciously, wondering afresh whether I'd brought any punk rock into the house, or whether I, too, might break out in a volley of unprovoked obscenities.

Up to my room, flick through *Melody Maker* (and hide a few 45s among the books beneath my bed). Gigs in London tonight. I needed to be among friends, even if they were strangers. December 1, 1976. It'll be like the day when Kennedy was shot, people will remember it for years to come. Where were you the night the airwaves turned blue? And you can say, "I was at the Marquee, or the Nash, or—"

. . . or the Golden Lion on Fulham High Street, to catch the second-ever performance by the Tom Robinson Band.

I'm not certain what drew me to that show. Possibly a faint affection for the occasional Café Society song I'd heard on the radio, maybe a dim awareness of the band's association with the Kinks' Ray Davies, whose genius would surely have rubbed off on his protégé. Or maybe it was simply the belief that anybody looking for trouble that night would be hunting down bands who sounded like punks. "Tom Robinson," on the other hand, could be a banker or a builder.

There were no antipunk vigilantes on the street, no police barricades set up around the venue to snare any likely-looking miscreants before they could make any further trouble. Fulham High Street was as deserted as it ever was once the sun went down and, although there was a sizable crowd in the Golden Lion, there were no more than two . . . no, make that three . . . people who looked like they'd even heard of punk rock. The rest could have been waiting for any pub gig, any time in the last five years.

But you could tell that something had happened despite that, broadcast through the thick silence that was underpinned by a groundswell of half-whispered conversation. *Did-you-see-it did-you-hear-what-they-said—I-can't-believe-that-happened—they-said-fuck.* No more than three hours had passed since the Pistols went off the air, and already the paranoia was sparking.

Few people would deny that the government only tolerated youth cults and cliques because they kept the kids from making serious trouble. The Pistols had stepped over the line. They *were* making trouble, and every time a police car passed the pub with its sirens on, you could feel the tension rise.

The Tom Robinson Band were rehearsing when the shit went down, and they needed to. Robinson had a stinking cold, one that no amount of Lemsip had been able to shift. In the end, he took to downing mouthfuls of Scotch from the bottle he'd won in a raffle a few days before. Worse than that, though, was the fact that the musicians didn't know the songs. Shit, they barely knew one another.

Across the six months since he first saw the Sex Pistols, Robinson's thoughts had been drifting further away from the pleasant but polite sounds that fueled the band he was then best known for, Café Society. He was tiring, too, of the audiences that seemed to be that group's sole constituency. Like their heroes, Café Society fans were respectable people. And Robinson insisted, "I hate respectable people."

It took him a few months to do anything about it, but when the realization came, in the middle of a sleepless night, it came hard. "I looked around and saw the Sex Pistols exploding all over the country, the Clash tearing the place apart, and here was I sitting in my bedsit, kidding myself. I knew I was never going to make it as I was. Having told myself that, I went back into a really calm sleep because I knew what I had to do, even though it would mean stabbing some good friends in the back." That was on October 12. The following day, he broke up the group.

The Tom Robinson Band emerged slowly. "I went around all my old contacts and started blagging gigs for a group I didn't have." A lot of them came through as well. The problem, as he told his diary, was that he didn't know who would be onstage with him from one show to the next. He cast around the circle of musicians with whom he customarily surrounded himself. Drummer Mick Trevisick had followed him on from Café Society; Anton Mauve, Bret

Sinclair, and Mark Griffiths were friends who agreed to help out when they could.

He'd already penned a handful of songs that he knew would do the new act all right: "Martin," "Grey Cortina," and a poppy rocker that looked like it might wind up being called "2-4-6-8 Motorway." But they were just the gravy around his true mission. The meat of the repertoire was the songs that shouted the loudest, that picked a political point and worried it like a sore.

The self-affirming "Glad to Be Gay" pointedly acknowledged that it was almost ten years since homosexuality was legalized in Britain, and queers and queer-bashing were *still* considered suitable material for prime-time television comedians. Robinson wrote the song relatively quickly. But he lived it every time he spent another long night listening to his gay friends lamenting the lives they were forced to lead, or manning the telephone at the Gay Switchboard, a crisis line for everyone who felt the need to call it.

Over the next few months, "Glad to Be Gay" would be picked up by the music press as the band's most singular rallying cry. To Robinson, however, its most pointed message was that Britain's gays weren't the only ones being singled out for discrimination. We all were.

Everywhere he looked, Robinson sensed "big trouble on the streets. And that's where the average music fan is. They're either still at school or just left school, and are in a boring job. Whatever music you make, you've got to be in touch with their lives. I could see they were going to want much more basic, more simple hard-hitting rock music." Robinson was determined to provide that.

The Tom Robinson Band, built around his immediate nucleus of players, debuted at Islington's Hope and Anchor on November 28, with everybody coming through in spectacular fashion. Three nights later, though, neither of his chosen guitarists could make it and Robinson spent hours plowing through his address book, looking for anybody who could step into the breach. Finally, he picked up the phone and called Wales.

He wasn't at all sure that Danny Kustow was the man he needed. No matter that he was one of Robinson's oldest friends; it was where they met, not when, that mattered. "I met Danny in a home for maladjusted children," he once told me. And what's more, he added, "it shows."

But he needed a guitarist, and Kustow deserved a break, if only for his persistence and his loyalty. Who else would bother hiking all the way from Presteigne to London, just to cheer on an old friend? Plus, you had to love his attitude.

Kustow flew to Robinson's side. He'd lost count of how many times he'd traveled to London, "each time asking Tom if he ever needed a guitarist, might he think of me. But he never once suggested that I might even dream of joining his band, he never gave me any sign or encouragement that he might need me as one of his guitarists. In the end, I only ever joined because one of the guitarists couldn't do it, and Tom said, 'Come along to a gig and do backing vocals.' That is how I joined the Tom Robinson Band, doing fucking backing vocals!"

Robinson kept the set simple. "It was a scratch band learning the set afresh at every gig, according to who turned up. So the set needed to be three chord, simple, repetitive songs that could be easily learned." A cover of the Velvet Underground's "Waiting for My Man," Dylan's "I Shall Be Released," and a handful of originals: "Up Against the Wall," "Right On Sister," "Motorway," and "Grey Cortina," a song that Anton Mauve positively loathed, but what choice did they have? The set was short enough as it was, particularly once Robinson dropped "Long Hot Summer," because "the arrangement would probably have been too fiddly for the band to have learned and played that night." And still Kustow remembers cornering Robinson just before they went onstage to lament, "Jesus, I haven't learnt all these songs properly yet." Robinson just smiled. "Don't worry, you'll be fine."

While the musicians stretched out, Robinson fought to reign in his own instincts. "The big danger is doing a gross-out and going over the top," he warned himself before the show. "Must stay in contact with that audience, and save any posing for during the singing. And make it a bit tongue-in-cheek. Really mustn't blow it."

He'd not played a show on such a knife's edge since July, when he took a one-man revue, Robinson Cruisin', out to the assembled hordes of London's Gay Pride week. There, however, he'd been preaching to the converted. Tonight, he knew what was at stake. "It's very important from the point of view of playing for real rock punters: a real audience and the chance of building a genuine following. That's going to be a bit dicey without Griff and Brett, but I really can't start worrying about that."

The support act, I don't remember who, came and went; the jukebox started up again. "The Boys Are Back in Town." "I Love to Boogie." Feel-good rock 'n' roll. The mood of the room was lightening a little. And then it darkened again, cold and silent, as the wail of a police siren drew closer.

Eyes flickered at one another. Hearts pounded. Had it started already? Was this it? The beginning of the clampdown, the authorities swooping to round up the punks, ship them off to detention centers? Eyes swiveled around the room. Who me? No, I've always dyed my hair green. That guy over there, though. I bet he says "fuck" a lot.

The siren drew closer. It was right outside now, its flashing lights reflecting through the windows. A pub full of frozen statues waited to see what would happen next.

Then the traffic lights changed and the car pulled away again; there was a collective sigh of relief, a bout of self-conscious smirking, and a snarl of "fucking pigs"; and the Tom Robinson Band wandered out onto the stage, and we could forget the fear again. Or maybe not forget it, but at least take solace that someone else was on our side.

But, even as the first few voices raised to sing along with "Martin," the cocksure confessions of a juvenile delinquent who didn't give a toss for whatever law and order dictated, still it was apparent that a Rubicon of sorts had been crossed, between the say-nothing, do-nothing, think-nothing status quo of everyday life, and the need to stand up and make your voice heard. And when Cassie and I caught the Tom Robinson Band again a few nights later, with the players settling down now, and the set bristling out, it was obvious that the Sex Pistols had merely fired the opening shot. The real revolution was still to come.

> "THE FILTH AND THE FURY! A pop group shocked millions of viewers last night with the filthiest language ever heard on British television. WHO ARE THESE PUNKS? Obnoxious, arrogant, outrageous . . . the new pop kids. They wear torn and ragged clothes held together with safety pins. They are boorish, ill mannered and arrogant. They like to be disliked."
>
> —*Daily Mirror*

> "I thought it was fantastic! Funniest thing ever! Totally unbelievable that any TV program at that time could let that happen. They must have known, it was the best promotion ever."
>
> —Bernie Tormé

* * *

It's not often that you meet a *bona fide* superstar at the bar of Fulham Greyhound, but that's where I found Martin Gordon, and he fulfilled many of the criteria by which I judged such deities at that time.

Two years earlier, Gordon was bassist with Sparks, positively *the* most exciting band to emerge in British chart terms since the heyday of Bowie, Roxy, and Bolan. Recruited following Californian band-leaders Ron and Russell Mael's relocation to London, Gordon was part and parcel of the fabulous unit that recorded *Kimono My House*, and then stormed the chart with "This Town Ain't Big Enough for Both of Us." As it turned out, this band wasn't big enough for both of them either, and, as swiftly as Gordon appeared, he disappeared, departing Sparks to form a new band called Jet, and then relaunch on a wave of excitement that was almost as pronounced as the one that launched Sparks. Almost, but not quite.

Two years, one LP, and a host of shattered dreams later, Jet had sundered, unmourned and largely unremembered. But was Gordon downhearted? No. Instead, he told me a story.

Jet's vocalist, Andy Ellison, didn't set out to get a record deal when he headed over to Camden Town one cold November morning; didn't even remember that he still had a cassette in his jacket pocket, left there from who knew when? But he was browsing through the albums at the Rock On record store when he recalled hearing that there was a small record company upstairs. He didn't know anything more about it than that, but he decided to go up there anyway and play them the tape. "It was," Ellison admitted, "a total chance thing."

The tape represented Jet's last will and testament, the store was the logical successor to the market stall that had borne the same name for so long already; and the small record company was Chiswick, half a dozen releases into its year-long existence, and still smarting at the speed with which Stiff had leaped ahead of it. What Chiswick needed, label head Ted Carroll determined, was a group . . . even a record . . . that would shake the label's pub rock constituency from its hair, as resolutely as the Damned had redecorated Stiff. He heard it that morning.

There were four songs on the tape, but Ellison needed play him just one, an ode to the joyous possibilities of the Kodak Instamatic camera, sensibly titled "Dirty Pictures." And "Ted was really knocked out. He wanted to release it right away, but he naturally assumed that Martin and I would be wanting to do everything on a big level like we had [in the past], but which Chiswick could never afford."

Ellison, after all, had a pedigree that almost matched Gordon's; a decade previous, he was the frontman for John's Children, a demented rabble of mods who cut a string of fabulous singles during 1966–1967, and whose guitarist across a couple of them was none other than Marc Bolan. The pair hadn't really spoken much since Bolan left the group, but his luster lingered on. Or, at least, Carroll thought it did.

Ellison was quick to disavow him of such sentiments. "I finally managed to persuade him that all we wanted was someone who would put the record out for us, and Ted was the first person I'd met who considered anything on the tape to be at all commercially viable. The money side of things didn't matter to us, because we were broke already, and we'd carry on being broke, but at least we'd have a record out."

The news couldn't have arrived any sooner for Gordon. The last few months had been hard. Home was a rented Gothic heap perched on the Harrow Road, so grim that the first time his mother saw it, she burst into tears. But the mice were friendly so long as you left food out for them, and the only time he was ever attacked by the rabbits that had taken over the back garden was his own fault entirely. One of them apparently objected to his impersonating its fevered digging for the benefit of a girlfriend, and urinated in his face.

"I was preoccupied with staying alive." A friend, topless model Stephanie Marrian, put Gordon in touch with "various very dodgy modeling and, unbelievably, acting, agencies," for whom he limped very effectively for a costume drama about the Napoleonic wars, enjoyed a few bit parts in *The Sweeney* and *Space 1999*, and even appeared, with an unconvincing moustache, alongside Glenda Jackson in *The Incredible Sarah*.

He kept such activities quiet from his musician friends, although he admitted that wasn't too hard as there weren't many of them. Jet's moment in the sun had long since passed—the one and only time I saw them, opening for Ian Hunter and Mick Ronson's first tour in March 1975, turned out to be the one and only time most people saw them; the musicians had been too busy trying to survive to indulge in any kind of social whirl since then. When I told Gordon that I was a Jet fan, he told me that he knew a doctor who could help.

The bulk of Gordon's time now was spent scouring the same Musicians Wanted ads in the back pages of *Melody Maker* that TV Smith had been posting, box after box of "bassist needed, no time wasters, must like (and here would be the name of some horrid band)." So Gordon would brush up on whatever horrid band it was, then trot along only to discover that the vacancy had already been filled. And it was a waste of time anyway because when he did get his foot through the door of another group, he immediately pointed out how dull their songs were compared to his own, and his tenure would come to an abrupt end.

Then Ian North called.

Like Gordon, New Yorker North was a graduate of the Sparks sphere of influence. But whereas Gordon played ultra-distinctive bass on their finest hour, North's involvement was confined to sharing the same manager while fronting glam tigers Milk 'n' Cookies. But the United States never had and never would bow down to worship the glitter that consumed the rest of the world, so rather than surrender to the inevitable and shatter on the spot, the quartet decamped for London, and broke up there instead. Now North was piecing together a new project, the modestly named Ian's Radio, and he wanted Gordon to broadcast alongside him.

The lineup was completed by the brothers Robin and Paul Simon (not that one), but it was not a happy time for Gordon. "We began 'working' together, if you can use the term to describe unpaid effort. I did my best to go along with Ian's *éminence grise* notions, but I wasn't a very good actor, as I had discovered in other, recent circumstances, and so it was rather unconvincing. He would trot out his rather workaday tunes, 'Girls in Gangs,' which was about girls going round in gangs, 'Rivets,' about falling in love with a welder, 'Model's World,' about the world of models—the word 'prosaic' springs to mind here—and I would pretend to be enthused by them."

In fact, he was more enamored by North's girlfriend of the time, with whom he was thoroughly enjoying a clandestine relationship.

But he grit his teeth and plowed on, through a handful of under-whelming demos, and a couple of equally unimpressive shows. "We had a couple of gigs, one supporting Ultravox! at the Nashville in November, another at the Speakeasy, where the grown-up rock stars would come out to play. But, unfortunately, they were all at home washing their hair on this occasion. Anyway, I'd been there, done that, during my time with Sparks, so it wasn't much of a turn-on and I frankly felt that I deserved better."

Neither was Ian's Radio wholly in tune with what was clearly bubbling up around them. While other groups—and their audiences—were becoming more street conscious and sharp, North was embarrassingly prone to donning a schoolgirl costume onstage, which Gordon would begrudgingly compliment with a bright pink jacket. At the same time, though, Gordon gracefully acknowledged that he wasn't exactly *au fait* with the Punk scene, either.

"I had the sense that there was clearly something going on, but I wasn't sure how (or even why) it would affect anything that I was involved with. There was punk action going on, certainly, and we all knew that, but actually there was no real discussion, because we didn't do discussion, we couldn't afford it, and analysis was also beyond us. We just waved a wet finger in the air to test the *zeitgeist* and began, unconsciously, but also uncynically, to play a little faster."

So Ian's Radio stumbled along, and then Andy Ellison called Gordon to tell him that Chiswick was interested in Jet. Just days later, Ellison, Gordon, and guitarist Ian McLeod were in Island Studios, remixing "Dirty Pictures."

Or intending to, anyway. It was December 2 and as soon as they arrived at the studio, having somehow avoided even glancing at the newspaper headlines that morning, it was clear that very little was going to be done that day.

The same scene was played out in offices and studios all across London. "Everybody turned up as usual," Gordon explained, "but the whole building was talking about the Sex Pistols. I hadn't actually seen it, but I soon knew every word. Not much actual work was done anywhere, as far as I could tell. There were knots of people in every corner, discussing the events, earnestly in the case of the executives, admiringly in the case of the musos. We adjourned to the local Island pub and decided that it was, on the whole, A Good Thing, then wandered back to the studio and carried on rehearsing." Finally, they got round to finishing off "Dirty Pictures." It felt like a new beginning, and it was.

Back at our record shop, the first customer of the day was a woman who marched in clutching a handful of singles, to demand whether we were the perverts who had sold this filth to her fifteen-year-old son. Will flicked through them. Leo Sayer, Queen, Elton John. "Well, yes madam, we may have sold them to him, but I don't think you'll find they are precisely the kind of records you think they are."

She didn't hear him. She was not, she insisted, having this kind of degenerate garbage in her house, and if we didn't take the records back right now, she would simply throw them in the dustbin.

Will smiled and told her to do whatever she felt most comfortable doing; then, once she had marched out again, the records still crushed into her pudgy paw, he told me that he would be manning the cash registers that day, and I should busy myself out back, checking stocks, following up on customer orders, and maybe giving the place a bit of a dust. I'm not sure whether he was trying to protect me, or protect his business, but clearly I'd be better off out of the way.

And so the day went on. Maybe three other people came in, two to warn Will off selling any punk rock to their children (without saying who their children were), and one to ask if we stocked the Sex Pistols record because if we did, then they would never cross our threshold again. Will later said he'd never seen the person before in his life, so it probably wasn't too great a loss.

The daily influx of schoolkids was another matter entirely, of course. The really hip ones had long since bought their copies of "Anarchy in the UK"; now came the rest, lining up at the counter

Radio Stars rarely dressed as conventional punks, but backstage, who does? Martin Gordon and Andy Ellison after a show. *Courtesy of Martin Gordon*

and each one demanding the same record. "I told you we needed to order up more," I grumbled as Will sent the eighth customer of the day away empty handed, but I knew why we hadn't. If a record wasn't showing any significant signs of movement after two or three weeks, it simply wasn't worth keeping more than a couple of copies on hand.

A police car stopped outside, coincidentally just as I'd finished telling Will about my night at the Golden Lion. We watched as its occupants sat for a while, then slowly eased themselves out of the vehicle and into the shop.

"Can I help you?" Will was politeness itself.

"Yes, sir. We were wondering if you'd seen—" They were on runaway kid patrol, and record shops were often regarded as a potential hangout for a lot of them. We hadn't, and they left. But the paranoia remained.

15

Down in the Sewer

MID-DECEMBER 1976

Cassie and a friend named Joe were heading home, waiting for the District Line at Hammersmith station, when a shout made them look around.

"Fucking punks!" A voice sailed over from the far end of the platform. She tried to see who was shouting, but there were enough people blocking her view that it could have been anyone. "Probably saw us coming down the escalator," Joe shrugged. "Idiots."

The first train through wasn't theirs, but it did empty the station, and when Cassie looked around again, three guys were standing at the far end staring down at them, taking it in turns to draw their fingers over their throats, and laughing to one another.

She nudged Joe. "Looks like trouble. Should we maybe go out and catch a bus?"

"Nah. I get this every time I go out. Fucking wankers."

"Well, don't do anything to provoke them." She could feel the loathing washing down the platform in waves toward them. People say that bullies tend to be motivated by fear more than anything else, and attack in the hope of affirming their own security. Not this bunch. They hated punks in the same way that a gardener hates weeds, or the police hated blacks.

"Look, when the train comes, let's get right down by the driver's compartment, OK? That way, if there is any trouble—" She felt the draft of an incoming train. "Right, remember what I said, right up by the driver's compartment."

They boarded and she tried to see whether the three guys at the far end had climbed on as well. This one platform serviced trains that went to three separate destinations. What were the chances that they were headed toward the third? Pretty good, it seemed. Five stops passed, and all the way she was holding her breath, listening for the telltale clatter of the connecting doors flying open as the trio made its way down the train. But finally Notting Hill flashed into view and, as the train slowed to a halt and the doors hissed open, she breathed a sigh of relief—then gasped as she turned around and saw the same three guys leaving the carriage next to them, grinning as they caught her eye.

Joe saw them as well. "Stay calm. Then, when we get outside, run."

They climbed the short flight of stairs to the surface level, aware of every step of the three men—and they were men, at least in their mid-twenties, maybe older—behind them. But when she and Joe ran, so did they, always a few yards behind them, but always there as they swung round the corner, dodged the traffic across the road, and then into the warren of backstreets that led back to the squat.

Their pursuers didn't gain, they didn't fall behind. It was like long-distance running. They just kept their pace, speeding up when their quarry did, slowing when tired limbs demanded it slow. But the squat was just around the next couple of corners and, dodging a bus, they were into the home straight. Which is when they ran smack into the trio.

"What's the hurry?" Two of them grabbed Joe, one caught Cassie by the arm and pulled her to him. She kicked backward, felt a moment's satisfaction as her heel connected with a shin, but the grip

didn't relax and now she was held immobile while she watched the
other two take turns punching Joe in the stomach. She saw his
glasses fly off and kicked out again, harder this time and squirmed
around to face her assailant as he pulled hard at her hair.

She was screaming now, and Joe was as well, and she didn't
know how it happened, but suddenly she was free, as her foot made
contact with a fleshy groin and her assailant leaped back. "I'm
gonna fucking kill you for that," he roared, but she was too far
ahead now, running around that last corner, but still hearing the yells
as all three piled into Joe.

She burst into the door of the squat, screaming into the front
room. "For fuck's sake, come on. They're killing Joe!"

Half a dozen Rastafarians rose as one. She heard a chair fall
over, and a record skip violently, and then they were outside again,
six hard Rastas with a hysterical white girl at their head, pounding
around the midnight corner to where the guys had Joe on the
ground, raining kicks into the tight little ball of flesh. Then they
caught sight of the new arrivals and, just for a second, Cassie
thought they might stand their ground. They didn't, but it didn't
matter. There was a roar and one of them was pinned to the ground,
and somebody—she thought it was Junior—took a running leap up,
and then down on his head, feet first and full weight.

Cassie skidded to the ground beside Joe, holding him at first,
then cradling him. She couldn't see his face, but in the half-light of
the streetlamp she saw dark smears of blood on her shirt and jeans.
"Christ, we need to get you to a hospital." She looked around to see
if anyone had maybe come out of one of the nearby houses to find
out what all the noise was. There wasn't a soul, just a blur of black
bodies as they tossed the three attackers from one to another, kicking
and punching and then slamming them down, onto the pavement or
up against a wall.

There was a cheer as two of them broke away, trying to run but
scarcely able to drag themselves out of harm's reach. But it wasn't

their escape that prompted the outburst. It was the sight of Linton standing at the very edge of the curb, arms raised and, squirming in the air above him, the third of the white guys, gripped so firmly by throat and groin that the screams she knew he was trying to emit were choked into a barely audible gurgle.

And what was Linton doing? He was waiting for a bus, the huge red bus that was now bearing down toward him . . . was almost level . . . was about to pass. With a grunt as loud as the engine, he hurled his load against it, a six- or seven-foot gap that the flying body crossed in no time, but which seemed forever as time slowed to a crawl.

There was a crash like she'd never heard before, flesh and bone meeting steel and glass, screams from inside the bus, the panicked cry of the conductor, and the screeching of brakes as the bus swerved to avoid an obstacle that had already smashed into it, mounted the pavement, came to a halt.

Cassie looked around. Linton, Winston, Junior, they'd all vanished, melted back into the night. Now it was just Joe and she, huddled on the pavement, and now lights went on around them and windows and doors flew open.

Passengers were staggering off the bus, dazed and shocked. The conductor was simply standing there, staring in horror at the broken . . . but not dead, astonishingly not dead . . . body that lay on the road, where it had rebounded after impact. Sirens howled somewhere out of sight, then burst into view, police first, then ambulances. She heard a woman's voice, one of the passengers. "It was the blacks. Saw him plain as day and black as night, just picked up the poor lad and threw him."

Someone stepped over to where Cassie still crouched. "Are you all right, dear? Is that your friend?" At first, she thought she was talking about Joe, then realized that she meant the man in the street. She shook her head, but no words would come out. An ambulance man appeared. "Gently." He tried to move her arm from around

Joe's shoulders, but she wouldn't let go. She couldn't let go. "Can't you see he's hurt enough already? Let him be."

"It's all right, we just want to take a look at him." The man rose a little, gestured, and two of his crewmates came over. One carried a flask; he poured a cup of tea. "You're all right. They've gone."

"Fucking coons. We should burn the lot of them out."

Cassie tried to protest. "It wasn't them. They saved us." She took a sip of tea, scalding and sweet. "It was them." She pointed toward the road, where two more ambulance men were gently rolling the groaning man onto a stretcher. "They attacked us. They saved us." She knew her words made no sense; could still hear people cursing the black bastards, heard someone else surmise that she was lucky she'd not been raped to death.

She wanted to shout and scream and tell them they'd got it wrong and later, at the hospital, sitting by Joe's side while a policewoman tried to piece together her story, she would do just that, asking them why they found it so hard to believe that three white men should attack two of their own, then be routed in turn by half a dozen blacks?

"Because that's not how it happens," the policewoman said. "I know, this has been my beat for three years. I see it all the time, the blacks hiding in alleyways, then jumping out, and they don't care who they hurt, or how badly. They took your handbag, I see. Can you tell me how much money was in it?"

Cassie looked at her blankly. They took her what? "I don't carry a handbag. Everything's in my pockets."

"Then that's what they were after." The cop nodded to a rip in her jeans. "Did that happen during the attack?"

"They didn't attack me. The black kids didn't attack me. Or Joe. I keep telling you, they were white. The guy who hit the bus, and two others. They followed us on the tube. Called us 'fucking punk rockers' and followed us, chased us—" and then she realized that nobody was listening anymore, not the policewoman with her three years on the beat, not the policeman who sat behind her taking notes, nor any of the others who'd been standing around, just itching for the order to go out and crack some nigger skulls.

"Punk rockers," said one quietly. "Fucking punk rockers." No longer cajoling with just a hint of sympathy, she could hear the same hatred in their voices as she'd heard on the tube station, and the same stifling wave of loathing and rage. "Yeah, look at the way she's dressed. Should have fucking known, wouldn't have wasted so much time if we had."

Cassie stood up. "Excuse me, is that it? We're punk rockers, so suddenly it doesn't matter what anyone does to us?"

The policewoman looked at her with what she obviously thought passed for a sympathetic glance. "It's not that, dear, it's just that resources are slim, especially around here. Of course, we can't spend as much time on every crime as we'd like, we have to prioritize, and I'm sorry your friend got hurt, but—" She paused, but Cassie never could decide whether it was for dramatic effect, or because she, too, couldn't believe the words that were coming out of her mouth. "But what do you expect to happen, if you go around dressed like that?"

* * *

Joe was not the only hospital case that weekend. The Sex Pistols' own career was in need of intensive care. Within twenty-four hours of the *Today* broadcast, the BBC had declared a blanket ban on "Anarchy in the UK"; the rival commercial broadcasters quickly followed suit. The single was still selling, but chainstore after store was refusing to restock it, registering their own "protest" against these foulmouthed monsters. At the EMI pressing plant in Hayes, the packing ladies announced that they would no longer handle the record. The "strike" only lasted a day, but it made the headlines anyway, perhaps the first industrial action of a strife-ridden year to win the approval of the national press.

At the other end of the country, in the northern climes through which they were now driving, the Sex Pistols' tour was in similar disarray. Like dominoes, the word filtered down that the shows were being canceled, either outright by local authorities, who refused to even countenance these self-proclaimed anarchists from darkening their doorways, or by proxy, with demands that the band "audition" for aged councilors before being given the go-ahead to play. It didn't matter that more than one rumor insisted McLaren was canceling many of the shows off his own bat, knowing that the media would never check such fine details. The system was seen to be exacting its vengeance, and punk was gaining its first martyrs.

But the fallout was affecting everybody.

It wasn't only the Sex Pistols who were having problems playing shows. Other bands were turning up at other venues to discover that a gig they'd been booked to play weeks before had suddenly been canceled. Some promoters blamed the breweries that held the license to the venue, or the landlords who owned the premises. Some blamed their immediate bosses; some blamed the local police. And some just blamed the sudden, massive lurch to the right that the general public had apparently taken, as though only a massive infusion of blind patriotism and brutal authoritarianism could place the country back on the paths of decency from which these punk shockers had suddenly sent it sprawling.

The first punks had already been attacked on the streets; the first pubs had already had bricks lobbed through their windows. And the first public figure had stepped forward to lead Britannia out of the darkness.

A few days after the *Today* broadcast, viewers of the decades-old *Opportunity Knocks* talent show were astonished when the program's aging host, Hughie Green, abandoned his traditional farewell in favor of reciting a piece of patriotic doggerel that he had composed especially for the occasion.

Performed with full orchestra and a military guard of honor, "Stand Up and Be Counted" railed against all the evils that were besetting the land, with the subtitled lyrics scrolling across the screen to make sure the message hit home. "Stand up and be counted: where the managers manage and the workers don't go on strike."

Green had always been known for his right-wing views (earlier in the year, he closed the show with a rousing chorus of "Land of Hope and Glory"), but even his bosses—who were as shocked by the outburst as Green's viewers—acknowledged that something must have pushed him over the edge. And there was little doubt as to what that something was. Green was a constant critic of television's apparent decline into obscenity and degradation. The Sex Pistols' *Today* performance would have been the final straw for such a demagogue.

EMI, too, were doing their best to ally themselves with forces of law and order, while pulling out every excuse they could think of to justify having even entertained the thought of contracting with the Antichrist. Their panic was contagious, too. Other labels were likewise trying to decide how they viewed this latest leprous plague, although not all of them viewed it with such terror and dread. Not if there was money to be made . . .

Was punk rock here to stay? In which case they should grab anything that even looked capable of sticking a safety pin through its cheek. Or was it just a passing fad, in which case they could just kick back and laugh at EMI's continued discomfort? Either way, it was a momentous decision, one that would require a great deal of thought and consideration. It certainly wasn't something that could be decided over a boardroom table, or a paper-strewn desk.

See you down the Speakeasy this evening?

Yeah, see you there.

Watching the venue filling up from the side of the stage, the Maniacs had never seen so many company suits clustered around the bar. "I found the Speak to be a kind of cool, dark, and intimate place, where you would get a more hip and happening punter," reflected Alan Lee Shaw. "There were few punks to speak of, it was still pretty much old-school rock bands." Which made it a very strange place for the wheels of industry to be so regularly greased, I always thought, but no matter. The Speak was where deals were done, dreams were born, stardom was schemed and, for a lot of onlookers, the Maniacs were about to offer them their first-ever taste of this new punk junk.

The Maniacs themselves had changed considerably since I last saw them; a change, Shaw admitted, that was down to an encounter with the Stranglers' Jean Jacques Burnel. "Des had befriended Dai Davies, who managed the Stranglers, and we got support slots with them at the Hope and Anchor, the Nashville, and somewhere else. There were seventeen people in the audience at the Hope, because the Stranglers still weren't that well known. But I remember Jean Jacques having a go at me for doing too many Velvet Underground covers, and saying we should do more originals. And, of course, he was right!"

Now the Maniacs' set was almost completely self-composed, with just the occasional nod of the head to their influences. But did the assembled heads of record-company-land even notice them? Of course not. They had their meetings and drank their drinks, and then agreed that they needed to discuss the matter some more.

See you at the Speakeasy tomorrow night?

Yeah, see you then.

Not every label was uncertain. Polydor chased the Clash for a while, financing some demos in mid-November before losing the band to CBS. CBS looked at the Stranglers, but something about the band's image just didn't sit right with the marketing team. Too old, too gray, too mustachioed. Finally, the label tried some market research, reportedly circulating a photograph around a sampling of their would-be audience—would *you* buy a pop record from these men? When the answer came back no, they passed on the Stranglers, and United Artists picked them up instead, then signed a deal to handle distribution of Stiff and the Damned—by which time "New Rose" had already sold four thousand copies by mail order and word of mouth alone.

RAK had another Vibrators single on the schedule, and there was even room for a few novelty records, as State uncapped the Water Pistols' "Gimme That Punk Junk" (home to the legendary lyric "anarchist anarchist anarchist a couple of local girls"), and Lightning unveiled the Punk label, to house the immortally named Matt Black and the Doodlebugs. With the festive season now bearing down fast, Black was inviting the nation's festive revelers to have themselves a Punky Xmas.

In the heart of Soho, meanwhile, the Adverts were being courted from a very unexpected direction.

As soon as he and Gaye arrived in London, Smith picked up a day job at a mood music company, an enterprise dedicated to providing background music for television programs and documentaries. Whenever a new order was received, Smith would locate the records among the mountainous shelves in the back room, slap them in an envelope, and take them across to the post office.

Now he was facing the curious possibility of bundling up his own albums like that. Moving a lot faster than many others in the media, Smith's bosses sensed the direction the musical wind was blowing; knew, too, that before very long, their mailbox was going to be bulging with requests for music to accompany punk rock documentaries. They'd fill those requests as well, even if it meant having to record the music themselves. And all eyes turned toward Smith. He was a punk; he had a band.

"There was a definite point when it looked like they were going to record the first Adverts album as a punk mood music album," Smith recalled. "They were offering us studio time to go in and record, we'd get a royalty, and the chance to go into the studio and put it out was a little bit tempting because you always think, 'Yeah, I could always make another one.'"

But you also had to wonder just how seriously anybody would take the group once word got out about what they'd done, a nagging doubt that grew through the day, and finally kicked into overdrive late that night, as he and Gaye sat in their one room, listening to John Peel on the radio. Punk rock was coming out of the nation's ears, if people only knew where to look for it. If and when the Adverts made an LP, they'd be making it under the same terms as everybody else. Their own.

Peel introduced the evening's show with a few words of warning. "I think you'll find this program's in rather marked contrast to the programs that preceded it because tonight, we're going to have a look at punk rock. Mind you, no two people seem to be able to agree exactly what it is, as is evidenced by the fact that somebody's been phoning us off and on during the day, and trying to convince us that our guests tonight, the Damned, are not punk rock, and punk rock fairly clearly means something very different to Americans. Anyway, we'll hear a lot of music that may be punk rock, and a lot that certainly is. And we'll start off with the Damned. Off you go and play, boys."

"OK, dad" came a voice from the tape, and straight into a storming version of "So Messed Up" that was birthed at the BBC studios eleven days before, as loud and thrashing as it ever was live, but clear evidence of exactly what Rat Scabies was always telling people: the fact that the Damned really could play their instruments, even when they were pretending through the song's chaotic close that they couldn't.

A slice of half-forgotten garage fuzz by the Seeds was next, a group, explained Peel, "that I used to hang around with in California in the 1960s, and they seem to be fairly crucial to the punk movement."

Hmmm. Crucial, maybe, inasmuch as they played with a certain primitive fuzz, but that was about it; there'd been a few music press writers recently sniffing around the possibility that punk was simply the heir apparent to a lot of old sixties sounds, the early Stones and Yardbirds, the American Midwest garage fuzz, and so forth. But unless you really wanted to base your musical predilections on the fact that it all sounded equally crunchy, such notions were one hell of a stretch.

Still, that did not deter Peel, as another slice of 1960s Americana, the Shadows of Knight, crackled out of the radio, before he returned to slightly firmer ground with Eddie and the Hot Rods. "Slightly" being the operative word. "A lot of people would argue whether Eddie and the Hot Rods are actually a punk rock band," warned Peel, "and the fact that they've achieved some degree of success would probably disqualify them in the eyes of some people. But they're on the cover of the latest issue of *Sniffin' Glue* and that's enough for me."

The Pistols were there, Peel bucking the BBC ban with characteristically lackadaisical flair, and the Saints, buoyed by Peel describing "I'm Stranded" as one of the best 45s of the year.

He skipped across to New York City, once a land of musical mystery and romance, but now the entire metropolis was an open book. Richard Hell's "Blank Generation" was newly released in the UK by Stiff, all choppy guitars and hangdog vocals; Television's "Little Johnny Jewel" spiraled through its myriad convolutions courtesy of the Ork label. There was room for the then-unknown Pere Ubu, Tuff Darts, and the Fast; a slash of vivid glam from the New York Dolls ("not one of my personal favorites," Peel conceded, "but considered highly influential by some authorities"). Iggy and the Stooges made a necessary appearance; the Ramones served up an inevitable curtain call, with Peel recalling how, the first time he played them on the show, he was bombarded by hate mail from his most loyal listeners. He didn't care then and he laughed at them now. Compared with some of what had become available since then, "it all sounds a little tame."

What continued to fascinate Peel, however, was the sheer vehemence that punk was arousing, and the strange sense of *déjà vu* that accompanied it. "It's always good when you find papers at both ends of the newspaper spectrum violently opposed to a new form of music. They used to do it in the days of the Rolling Stones and the Who, and they used to do it in the days of Elvis Presley and Bill Haley as well. I'm not saying that these sort of bands are the new Whos and Rolling Stones . . . but I'm very glad that they're there, because they bring an injection of energy and crudity into a rock scene that's been painfully smug and complacent in the last few years.

"At the age of thirty-seven and weighing just a little bit over thirteen stone [182 pounds], I'm not about to dress up as a punk or change my hairstyle or anything, unlike one or two media people who appear to be attempting to effect the lifestyle and the appearance of punkdom. But I'm very grateful to the bands and the people who make the music (or most of them anyway) for the excitement and heated debate and general bewilderment they've brought back to the rock scene. It's been much missed."

And, in bedrooms and bedsits across the UK, the people who knew punk, the people who hated it, and, most of all, the people who were making it, listened to Peel, considered his selections and understood instinctively that he'd just drawn a very thick line in the sand.

Johnny Rotten may already have rechristened the veteran giants of 1970s rock as "boring old farts," but *he* was hardly going to say anything else. This, however, was John Peel. John Peel, the man who once encouraged his listeners to sit through umpteen minutes of Lynyrd Skynyrd's "Free Bird." The man who allowed his audience to bliss out by playing entire Mike Oldfield albums end to end. Who could swing from a Burning Spear opus to some Soft Machine jazz-rock with barely a pause for breath. The one deejay you could turn to and know that he hated the current Top Thirty singles chart as much as you did. If he'd had his head turned by this new punk rock thing, then nothing was sacred. By the end of the week, the handful of demo tapes that usually landed on his BBC desk had been transformed into an avalanche, and almost all of them were styling themselves punk rock.

Peel listened to them all.

"It's impossible to overstate John Peel's contribution in championing punk on the airwaves," Alan Lee Shaw confirmed. "He was pretty much the only deejay to promote punk in the early days, and his shows were a must if you wanted to hear the latest punk 45s. He was also a regular at punk gigs, you would see him in the audience on numerous occasions. Peel was a one off, a real man of the people."

And the boring old farts could all fuck off and die.

16

Pogo Dancing

JANUARY 1977

SOUNDTRACK

"Bionic Dread"	Dillinger (Black Swan)
"Dangerous Rhythm"	Ultravox! (Island)
"Dreadlocks Party"	Little Joe (Belmont)
"Dreamland"	Bunny Wailer (Island)
"False Teaching"	Junior Murvin (Well Charge)
"Gorilla Got Me"	Gorillas (Chiswick)
"Grip"	Stranglers (UA)
"Judas the White Belly Rat"	Lee Perry (Upsetters)
"Natty Sing a Hit Song"	Dillinger (Arab)
"Plante Comme un Prive"	Asphalt Jungle (Skydog)
Ramones Leave Home LP	Ramones (Sire)
"Rockers"	Tappa Zukie (Klik)
"Soldier and Police War"	Jah Lion (Island)
Spiral Scratch EP	Buzzcocks (New Hormones)
"Teenage Head"	The Snakes (Dynamite)
"Things and Time"	Wailing Souls (Well Charge)
"Three Babylon"	Aswad (Island)

We took a right out of Covent Garden tube station, crossed over the road, and Neal Street was directly ahead, fenced on either side by the towering, dark brick buildings that had somehow escaped being blitzed to oblivion (plus a handful more that still bore the scars), and which now left the street in shadow, even when the sun was up.

It was even darker now. London nights start early in winter, and the weeks around New Year's were as black as it got. Even the streetlights weren't sure what to do, while the handful of offices that still clung to life kept their glow to themselves.

The only life seemed to percolate from the occasional pub and the late-night Wimpey Bar on one corner. Up until a couple of years before, Covent Garden was home to the country's biggest fruit and vegetable market. But, as the London streets grew more congested, and the necessary lorries and vans found it harder to get around, the market upped and moved to Nine Elms, on the other side of the River Thames. The Covent Garden market buildings would survive, and there was talk of redeveloping them into a tourist plaza. For now, though, the place was one vast, semiderelict building site, corrugated metal fences and precarious-looking scaffolding surrounding and surmounting the hollow warehouses and empty offices, while the stench of rotting vegetables permeated every surface, and the only flash of color was the graffiti splashed across every wall.

Millwall Rule OK. Football supporters passing through as they enjoyed a night on the town.

Dyslexia Rules KO. Comedians following a few days later.

George Davis Is Innocent. A dangerous armed robber, or the victim of a police frame-up? The campaign to have George Davis's conviction overturned was one of the defining features of mid-1970s London, and the spray paint clung to every surface even after his conviction was declared unsafe and overturned in May 1976.

Arsenal Skins Kill Millwall Scum. The football supporters were back.

NF. Oh look. They can spell.

We were on our own.

Welcome to the Roxy, London WC2.

We saw the beginnings of a crowd; or, at least, a motley gaggle of stragglers that was slowly resolving itself into something remotely resembling a queue. We did a quick headcount to make sure the place wasn't going to fill up before we got to the entrance, and walked in. A little hole on the right hid the cashier away.

"A pound."

"Thanks."

In we went. On the left was a seating area, on the right there was a bar with some stools. Past the cloakroom and the graffiti-smeared toilets. There was a staircase at the end of the bar, leading down to the basement and a dance floor fit for two hundred fifty, three hundred bodies at a squeeze.

We swept through. "Who sits down for punk rock?" TV Smith sniffed as Cassie and I clip-clopped down the sticky stairs. We could see the stage from about halfway down, and a musician or two checking their leads for the last time, before they took the plunge. There were no roadies to be seen, or very, very few. Those that did affect that lofty title were merely friends of the band, thrilled to be playing their own part in the drama.

We made our way to the bar, tried to decide between the two beverages on sale, Breaker malt liquor, or Colt 45. In cans. Around us, a handful of familiar faces were pleading poverty with the bar staff. "We never had any money," Smith reflected. "So we'd have to try to get people to buy us one, or go without. You'd have to hope a journalist or a manager or someone who'd just cashed their dole money would take pity on you." Over at the deejay booth, Cassie was talking with the tall Rasta who spun there. She knew Don Letts from his day job at ACME Attractions on King's Road, where his collection of reggae records was the permanent soundtrack to any shopping expedition. It was one of his coworkers, accountant Andy Czezowski, who was running the Roxy, after being tipped off to its availability by Gene October; Czezowski was managing the Damned at that time, and he had his own rehearsal space, too, "a place he'd rented under some railway arches in Greenwich." According to October, "it was real run down but he just put a stage at one end and everyone used that. Andy fancied getting involved in a punk club and said to me, 'Gene, if you spot anywhere you reckon could be a good venue, let me know.' So I did."

The Roxy hadn't always been a punk club; it hadn't always even been a music venue. In its earlier guise of Chaguerama's, the original owner, reggae producer Tony Ashfield, staged a handful of gigs there during the very early 1970s, proggy combos like Stackridge and Egg, and various visiting reggae artists. (The club was named for Chaguaramas Bay in Trinidad, a little oasis of Caribbean sunshine in the dismal desert of London.)

But the club was better established as one of the capital's leading gay venues, and that was a sight to behold, its bright and beautiful clientele rubbing shoulders with the then-thriving Covent Garden market men and barrow boys as they made their way to Neal Street.

Exclusive in a run-down and seedy kind of way, foreboding in a dark shades and leather manner, "Shaggers" had already been discovered by the Bromley Contingent, one of a network of London gay clubs and pubs where their flamboyant outrage could pose and preen to its heart's content, without fear of censure, complaint, or worse. Other gay clubs—Louise's, the Bird Cage, the Sombrero, and the Catacombs—all welcomed anyone with a taste for the unexpected, and a distaste for the discos and nightclubs where the "normal" people went. But Shaggers had an ambience all its own, and a deceptive one as well. I went there with a friend one evening in 1975, midway through the school summer vacation, balked at the price of even a soda, and wasn't too crazy about the music they were playing. So we left, and it was only later that we discovered that we'd spent an hour in a gay club, and hadn't even realized it.

"Well, you were at an all-boys' boarding school," Cassie remarked when I told her the tale. "It probably seemed quite normal to you."

October continues his story. "It was owned by a couple of Swiss geezers, millionaires, the kind of guys who would drive round Piccadilly in a Rolls-Royce and pick up guys off the street. I went in there for a drink one night, and the place was empty. Loads of advertising, they'd spent a lot of money on it. I went there because I liked the guy who worked behind the bar. And the minute I went in there, I said, 'Bloody hell, you've only got five people in here and it's a Friday night. You must have spent fifty grand advertising—what's going on?'"

What was going on was a petition arranged by local residents and businesses, complaining about the class of person who descended upon their neighborhood on the way to Shaggers. The club had survived one closing order, but the ninety days' extension that was granted on appeal would be up at the end of the year. Unbeknown to October, the club's owners were desperate either to sell the premises and move on, or find somebody else who would rent it, and give it a whole new identity.

He made his pitch. "Listen, I've got a band and we need some place to play. Fancy it?"

They did.

October was right—Chelsea did need a gig—and, in the wake of the Pistols debacle, so did a lot of other groups. By the end of the evening, October had the answer to all their prayers.

Of course, things didn't work out quite as October planned. Manager Czezowski bailed on Chelsea within weeks of becoming their manager; or, rather, he bailed on October. Little more than two weeks after Chelsea's first show, October awoke to discover his entire band—Billy Idol, Tony James, and John Towe—had quit to form their own group, named Generation X after a trash 1960s paperback that Tony James found under Idol's mother's bed.

It was they who had the honor of igniting the newly rechristened Roxy—a name hoisted upon the venue by the Shaggers management, to prove to their neighbors that the gay club had gone. Of course,

John Towe . . . ex-Chelsea, Generation X, Rage, and the Adverts, and that was just within the first eighteen months of punk. *Author's collection*

what they were proposing to replace it with was not likely to strike the sensitive locals as much of an improvement.

Helmed by Czezowski and business partner Barry Jones (the owner of the four-track studio where the Damned cut their maiden demos), the Roxy staged its opening night on December 14. October was not even present. Czezowski barred him from entering the venue he'd discovered. It opened again the following night, for a special performance by the Heartbreakers, and it was the success of those two shows that convinced Czezowski that he could make a go of the place. By the end of the month, he had negotiated a new deal, taking over the club for the next three months, for £350 a week.

On New Year's Day, it was the Clash's turn to headline the Roxy, with October now restored to favor, and introducing a new Chelsea lineup to the stage—Bob Jessie, Martin Stacey, and a former Stranglers roadie named Carey Fortune. But these first nights at the club were tentative. Word of its existence had yet to spread far afield, and audiences were more likely to comprise the different bands' friends and acquaintances than a general cross-section of punkoid youth.

Photographs of the place depict a liquid jigsaw of multihued humanity flowing across the dance floor, but it really depended upon who was playing that night, what counterattractions could be found around town, and, ultimately, whether you stood near the front, where the hardcore tended to assemble, or lurked at the back where the rest of us went.

There were far more jeans and T-shirts on show that first evening than the bondage trousers and safety-pinned bin liners of later lore, although a growing sense of momentum was certainly afoot. TV Smith fondly recalled how the crowd "started off with a bunch of misfits, people who'd raided their local charity shops and put some kind of outfit together, and small pockets of people who'd spent a lot more time on their image and were dressed to shock"; Cassie preferred to think of it as one of the few places in London where you could wear the last clothes you had left before doing the laundry without somebody making remarks. And those faithful old electric blue satin flares crossed the room on more than one occasion.

Bernie Tormé loved the Roxy. He was throwing himself into the punk scene with abandon now, not only impressed by the rebelliousness of the music, but likewise by the sheer freedom of expression. The Elton John shoes and paisley shirts had long since been binned, and with them, all dreams of a career in heavy metal. "There was something happening, something with kids and energy. It was difficult to put it in a box. There was little similarity between the Stranglers, say, and the Damned, or either band and the Pistols. Or the Clash. Musically they were not similar, it was more of an ethic and clothes, really.

"It was very diverse, because there were a lot of people coming in from completely different directions, partly opportunistic, but everyone believed in the ethic, I think. Of course, you ended up with the Punk Mind Police West London Savanarola Division, in a short space of time—'this was,' 'this wasn't,' 'this should be considered as,' 'this not,' but actually anything that called itself punk initially was punk. That's how it worked."

"Being in a punk band at the time, I felt we had at last found a voice and all was expression," continued Alan Lee Shaw. "All was a blast, and all behavior felt acceptable." Away from the near-nightly pilgrimages to the Roxy, he recalled regular Saturday sojourns to Portobello Road, dropping in at the Portobello Gold or the Lonsdale pubs "to check out like-minded punk movers and shakers. Then a trip to the Rough Trade record shop for the latest punk 45 releases, and then on to the numerous second-hand clothes stalls to acquire some cheap duds that we could cannibalize into punk ware. I had an old Austin Reed jacket and a pair of black leatherette strides that served me well. I didn't go in for the full-on studs and safety-pins-through-the-nose story. Although I do remember having a chain around one boot at some point."

But, he conceded, however it was dressed, "punk must have come across as very threatening and subversive to the old guard." He knew, as we all did, that its violent, ugly side was, for the most part, all bravado, "a celebration of individual freedom, angry and vocal." But individuality was not something that the establishment had ever been inclined to encourage, for that way lay anarchy—in the UK or elsewhere. Punk was throwing down a direct challenge to that orthodoxy, and the Roxy was to become that challenge's nerve center.

Eventually. For now, it was just a place to go.

If what would become history's vision of punk costuming and attitudes were in a minority, so was any suitable music with which to entertain the masses. As the Roxy's resident deejay, Don Letts was responsible for keeping the audience happy in between bands, and he quickly found himself facing an impossible dilemma.

How many true punk records had been released by the end of 1976? John Peel highlighted most of them in his show, and played no more than twenty. I could go through my record collection, or the boxful of 45s that sat on the counter at work, with "Punk Rock" scrawled across it in Biro, and pull out maybe a dozen more. The Ramones and the Patti Smith Group. "New Rose," "Anarchy in the UK," "We Vibrate," and "I'm Stranded." A couple of others were on their way; the Buzzcocks' *Spiral Scratch* EP appeared in mid-January. But still it wasn't enough to fill the gaps between and around the live entertainment, so Letts began looking further afield.

Once a week or so, he headed out to the same record shops that I used to visit, in search of ideas for new things to stock. Rock On in Camden Town, of course; Lightning Records on Praed Street; and Rough Trade on Kensington Park Road, the holy trinity of worthwhile emporiums, and the pulsebeat of fresh esoterica. It was in one of them that I first heard the long-mothballed debut by Jonathan Richman and the Modern Lovers in its entirety, Velvet Underground organ and Richman's dissonant vocal coming together in the utterly anthemic "Roadrunner." There, too, I first encountered schoolgirl Arianna Foster, now rehearsing her promised Slits, and dividing her time between Rough Trade and the reggae specialist Dub Vendor on Ladbroke Grove. Like me, she still looks back and marvels at "a pile of records like a mountain, a mountainside. Piles and piles of records and sleeves and everything thrown down on the ground and piles of papers and piles of scattered girls running around. I don't know how they sold records like that!"

But they did, and Letts picked up heaps of them. The first time Mick Farren's "Lost Johnny" scorched your eardrums, the acerbic missing link that pitted the spirit of 1960s rebelliousness firmly into the heart of 1970s discontent, it would probably have been at the Roxy. Nick Lowe's seething revision of the Feelgoods' "Keep It Out of Sight." The MC5's "Looking at You." The Snakes' swampy revamp of the Groovies' "Teenage Head."

And there was reggae. Lots and lots of reggae, because the mid-1970s were a fertile, febrile time in Jamaica as well, as the Roots movement that had been percolating for a few years now arose to take the societal bull by the horns.

Letts explained. "To me, the reggae thing and the punk thing, it's the same fucking thing. Just the black version and the white version. The kids are singing about change, they wanna do away with the establishment. Same thing the niggers are talkin' about. 'Chant Down Babylon.' It's the same thing. Our Babylon is your establishment, same fucking thing. If we beat it, then you beat it and *vice versa*."

The music was marvelous. Dillinger's "Natty Sing a Hit Song" and "Bionic Dread," Little Joe's "Dreadlocks Party," Junior Murvin's "Police and Thieves" and "False Teaching," Lee Perry's "Judas the White Belly Rat," Trinity's "Natty Tired fe Carry Load," Jah Lion's "Soldier and Police War." And "Three Babylon" by Aswad, a bunch of Ladbroke Grovers who'd just been picked up by Island Records, the first homegrown reggae act ever to land a major label deal.

Protest and prophecy were everywhere, even without *Two Sevens Clash* to stir the prospect of apocalypse into the pot. Bob Marley was on the run, recording in the United States to escape the assassins who almost killed him in Kingston a few weeks before Christmas, and preparing what would become his most defiant LP yet, *Exodus*. Prince Far I was barking Armageddon, Jacob Miller was musing on the tenement yard. If any music could soundtrack the still-formative rumblings of punk in the days before the record labels pounced and gave a deal to every spiky-haired ragamuffin in sight, it was reggae, and the Roxy crowd responded with glee. Soon, Letts grew tired of repeating, he was receiving requests not to play anything that might be classed as punk rock, because there'd be enough of that onstage later on. People wanted reggae, and the heavier the better.

"He was very sussed, Don," Gene October laughed. "People also used to bring in their own records, stuff they'd discovered, and ask him to stick it on. But he was having a good time, getting stoned and playing his reggae. His mates used to sell blow to the punks. And he filmed all those bands on a handheld camera, because he knew there was something going on here."

Back in the early days of the New York scene at CBGBs, Ivan Kral filmed everything he could, the formative days of all the acts that would soon be erupting out of the city: Television, the Ramones, Blondie, the Talking Heads, Wayne County, the Dictators, everybody, and then cobbling all the footage together into the seminal documentary *Blank Generation*. Now Letts was doing the same, and his Super 8 was ubiquitous.

He, too, talked vaguely of making it into a movie but for now he was simply making a visual record of a moment in time, capturing performers who, at that stage, had no idea of whether they would ever be given another chance to physically record what they were doing.

"I looked around," Letts explained, "and all my friends were picking up guitars, and soon the stage was full up. What I loved about punk was that they didn't try to encourage a fan mentality. They said, 'You can have a go, too, if you've got an idea and a motivation.' So I picked up a Super 8 camera."

There was no shortage of subjects for him to be capturing, nor for the handful of other enterprising auteurs who would soon descend upon the city. Across the first two weeks of the Roxy's existence, Chelsea, the Clash, Slaughter and the Dogs, the Jam, Wire, the Lurkers, the Heartbreakers, the Vibrators, and Generation X all crossed the stage, and Czezowski was constantly on the lookout for more, as TV Smith found out when he called the Roxy from work one afternoon.

"Hi, John Towe told me about the club, I was wondering if my band could play there sometime?"

"I dunno. What's the name of your band?"

"The Adverts."

"OK."

And that was it. No audition, no rehearsal, no "have you got a demo tape and I'll give it a listen." Just "great, see you on January 19. You're opening for Slaughter and the Dogs."

What Smith didn't know, and what Czezowski didn't tell him, was that John Towe had already made him aware of the Adverts; that he had, in fact, already penciled them in for another Roxy show, four days earlier, opening for Generation X. One moment, the Adverts were standing staring at the rehearsal room walls, the next they had two gigs in the space of less than a week.

"I'll always remember the Roxy for being my first 'real' gig, playing in front of people who were into the same kind of bands and

MEMBERSHIP CARD

The ROXY

Disco Club

41-43, NEAL STREET, COVENT GARDEN, W.C.2.

Name. DAVE THOMPSON

No. 3310

Date of expirey

Signature

3310

Not as exclusive as it looks, I seem to recall these being handed out to anybody who asked for them. Note the subtlety with which the club's true musical intentions are disguised beneath the promise of mirror balls and polyester strides. *Author's collection* music as me," Smith told me. "Before that, playing with [his last group] Sleaze in Devon, it was a pretty random bunch of people, most of whom were into local rock bands and tribute bands to Free or Deep Purple. Getting out on stage to people who knew about Iggy and the New York Dolls and the Ramones and the Sex Pistols was a whole different experience. Before, I didn't really care what the audience thought because I went on stage assuming they wouldn't like it. But at the Roxy, it mattered.

"Some of the most exciting early gigs I remember were from the Damned. I also loved the chance to see some of the American bands

"My God, there're photographers everywhere!" The Adverts hit the boutique circuit. *Courtesy of TV Smith*

like Wayne County and, of course, the Heartbreakers. Then again, a really important part of the Roxy was the unexpected little bands who would never have got on a stage anywhere else, like Johnny Moped."

The Adverts also fit into that category, at least if their maiden appearance in the *New Musical Express* was anything to go by. "The Adverts were chronic," condemned the reviewer. "There wasn't a hookline or riff in earsight as the singer raged and ranted unhearable lyrics. The best thing about them was their female bass player."

"Not bad for your first piece of press," smiled Smith. "It's a strange combination when you get your first review and it's the worst review you could ever have. I was quite impressed how much the journalist hated us. It did hurt a little, but he hated it so much that you do feel this switch. I really must be doing something right! Because when you've done something in good faith and someone takes that much offence to it, or misunderstands it so totally, it must be right! Much better that someone comes to your first gig and says you're chronic than they come and say it was 'all right.'"

1 7

Beat on the Brat

EARLY FEBRUARY 1977

SOUNDTRACK

"Borderline"	MC5 (Skydog)
"Gatecrasher"	Gorillas (Skydog)
"I Can't Explain"	Flamin' Groovies (Skydog)
"I Got Nothing"	Iggy and the Stooges (Skydog)
"I Remember You"	The Ramones (Sire)
"I'm a Punk"	Norman and the Hooligans (President)
"IRT/Stanley"	Snatch (Bomp)
"Ital Dish"	I Roy (Sunshot)
"Leaving Here"	Motörhead (Skydog)
"Man in Me"	Matumbi (Matumbi)
"Neat Neat Neat"	The Damned (Stiff)
"Piss Factory"	Patti Smith (Sire)
"Roots Train Number 1"	Junior Murvin (Black Art)
"Smile Jamaica"	Bob Marley and the Wailers (Tuff Gong)
"Suicide Jockey"	Tyla Gang (Skydog)
"X-Offender"	Blondie (Private Stock)

So far as the media were concerned, punk's most natural foe was the Teddy Boys, fossilized remnants of Britain's rock 'n' rolling past who had been prowling the fringes of youth culture forever, lashing out at anything that didn't fit their own narrow acceptance of what decent music and a respectable appearance should be.

Malcolm McLaren had a finger in that pie. A couple of years earlier, Sex (or Seditionaries, as it was renamed in the aftermath of the *Today* show) was known as Let It Rock, and specialized exclusively in Teddy Boy clobber. The day McLaren abandoned that line in favor of more esoteric wares was the day that the Teds declared unrepentant war. It just took them a while to work out what to do, although every time you passed the store, the knot of disconsolate Teddy Boys hanging around outside would seem to be a little larger, every one of them holding their roll-up cigarettes between forefinger and thumb, mouthing "be-bop" to each other by way of secret code, and leering disgustedly at the new range of clothes. Then they'd congratulate themselves for their daring with smirks, and take another drag off their cigarettes.

Slowly, however, they progressed to more physical shows of violence, jostling customers on their way in or out, or occasionally heaving a projectile through the store's plateglass window (hence the white boards and fencing that McLaren was eventually forced to erect).

There was a difference, however, between garbage cans thrown through a shop window, and the same principles of velocity being employed on a human body; and a difference, too, between the traditional Teddy Boys with the slicked-back hair and crepe-soled shoes, Edwardian jackets, and bootlace ties, and the new breed of thug now creeping into view; namely, any middle-aged-and-under gent with enough surviving testosterone to run with a baying horde, and enough pent-up, boozed-up anger to lash out at anything that moved.

Just weeks after her late-night encounter in Notting Hill, Cassie and I were chased from one end of Oxford Street to more or less the other, a mile-long dash that we would probably have completed in record-breaking time if we hadn't had to dodge around however many hundreds of Saturday afternoon shoppers were out that day, not one of whom looked like they'd even noticed us, let alone the half dozen or so yobs who pursued us, at least one of whom was carrying what looked like an iron bar.

We knew better than to resort to the most obvious means of escape, ducking into a store in the hope that the gang would just sail past us. More likely, they would simply wait on the street until we were turfed out for loitering. We discarded taking any side streets, too, for fear that if we were finally caught, there'd be even fewer people around to maybe stop a murder. So we just ran, and didn't stop running until we finally reached Marble Arch, just as a bus slowed down at the traffic light. We leaped aboard, thankful that London Transport still hadn't got round to replacing the old-style buses, with the open platform at the back, with the new-fangled models with doors. The bus pulled away as our attackers reached the corner, but we kept our heads down regardless. The trouble with London buses was, they usually traveled in packs—you could wait half an hour for one to arrive, and then three would turn up at once. The last thing we needed was for our pursuers to leap on the next one.

We were fortunate. We got away. A lot of other people didn't, and the only consolation for the police and doctors who had to patch up the wreckage was that the victims were usually punk rockers, which meant that they usually deserved it. Even the local newspapers didn't really bother commenting upon the rising tide of admissions to the neighborhood emergency room. Another punk with his head stove in? Serves the stupid bastard right.

Chelsea was one of the first bands to run into a deliberately orchestrated antipunk bashing. The new lineup's debut performance out of the way, Gene October booked their second and third gigs for the same night, with two performances at the Hope and Anchor pub in Islington. But, though the first set passed off with nothing less than triumph, the second was canceled with just five minutes notice, as an army of Teddy Boys descended upon the basement room where the stage was set up, and began knocking people about. The police were called, Chelsea packed up, and the Teds wandered off to celebrate.

"There was a lot of violence, but it was never from the punks, never from us, but the local thuggery hanging about outside or the local football squad," Rat Scabies recalled. "You have to remember the cops and everybody turned their backs on everything. We did shows where cops would just drive away while five hundred people trashed our van. But it wasn't the punks that were doing it, it was more like gang warfare. If you weren't a punk, you went and hit one. And that became if you were a punk, and you saw someone that wasn't, then they'd better look out, because if they gave you any shit, you'd hit *them*."

Nils Stevenson, manager of the slowly re-forming Siouxsie and the Banshees, was caught very early on. "When I was first dressing up in ripped clothes and spiky hair, people used to get out of my way in the street. Then as soon as the word 'punk' was coined, it was the reverse, people were 'Oh, he's not a nutcase, he's a punk rocker. Let's beat the fucking crap out of him.'"

Still, at least we had Cassie's housemates to put everything into perspective for us, after we'd finished relating our Oxford Street adventure. "At least you have one thing to be grateful for," laughed Winston. "You're not black."

Not much had changed around Notting Hill since the carnival ended in bloodshed and riot, back at the end of August. It was still the happy hunting ground for any number of predatory racists, and not just the Hill either. Any area with a sizable immigrant population was regarded as ripe for a kicking and, again, the majority of incidents went completely unreported.

A friend of a friend might tell you about something he'd seen, a gang of whites kicking the shit out of some defenseless Pakistani at a bus stop late at night, and nobody could miss the growing tide of

National Front graffiti, which was sprouting up all over the city—early one morning, making my way home just a couple of hours before I needed to get up for work again, I watched a Sikh shop owner out on the sidewalk, with a broom and a bucket of water, trying to wash a vast "Blacks Out" slogan from the brickwork. Passing by again that same evening, the same words were back and even bigger.

Nobody cared.

Or maybe they did.

Again back in August, Eric Clapton sparked a storm of protest after demanding to know whether there were any "foreigners" in the audience? "If so, please put up your hands. I think we should vote for Enoch Powell." Onstage at the Birmingham Odeon, in the immigrant heart of Britain's Midlands, the guitarist formerly known as God openly pledged his support to a right-wing politician best remembered for back in 1968 advocating the forced repatriation of Britain's black population before they slaughtered us all in our beds.

It was August 5, 1976, and the very next week, outrage surrounding Clapton's outburst prompted the three major music papers to publish an open letter announcing the formation of "a rank and file movement against the racist poison in music." The signatories urged "support for Rock Against Racism." Over the next seven days, the letter drew 140 responses from the public.

But it was not Clapton whom these people were reacting against; or rather, it *was* Clapton, but it was a lot of other stuff as well. As Britain slid further down the pan, and homelessness, inflation, and unemployment skyrocketed, so people began casting about for a scapegoat. They found it, as they so often do, in the immigrant communities that the right-wing politicians claimed had been inundating the country for more than twenty years, and corrupting the so-called British way of life as they did so. It was the National Front whom Rock Against Racism would most visibly be targeting, because it was they who were spilling the most poisonous bile. But it was the mass of people that lurked behind the Front whom they hoped to reach, the vast and, for the most part, unattached hordes who didn't like politics, but didn't much like the darkies either.

It took the new movement just three months to put its mouth where its motives were, and organize its first live event, taking over the Royal College of Art for a cold winter evening with blues singer Carol Grimes and the reggae band Matumbi. "From the beginning," one of the organizers, Roger Huddle, explained, "we wanted a DIY organization. We wanted local bands and anti-Nazis to come together and make it impossible for Nazi ideas to get a grip."

That first gig was barely attended beyond the RCA's own student population, and scarcely publicized either. But it was never intended to be. It was a toe in the water, an attempt to figure out whether or not Rock Against Racism was even capable of putting together a concert; of finding a venue and booking a show, of printing up literature and engaging an audience. And of doing all of these things without appearing to raise itself above the people it wanted to help.

Grimes was living in Westbourne Grove at the time, itself a virtual adjunct to Notting Hill, and close by one of the black community's favorite haunts, the Mangrove restaurant. Usually in the company of Winston and the others, Cassie and I had eaten there several times, usually conspicuous as the only white faces in the place, but welcomed regardless by manager Frank—even on those occasions when you could have forgiven him for slamming the door in our pasty white faces.

The local police loved the Mangrove. Not for the food, not for the ambience, and certainly not for the company of its patrons. They loved it because whenever they needed to get the arrest figures up, they could just descend on the Mangrove and round up its customers. The hapless diners might not even have been doing anything wrong. They were there; that was enough.

The Mangrove brought Carol Grimes into Rock Against Racism's orbit. From her window, she could watch the raids in all their regularity and, being interviewed by one of the music papers that summer, she happened to mention her horror. Red Saunders, one of the signatories to that original Rock Against Racism missive, read the article and got in touch. Grimes would become one of Rock Against Racism's leading spokespersons.

"The whole Rock Against Racism thing did more than just challenge racism," Grimes was insistent. "It made the idea of black, brown, and white united something real, and that together we could tell the fascists to 'fuck off.'"

At that first show, "people who had come to hear my blues went away having been exposed to reggae." But as Rock Against Racism spread its wings and began putting on more shows, "people who had gone along because they were into reggae came away thinking that punk had something to say."

Soon Rock Against Racism's eclectic blend had a presence at almost every show we attended, regardless of whether or not the organization was staging it. It might be a stall set up at the back of the room, distributing literature and selling badges or T-shirts, it might be merely a couple of people in the street outside, handing out leaflets to the crowd. Whatever. Rock Against Racism was growing in strength and recognition all the time.

Some events raised money, some raised hackles—the National Front regularly had some picketing presence wherever the Rock Against Racism banner was hoisted. But all raised awareness, and they did so at precisely the right time. Because violence was increasing at exactly the same rate, against blacks, against punks, against anybody who appeared to be disturbing the status quo that had held Britain in its right-wing thrall for so long. Rock Against Racism was the voice that would shout back at them.

Of all the bands drawn into Rock Against Racism's sphere of influence, the Tom Robinson Band was the most vociferous. As Kustow recalled, those earliest days were "weird. I remember playing the Red Cow in Hammersmith, the Nashville in West Kensington, the Kensington Pub. They were the very first TRB gigs at the very tail end of 1976, very raw, unrehearsed gigs with simply a drum kit, Marshall 50 watt 4 x 12s, a cheap bass guitar, and a very dodgy, small PA system."

The "classic" lineup, with Robinson and Kustow joined by keyboard player Mark Ambler and drummer Brian "Dolphin" Taylor, debuted at a packed Sir George Robey pub in Finsbury Park in the New Year, before embarking upon a string of three- to four-week residences at any pub or club that would have them. "We had no money to rub between us," Kustow says. One night, seated in a café eating dinner, the guitarist unthinkingly ordered a second hamburger. "Tom [got really] pissed off with me. I should have made do with just one. We were hungry in every sense of the word."

What sustained them was their belief in the songs that were now pouring out of Robinson, and the sense that the causes he espoused, and the dangers of which he warned, were shared by an ever-growing army of people.

"Glad to Be Gay" remained the music press's chief point of entry into their world, and would dominate most mainstream commentaries on the group. But it was the horror show that the musicians took the greatest pride in, Robinson's musical document of the kind of postapocalyptic universe that would erupt should the National Front succeed in their aims; a world in which carrion crows feed on corpses on the motorway ("You Gotta Survive"), the military elite SAS replaced the police on the beat ("The Winter of 79"), and the right-wing rich were huddled in their country houses, waiting for the all-clear to sound ("I'm Alright Jack").

All leading up to what became the most haunting lesson of the entire age. "Power in the Darkness" was (and remains) a reminder that government is *not* the right of the minority to control the lives of the majority; that far from people being afraid of their leaders, it is the leaders who should be afraid of the people.

When the song begins, it seems to be little more than a tightly constructed rabble-rouser, built around a singalong chorus and verses that simply document the freedoms that you endanger every time you put an X on a ballot sheet. Midway through, however, the timbre changes. A news broadcast filters through the rock 'n' roar, a party political broadcast from whichever right-wing demon you fear most, an impassioned demand for a return to "the traditional British values of obedience, discipline, morality and freedom" that hallmarked the Golden Age that the past had now become.

The Tom Robinson Band knew they'd never get a hit single with "Glad to Be Gay," but they released it on an EP regardless. It made the UK Top Twenty.
Author's collection

The mark of the resistance. TRB's logo was soon appearing all over the country. *Author's collection*

Six months earlier, Hughie Green's "Stand Up and Be Counted" touched upon the fear that the Communists were about to take over his beloved country, while acknowledging that they were only the best organized of the rising rabble. "Power in the Darkness" outlined the forces that Green left unsaid, and demanded that Britain be rid of them all. "Freedom," it insisted, was a world free of "Reds . . . Pakis . . . the Unions, prostitutes, pansies and Punks, football hooligans, juvenile delinquents, lesbians and left-wing scum." Everybody, in other words, who was standing in front of the stage, listening to the song.

Some nights Robinson would perform the tirade; other nights, he would have a masked guest step up, your average middle-class, middle-aged, smartly suited, ultra-conservative dickhead. Then, at the end, the mask would be removed to reveal a black man. It caught people by surprise every time.

But the theatrics could not disguise the thinness of the ice upon which the Tom Robinson Band was skating as they pushed their message into landscapes that took them far from the comfortable realms of punk rock. Had they been content to spend their career at the Roxy, the Tom Robinson Band might never have seen a fist raised in anger, beyond that clenched in defiance upon their backdrop.

But they weren't. The Tom Robinson Band played wherever they could, until the Roxy was pretty much the only place they *didn't* play. Universities, prisons (like the Sex Pistols before them, the Tom Robinson Band performed at the Chelmsford lockup), strip clubs,

Tom Robinson onstage with Aswad's Brynsley Forde.
Author's collection

brothels, pubs, clubs, and what Kustow described as "toilets up and down the country," the suburban hideaways where unreconstructed Englishmen could still go to sink a pint and throw some darts and hold forth to one another about how . . .

. . . *well, you know I'm not a racialist, but the darkies are taking all the jobs, and you can't even go for a piss anymore because the toilets are full of homos, and there's weirdoes hanging out on every street corner, and the women are all squawking on about equal rights, and you can't kick your cat or smack your kid without some liberal do-gooder making a fuss. The whole fucking country is going to the fucking dogs, and then you turn around . . .*

and what's that up there on the stage?

A git with bright red cockatoo haircut, a curly haired poofter with a Gay Pride badge, and cop a load of the rubbish they're singing, mate. I'll give you "sing if you're glad to be gay," you fucking poofter, at the same time as I ram your fucking teeth down your fucking throat.

Nightly, Kustow would warm up by looking out at the audience, and feeling "so very scared of going up on that stage with all those seemingly heavy dudes propping up the bar out there, especially knowing we were about to do a song called 'Glad to Be Gay.' All those heavy dudes in their leather jackets with their birds, how would they take it?"

But it didn't stop the band.

Normally, the sheer weight of numbers, the growing army of Robinson supporters against a handful of genuine troublemakers, served to keep the peace in the club. You couldn't always rely on appearances either. One night, Cassie and I were part of an audience rendered thoroughly uncomfortable by the sight of a dozen or so burly lads clad in the blue of Chelsea soccer team—home to one of the most notorious, and most bigoted, hooligan firms in the capital. By the end of the show, though, at least half of them had their arms in the air, bellowing "Glad to Be Gay" as lustily as the most partisan audience.

Which proved, as Robinson smiled afterward, that you could never judge a hooker by her lover. It didn't matter whether people understood what they were singing, he said. What was important was that they *thought* about understanding. As with so many other prejudices, it is not hatred that is the enemy. It is ignorance.

Echoing what became a mantra within Rock Against Racism's own literature, Robinson explained, "Motives don't matter. It's the end result that matters. If you see a guy starving on the street and you give him a quid just to impress your girlfriend or boyfriend, it doesn't matter. 'Cuz at the end of the day that guy's still got the quid." Onstage, that lesson hit home with stunning accuracy.

Outside of the clubs, however, the musicians made a sitting target. "I suppose we weren't really a punk band like the Clash, the Pistols, or the Buzzcocks," Kustow conceded. "But we had all the punk sensibilities, and I felt we were a punk band. After all, I did have red hennaed spiky hair, and yes, we were accepted by the punk audiences." Which automatically meant they were not about to be accepted by many other people. The guitarist grew almost accustomed to "huge menacing vibes when I was on the street, or in pubs. I do remember cars driving by, and windows being rolled down, and awful things screamed out of those windows."

One evening, he was waiting for a train at Highgate tube station, resplendent in his spiky red hair and a long feather earring, when "a rocker guy with a big quiff came up to me and said, 'Oi, are you a punk rocker?'"

Kustow nodded, and that was all his interrogator needed to know. "He said he was gonna push me onto the tracks." In the end, the crowd of people standing around them dissuaded the thug from carrying out his threat. But Kustow was convinced that this was the only reason.

Robinson's outspoken militancy continued to transform a hard-working rock band into a magnet for every bigoted hatemonger there was. Scuffles in the street outside, a skinhead reacting badly to being handed a Rock Against Racism leaflet were commonplace. Kustow continued, "There was trouble and aggro with some of the audiences, the usual throwing of beer cans, spitting, gobbing, and hecklers, and I do remember Tony Howard, our manager, coming up before one gig telling us there was gonna be extra security because there was a bomb threat made against us."

The agenda set out by Rock Against Racism's founding principles, and which was then spread around the nation by Robinson and so many other musical crusaders—the Clash, Sham 69, Generation X, and more all threw their weight behind the organization—was to change little over the years, because there was no need for it to do so. As another of the organization's cofounders, David Widgery, explained, "The music came first and was more exciting. It provided the creative energy and the focus in what became a battle for the soul of young working-class England."

Indeed, you only had to be involved in the punk scene, no matter how peripherally, to feel yourself part of Rock Against Racism's larger aims. As the harassment grew, punk increasingly saw itself as the sound of the rebellious streets, and though its blood ties with reggae were only partially forged through a mutual distrust of the establishment, they were cemented by the establishment's heavy-handed attempts at repression.

Young Rastas always were an easy target for opportunistic police, accepting their lot with far more weary resignation than most white kids could have mustered. "I should have known better than to go to Oxford Street on a Saturday afternoon," was all you heard from Aswad drummer Zeb, after he was pulled up by the police on the capital's busiest shopping street.

But now young punks joined them on the wanted list, falling victim to Scotland Yard's sudden love affair with the so-called Sus law, a nineteenth-century social control legislation (section four of the Vagrancy Act 1824) that gave the police the right to stop and search anybody they "suspected" of having been involved in a crime—whether or not an actual crime had been brought to their attention. Two years ago, Sus had scarcely been heard of. Now you couldn't shut it up.

I remember walking home late one night, down some distinctly darkened side streets, aware all the while that I was being followed. I'd stop, they'd stop; I'd trot, they'd trot; I'd turn around, they'd vanish into a convenient doorway. But finally I caught a glimpse of these persistent stalkers and, I assumed, would-be assailants. Two beat cops, obviously bored with their usual route, waiting to see whether I might commit a crime. Another time, hitchhiking some place or other, I was stopped and searched by the side of the highway. Frisking me first for weapons, the officers then turned their attentions to the possibility of drugs, not only examining my cigarettes, but even squeezing out the toothpaste tube that I'd conscientiously packed in my rucksack. I came so close to reminding them that if I'd been able to afford drugs, I'd scarcely be trying to cadge a lift by the side of the A-13.

The sense that the police were as much a part of the problem as the National Front escalated. One side attacked you with stones and bottles, the other with their own peculiar interpretations of law and order, but ultimately both had just one end in sight. Yours. And so the anger grew; fear bred ferocity; beatings bred revenge. And leaking through the cracks that were now splitting the veneer of a civilized society, stirring the pot and finding ever more volatile ingredients to throw into the bubbling ferment, there were the vigilante newspaper journalists who patrolled the streets in ink-stained packs, serving Queen and Country with accusation, innuendo, and incitement.

18

Dandy in the Underworld

LATE FEBRUARY 1977

The best press the Roxy received during its earliest weeks came from the most unexpected source imaginable. Robert Plant, John Bonham, and Jimmy Page of Led Zeppelin, kingpins of the dinosaur scene that punk was apparently born to destroy, followed up their encouragement of the Adverts' first rehearsals by dropping by to catch one of the Damned's Monday night residencies. And it was an indication of just how heavy was the impact of their band (and so many like them) upon all our lives that not a soul in the room stirred in their direction to tell the trio what boring old farts they were.

Confession time. Long after the fact, it became very fashionable for people to claim that they had ditched their entire prepunk record collection the moment they heard the Sex Pistols for the first time. And maybe some people did. But I never went home empty-handed after an afternoon spent second-hand record store shopping, and I still have the scratchy old progressive rock LPs to prove it. I can honestly say that I never felt so betrayed or disgusted by the artists I was listening to before punk came along that I stopped paying attention to what they did afterward.

Well, not often, anyway. I did spend several days of mounting excitement awaiting the release of Emerson Lake and Palmer's *Works*, their first new studio album since the monumental *Brain Salad Surgery* almost three years before; and I hated practically every minute of it. Genesis, too, let me down badly, the moment they traded Peter Gabriel in for Phil Collins. But Gabriel went off on a solo career, and his debut album, in spring 1977, was as great as it should have been. Maybe even greater.

Who else? Bowie rarely disgraced himself in those days, and *Low* was no disappointment. I loved the Stones' disco album, the still-supreme *Black and Blue*, and it didn't matter what Johnny Rotten's T-shirt insisted, I enjoyed Pink Floyd's *Animals* as much as anything else they'd done. And so on.

Zeppelin, on the other hand, had never been a particular favorite; back at school in 1975, I outraged every music lover in earshot when I declared that the band's greatest moment was the mock-reggae "D'Yer Maker," even as *Physical Graffiti* was pronounced the finest album ever made. But I came to love "Kashmir" and I often wondered what would happen if Don Letts had spun Zeppelin's "Trampled Underfoot" at some point in a Roxy evening. The frenetic speed, the breakneck energy, the relentless rhythm . . . you could pogo to that, and no mistake.

So, punks liked Zeppelin, and Zeppelin liked punks. "I was really impressed by them," Plant enthused after the Damned finished playing. "I like to see new bands, see what they're doing, how good they are. You ask me if it reminds me of when we started out, but it doesn't. It reminds me of when we were rehearsing this afternoon." That was also the evening John Bonham got up to jam with the Damned, and wound up being thrown off the stage, a fat, abusive drunk whom the club management failed to recognize, and whose bandmates were too busy laughing at to intervene. His last words as he was pulled onto the dance floor were, "This is a fucking great band."

Neat Neat Neat
The Damned

The Damned's second single, titularly similar to their debut album, but who are those bagged men on the sleeve? *Author's collection*

Other superstars were less in tune with the times. Mick Jagger realized something was going on when he picked up the *New Musical Express* to learn that Howard Devoto had left the Buzzcocks, just eleven gigs into their career. "*Who* leaves *what*?" he demanded to know. And the rumor mill still buzzed with the names of the artists who purportedly wrote letters to A&M, during that brief week when the Sex Pistols were numbered among their labelmates, demanding that the cancer be excised. Peter Frampton, Karen Carpenter, Rick Wakeman, Supertramp—the list was almost as long as the label's roster, and most of them have denied being party to it since. At the time, though, if you needed a reason to hate Joan Armatrading, here it was.

But Freddie Mercury was delighted to meet Sid Vicious, even if he did insist on renaming him "Mr. Horrible," and Status Quo's Rick Parfitt told me how he loved the energy, even if it did all make him feel very old. "I was quite surprised when I went to the Marquee one night. Punk was just about to happen, and I saw this whole different energy in the audience, I'd never seen this before, these weird-looking creatures—they were weird-looking creatures to me and I was only thirty years old! I'd seen audiences go wild before, but not like this. It was quite amazing."

He certainly got off a lot lighter than bandmate Francis Rossi. "I remember mixing *Rocking All Over the World* in the Marquee studio. There was some punk band recording next door, so Rick and I went to have a look. This punk turned round and said, 'Fuck off Rossi, you boring old fart.' I was stunned. I was twenty-seven."

But if you felt as though you were a part of the scene, then you were. TV Smith recalled, "Over the opening weeks, the crowd got bigger and began to merge into the standard punk look—Ramones look-alikes and Sex shop customers. For early gigs, where not too many people were in the audience, they tended to stand back from the stage while the bands played and not give much response. But as the gigs got more crowded, everyone was pressed together, and the place became a sweatbox, that's when the atmosphere in the club got really exciting."

"My favorite memories of the Roxy would be just being at the most happening place at the time," Alan Lee Shaw agrees. "Punk was exploding, and you just had to be where it was at. The Roxy was the epicenter. There were other places, such as the Nashville, the Red Cow, the Hope and Anchor, the Kensington, and so on, but most were old pubs and you would see a mix of pub rock as well as the new punk rock bands. The Roxy was just for the emerging new bands on the punk scene, so it seemed kind of special and cool. Be there or be square. All new music trends down the years have had venues where new movements kick off and for punk, the Roxy was synonymous."

Shaw was there on Valentine's Day to catch the Damned, fresh from recording their *Damned Damned Damned* debut LP, and he arrived in time to catch the Adverts as well, as they staked their claim to become one of the venue's most regular acts. TV Smith recalled, "In the first couple of months in 1977, we played the Roxy many times, but only a handful of gigs in other venues, usually as support slots to bands like the Stranglers, that we got offered because they'd seen us at the Roxy."

In fact, the Roxy would be the venue for almost every significant event in the Adverts' early life. It was there that Brian James first saw them play, and promised to do all he could to help out—the Valentine show was among the first fruits of his largesse. It was there that journalist Barry Miles first encountered them; he introduced the group to their manager, publisher Michael Dempsey, and later produced their third single, "Safety in Numbers."

And it was there that Stiff supremo Jake Riviera concurred with James's enthusiasm, and offered the Adverts their first record deal.

Stiff was not the first label to court the Adverts in the weeks since Smith turned down the advances of the mood music company. First on the scene was Mark P, founder of *Sniffin' Glue*, in his capacity of A&R man for American-born entrepreneur Miles Copeland. Operating out of an office in Dryden Chambers, Oxford Street, Copeland was in the process of creating an empire around punk, an operation that included publishing (S[niffin'] G[lue] Publications), tour promotion, artist management, music publishing, distribution (Faulty Products), and no less than three record labels: Illegal, to be led off by his brother Stewart's new combo, the Police; Deptford Fun

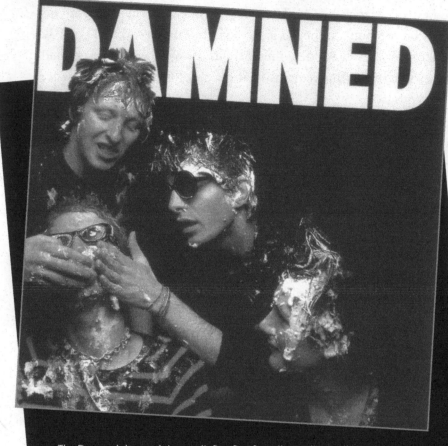

The Damned damned damned's first first first album album album. Early pressings arrived with a photograph of Eddie and the Hot Rods on the back sleeve, placed there in error and to give future collectors something else to dream about. *Author's collection*

City, which would focus on a South London act called Squeeze; and Step Forward, soon to flower as home to Chelsea, the Menace, the Cortinas, the Models, and Sham 69.

Smith asked for time to think about it. There was something about the setup that left him cold, something that reeked of empire-building monopolies, conglomerate leviathans, institutionalized monoliths. Which is when Stiff Records stepped in.

Jake Riviera "came running up to us with a very thin contract, and said 'sign here, I'll make you broke,'" Smith recalled. "We believed him and he did." But the Adverts went into the arrangement knowing that there wouldn't be much money in it. It was an exposure deal. "Jake knew he was picking up on a lot of bands who would go onto other labels once their first record was out, and he modeled the contracts on that." Certainly there was no question in Smith's mind that Stiff was right for the Adverts. The following week, Smith and Gaye were seated in Stiff's Alexander Street offices, looking over a two-page contract to record one single. "We signed it there and then. We'd only done about five gigs. We were thrilled to be on Stiff Records."

It was Riviera who suggested that the Adverts record with Larry Wallis, kingpin of the latest incarnation of the Pink Fairies, but solo ever since he was cornered by Riviera and Nick Lowe at Dingwalls one evening. "They made me the proverbial offer I couldn't refuse," Wallis explained. "'Why don't you give the Fairies a rest and get modern?' It was a 'come in with us on this new adventure' kinda thing, and so it began."

It was an inspired marriage. No matter that the Fairies had been around in one form or another since the end of the 1960s, still it was growing increasingly difficult to overlook their influence on a lot of what was now going down, both musically and in terms of the "fuck you" attitude with which the Fairies had spent their entire careers taunting the establishment. Captain Sensible and Brian James certainly professed an undying love for the band and, while other musicians were more circumspect, you'd often spot a Fairies album snuggled away in their record collections.

But Wallis had no intention of being held back by nostalgia. Enthused by the atmosphere of undiluted creativity and madcap enterprise that was Stiff Records, he flew into action. "One thing

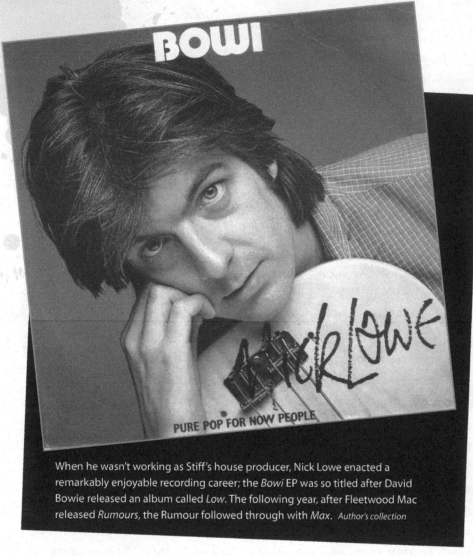

BOWI

PURE POP FOR NOW PEOPLE

When he wasn't working as Stiff's house producer, Nick Lowe enacted a remarkably enjoyable recording career; the *Bowi* EP was so titled after David Bowie released an album called *Low*. The following year, after Fleetwood Mac released *Rumours*, the Rumour followed through with *Max*. *Author's collection*

about being with Jake was, he made things happen, and they happened fast." One Friday evening, while watching Angie Dickinson in *Police Woman*, Wallis wrote a song called "Police Car." He played it to Riviera on that Sunday, "and, somewhere around Tuesday, me and a couple of Hot-Rods (bassist Paul Gray and drummer Steve Nicol) went into Pathway studio to record it. About five minutes later, it was in the shops. What a deal!"

larry wallis police car

Inspired by American TV, but wholly locked into the mean streets of London, Larry Wallis's "Police Car" remains one of the most sinister automotive songs ever recorded. *Author's collection*

Now Riviera was calling him up and telling him to be back at Pathway the following week. He was producing the first single by the Adverts. Wallis simply nodded. "Bless him, Jake rarely asked anybody anything. He *told* them."

Wallis was not completely inexperienced. He'd self-produced "Police Car," and having written much of the Fairies' material, "when it came to recording I always knew what I wanted—y'know,

'2,000 guitars, all with echo please.' But the Adverts was the very first 'I'm a hero/I'm the goat' situation, and I found it terrifying. Not only was I at the helm of a studio, I also had an engineer and four tiny, young, expectantly upturned faces asking me, 'Please sir, what shall we do now?' Gaspo! But it all worked out OK."

Smith was equally pleased with the partnership. "We didn't even know what a producer did, but 'Police Car' was a good record and we liked Larry straightaway—despite, or maybe because, he looked like an old hippie. We still weren't clear why we needed a producer; until you try it yourself, you don't realize how difficult it is to 'capture the sound of the band,' which is what Larry did. He knew his way round the studio and we knew, while we were downstairs running through it a few times, he was the one upstairs saying 'that's the take.'

"We had the day at Pathway, set up, we did the b-side ["Quick-step"] first which took a couple of run-throughs, then 'One Chord Wonders,' and that was it. The rest of the day was Larry mixing. We didn't try to do overdubs or make it sound slick. He took the band and captured the sound as we were." The sound of the Roxy Club at its peak. And that was a wonderful thing to be able to take home with you and play in the sanctity of your own bedroom. Because while you might miss the crush of the crowd and the smell of the beer, you were also out of range of something else, something that became so synonymous with punk rock that, long after people had forgotten why it started, they were still duty-bound to maintain the tradition.

I love this band. I think I'll spit at them.

When did it start? When did punk audiences first decide that a flying projectile of snot was a suitable way of showing their support? Reports from the Sex Pistols show in Manchester, one of the few dates on the Anarchy tour to take place, insist the audience show-ered each of the performers in "gob"; earlier than that, claims that Johnny Rotten occasionally spat at his audience, who reciprocated in like-minded fashion, may or may not have been apocryphal. I never saw anybody do it until the Clash played the Roxy. But once the beast had been unleashed, there was no way to cage it again. Plus, the more an artist begged the crowd to stop, the more spit they would proceed to unleash.

"The dawning of the age of gob was always a tough one," Martin Gordon affirmed. "Dirty Pictures" was still awaiting release, the band was still awaiting a name. But he would quickly become wearily familiar with the roadcrew handing him a never-ending supply of towels, with which "to wipe the gob off the bass, as it was impossible to play. This I did not encourage, as you can imagine. Where it came from and the significance of it, a sociologist will have to decode. I presume it relates to equality, but there might have been another way of better expressing it, or at least one which didn't involve so much laundry."

"I hated it," TV Smith agreed. "I think everyone hated it, nobody liked it. But before you had a chance to say anything about it, it had become part of the ritual and you couldn't say anything because all it would do was bring more spitting and I knew, most people knew, that the spitting was a sign that they liked you. It'd be like telling people to stop applauding. And, if you're involved in an alternative art scene, then the audience has their own right for their alternative means of expression. But even if I justify it like that, it's still disgusting."

And if spitting was bad for the homegrown talents whose own careers developed hand in handkerchief with the barrage, it was even worse for anyone who had never encountered it before.

19

Storm the Gates of Heaven

MARCH 1977

SOUNDTRACK

"China Girl"	Iggy Pop (RCA)
"Here I Come"	Dennis Brown (Observer)
"Hold Back the Night"	Graham Parker and the Rumour (Vertigo)
"I Might Be Lying"	Eddie and the Hot Rods (Island)
"Immanuelle God Is Coming"	Dennis Brown (DEB)
"Less than Zero"	Elvis Costello (Stiff)
"Love Jah Jah Children"	Big Youth (Chanon Jah)
"Love—Building on Fire"	Talking Heads (Sire)
"Marquee Moon"	Television (Elektra)
"Money"	Delroy Wilson (Morwells)
"Native Land"	I Roy (Thing)
"Outside View"	Eater (The Label)
"Riverboat"	Big Youth (Negusa Negast)
"Set the Captives Free"	Gregory Isaacs (DEB)
"Sticks Man"	Black Slate (Slate)
"Three Black People"	Burning Spear (Island)
"Tribal War"	Trinity (Nationwide)
"Two Sevens Clash"	Culture (Joe Gibbs)
"White Riot"	The Clash (CBS)

New York came to the Roxy over the first weekend in March.

The U.S. scene continued to reverberate strongly in London. No matter how many domestic contenders were now slipping into place, still the imagery that flowed in from across the Atlantic continued to captivate, all the more so since it became apparent that most of the bands were just as good as we'd always been led to believe.

The Ramones and Patti Smith were established now, and the Heartbreakers had all but been adopted. Even the British government had abandoned its attempts to deport the group for overstaying their visitors' visas. Richard Hell, Television, and Blondie were shaping up to deliver their long-playing debuts, while a follow-up to the loathsome *Live at CBGBs* collection had just materialized in the shape of *Live at Max's Kansas City*, and this time there were no disappointments. Pere Ubu, Wayne County, and Cherry Vanilla led the way, and it was the Max's disc that the Roxy had eyes for, by adding to its musical fission the art and influence of David Bowie.

Both County and Vanilla were valued members of Bowie's entourage during his years of greatest glam rock importance, Vanilla as the vivacious press officer who made certain that His Ziggy-ship's name was on everybody's lips, County as an electrifying self-styled freak show who made Bowie look like an underdressed art school dropout. Together the pair had launched vibrant careers far from the superstar's stifling influence, and both were now coming to London.

James Stevenson paid his first visit to the Roxy that weekend, partly to catch the Americans ("The whole New York punk thing is what got me into punk in the first place"), but also as a fact-finding mission. He'd spent the last few months in a band called Metro . . . the previous week they played the Ad Lib, next week it would be the Rock Garden. But time was running out. He lost his Les Paul guitar following the Ad Lib show, when someone lifted it out of the van, and Metro were losing their name. A rival Metro had just emerged, with a record deal, an album, and a sonic single called "Criminal World."

ZigZag's infamous welcome to Cherry Vanilla, Wayne County, and the Heartbreakers—infamous because at least one major chain of newsstands banned it from their shelves. Wonder why? *Author's collection*

There was no way Stevenson and Co. could compete with that. They would be known as Inter-City now, but they weren't happy about it; a change of name was the kiss of death for an act that relied on word of mouth to fill shows. It was time to move on. A few days earlier, Stevenson and Metro bassist Henry Badowski responded to an ad in *Melody Maker*, seeking players for the next incarnation of Gene October's Chelsea. The auditions would be held next week. Tonight, their maiden trip to the Roxy, was their chance to find out exactly what they were letting themselves in for.

Stevenson was thrilled. "It was, by and large, a completely punk audience. You'd get the odd straight person checking it out, but on the whole I think most people were scared to go in. I always felt it was friendly. What I remember best is just how personal and intimate it was. It had the feeling of being an exclusive club—quite the opposite of its intention. It could get really hot and dirty. But that all added to the vibe.

"By the time I started going to the Roxy, most of the 'A' division groups had already been and gone, moved on. The first show I went to was to see Wayne County; I thought he was a great performer and I loved his guitarist Greg Van Cook. He was a really nice guy—more rock than punk as a player—and Wayne was always entertaining."

It was not County's first visit to the Roxy. He'd passed by a handful of times already since moving to London in February, but even before then, he knew it well. "I remembered the club from when I visited in 1973, when it had been a gay club, and I'd seen Hinge and Brackett [a riotously popular drag duo specializing in arch Gilbert and Sullivan recitals]. It had certainly changed since then." The first thing he saw on this visit was "a guy sitting at a table, slashing his arm up with a razor blade."

He'd met me before as well, during that same long-ago visit, although I doubted he'd remember it. Bowie was playing the Marquee, filming the *1980 Floor Show* television spectacular, and I was sidling around the assembled superstars when County hove into

A Roxy flyer for March 1977. Not every show on the handbill was played—financial difficulties saw a week or so of shows canceled later in the month, including what would have been the Roxy debut by Iron Maiden. Yes, *that* Iron Maiden. *Author's collection*

view, resplendent in a bright red nightdress, with a huge blond Afro and a metal handbag. I asked for an autograph and we wound up talking for what, to my astonished thirteen-year-old mind, seemed like ages. That's what I told my diary, anyway. But I was impressed then, and I was about to be impressed now, almost four years later.

County was breathtaking. London had never seen anything like him. A transsexual in the first stages of a sex change, he had halted his hormone treatment when he first relocated to England, "so to all intents and purposes, I was just a punky boy with a big nose and too much makeup, which is a lot less threatening than a drag queen with real tits." But still a scene that had only ever flirted with androgyny and gender confusion reeled before County's onslaught.

That first night at the Roxy, with his Electric Chairs sparking behind him, County took the stage in full drag, thick makeup and a long blonde wig, and a dress that was more rips and tears than fabric. A quick change of wigs brought out another festooned in condoms and garbage; a dress change revealed a tattered garbage bag, with old Roxy handbills pinned to it.

With an array of onstage sex toys to illustrate his lyrics, and a hatful of songs that screamed outrage and obscenity, even the most hardened Roxy crowd member was initially lost for words. People didn't know what to do or where to look. Later, people would say he brought a toilet bowl on the stage with him, and ate dog food out of it in lieu of shit; or that he let more dog food drain from the back of his pants. No. That was wishful thinking, and some distorted recollections of a few old press reports. But tonight was just as memorable.

So, forget the music, watch the show? Again, no. The music was thrilling as well, a taste-defying succession of garage pop anthems with names like "If You Don't Want to Fuck Me Baby, Fuck Off," "Toilet Love," "Cream in My Jeans," and "Bad in Bed." He even brought out the Patti Smith impersonation that Ivan Kral had warned me about, complete with a matching "The Boy Jerked Off on Johnny" recital.

If you wanted to take things dreadfully seriously, you could probably sniff and say there's nothing especially clever about starting a song (or even titling it) with the words "I got fucked by the devil last night." In terms of what punk was "meant" to be, however, the destruction of taboos, the removal of barriers, the ultimate liberation of the spirit from the strictures of society, County was so far ahead of the pack that, for many people, it wasn't even worth trying to catch up.

"I always felt the kids at the Roxy were playing a role, that a lot of the outrageous behavior was only for show," County once told me. "But the atmosphere was really great. It was energetic, all about jumping around and sticking your tongue out and spitting. As my whole act was based around being obnoxious, I felt right at home."

Even on the nights (and there would be many) when audiences were not prepared to get into the swing of things, County enjoyed himself. First he would wait out the opening hail of abuse, then dodge around amid a barrage of empty beer cans. Then a few full beer cans. Any other performer would cut their set short and leave the stage at that point, but County simply turned everything back upon his detractors. By the end of the show, they were ready to kill him, and County loved every second of it. "The punks respected me for being real and not afraid to be myself. I had nothing to hide. I did not give one piece of shit what anyone thought about me, and they respected me for that. I got away with murder!"

Cherry Vanilla, the following evening, was equally thrilling. Especially if you'd spent the last four years waiting to get this close to her again. Again in 1973, again thirteen years old, I once met her outside Bowie's old management offices in Gunter Grove, Chelsea, while hanging out with a bunch of other Ziggy freaks. I got another autograph (God, I wonder what happened to them all?) and a peck on the cheek, and I was madly in love with her from that day forth. She repaid that devotion one hundredfold.

Vanilla's own initial impressions of the Roxy were not promising. No matter how great she'd heard the Roxy was when she was home in New York, the reality was like walking into an outside toilet and discovering there was no paper. Black pipes suspended over the stage dripped condensation, the walls were wet to the touch, and the stage was so low that you could smell the audience's breath.

The sound system was scarcely top of the range, which meant "we could hardly hear ourselves in the monitors," and then there was the spitting. Wayne County had relished it, encouraging the crowd to spray ever more out at him, and then rushing around the stage, to make sure that the globules enjoyed maximum impact. Cherry, however, was caught completely off guard. "The arcs of spit flying through the air freaked me out a bit, until somebody told me it meant the crowd liked us. Still, it seemed pretty disgusting to me."

Other shocks. "First thought: this place is a complete fire trap. The stairs, which seemed to be the only way in and out, were packed with people and all of them were smoking. When the music started (can't remember what band), everyone rushed closer to the stage. Second thought: if there was a fire, the performers would be the last ones out. But the vibe was pure rock 'n' roll, and I soon forgot about my safety, and everybody else's."

We had Miles Copeland to thank for bringing her over, setting up a short UK tour and giving her his kid brother's Police as both a support act and sidemen. But you didn't pay any attention to them. It was Cherry who captivated.

She had the most amazing eye contact. Every so often, you'd see her glance meet one of the audience and, whoever he was, he'd melt. The Roxy melted with him. She knew it as well. "When I'm on stage, what makes me hot is to think that I'm fucking. The energy you get at orgasm, I try to reach that with my music."

Not that she flaunted it *too* much. "The way people write about me sometimes, you'd think I had an act where I got on the floor and shoved dildos up my cunt," Cherry snarled. "Which I've never

Cherry Vanilla at home in her Chelsea apartment.
Courtesy of Cherry Vanilla.

done." What she *did* do was project an eroticism that blasted all manner of imagery into the watching impressionable mind. Posters for the show pictured Cherry clutching a bright red dildo. The original photograph featured nothing more phallic than a microphone, and the first she knew about the switch was when she saw a copy of the poster inside the club. But she didn't object. "The excitement was huge," she punned, presumably none too accidentally.

A devastating performance was pure high-energy rock 'n' roll. Cherry took the stage with a solid clutch of songs that may or may not have been strictly autobiographical ("Little Red Rooster" could have been about a certain Mr. B.; "Bad Girl" might well have been her statement of intent), but which felt as though she meant every word, an electrifying storm that might have looked brazen, but was brimful of subtlety, too.

It would have been too easy for her to play the sex kitten with the kiddies. She preferred to make them work for their fantasies, and only occasionally nudge them in the desired direction, little things like appearing onstage sporting a T-shirt with "Lick Me" picked out in sequins and stars, then spending half the show trying to stop the front row from taking her up on the offer.

But even that, she was adamant, wasn't her first choice of costuming. She'd only flown in from New York the day before her UK debut show in Newport, Wales; the tour reached London three days later, and she was still armed only with whatever she'd stuffed into her suitcase before she left home—dirty clothes, mainly, because she'd not had time to hit the launderette any place else. "We didn't have any money, so my band were not decked out in the latest of punk fashion, and the only clean clothes I could pull from the bottom of my bag were a pair of underpants and my "Lick Me" T-shirt. Little did I know that the T-shirt would be the most photographed thing I ever wore!"

It didn't matter. Cherry Vanilla was the sexiest, gorgeous-est, and most glamorous thing on earth, and the Roxy treated her like a queen. "This was one of those rare historical moments that would go down in musical history. Punk was peaking, especially in London, and the Roxy was the place to be. And I was not only there, but playing it. I couldn't believe my good fortune." She was even prepared to overlook the state of the bathrooms, although it had to be admitted that those dark pits had their uses, above and beyond their stated purpose.

Wayne County purred, "One of my strongest memories of the Roxy was going into the men's room, and being told by a cute young man that I was in the wrong toilet. I knew right then that I was going to love the London punks, the Roxy, and the British in general. I was knocked out by the reaction I got."

He was knocked out by what he discovered taking place in the toilets, too. Rarely cleaned and never policed, the Roxy bathrooms became the center for all and any activities that could not be conducted on the dance floor, from surreptitious drug-dealing to undercover sex, and on to a variety of weird and wonderful experiments involving either or both.

"There were a lot more different sexualities floating around than people actually knew about," County discovered. "People just kept their mouths shut about their sexual preferences." Sid Vicious wondered aloud whether he might be gay, cornering both County and his fellow New Yorker, Heartbreakers manager Leee Black Childers, on the subject, but he was by no means the only one. The Roxy bathroom, for many young uncertainties, was the place where they first learned the reality behind their private fantasies.

However, even if the sexual spirit was willing, County was convinced that the flesh was invariably weak. "A lot of the kids were on that fucking awful cheap speed, sulphate. That stuff would knock your head off, and give you the shits to boot! I remember overhearing a conversation between some punks about how much they loved sulfate, but it was impossible to get a hard on with it. I think that is one reason all that 'anti-sex' stuff started. No one could get a hard-on, so the sex was way down their list of priorities."

"Amphetamine sulphate and strong cider *were* the drugs of choice," Alan Lee Shaw agreed. "Which fit perfectly with the aggression and speed rush of the music; although, having given one that marvelous feeling of euphoria and invincibility, the comedown could be gut wrenchingly awful. Pot and harder drugs were not really conducive with punk to start with, because they slowed you down."

But those other substances floated around regardless. The Heartbreakers were solid supporters of heroin, later boasting that they were responsible for giving great swathes of British youth its first taste of the drug. But nothing could dislodge speed from its throne, nor protect its users from the inevitable fallout. It only needed one speed freak in the back of a van to bring chaos and collapse to a gigging group.

"I knew a lot of people who were using speed in the punk circuit," TV Smith acknowledged, "and I saw the chaos it brought. I saw it as causing a lot of social disruption and stifling creativity. It broke down the interaction that you need to be in a band, you don't need someone who's overindulging all the time."

* * *

The New York festival was not the only American show in town that weekend. Another legend was prowling the London streets and, like County and Vanilla, the sheen of Bowie stardust was sprinkled heavy across his reputation.

zigzag '70

Jan. 1977   30p. $1.50

GY POP
he stooge
steals the stage

RY COODER
On chicken skin
Mex Music

ILS LOFGREN
The Rocking Athlete

ACKSON BROWNE
s about The Pretender

Monthly since the early 1970s, *ZigZag* once had the kind of reputation that prompted *Sniffin' Glue* to recommend spitting inside an unsold issue, to horrify the hippie who did eventually pick it up. Things later changed dramatically, but even before then, when the magazine covered an act you cared about, the ensuing feature was generally priceless. *Author's collection*

In 1973, Iggy Pop and the Stooges released *Raw Power*, an LP that more than either of the group's earlier records, absolutely prophesied the spirit of punk. John Peel acknowledged that when he included "Your Pretty Face Is Going to Hell" in his punk rock special; Gaye Advert confirmed it when she glued the album's cover photograph to the scratchplate of her Gibson bass; and TV Smith nailed it firmly into legend one night at the Roxy, arguing down no less an intellect than Colin Newman of Wire over what was the best album ever made. It didn't matter what Newman threw out there. Smith hit back with *Raw Power* every time.

At eighteen, Smith could not even begin a new day without first listening to *Raw Power*. "'Search and Destroy' was certainly *the* song, so blistering and it's totally unlike any other record has ever sounded. Dirty guitars mixed right up, jagged and raw. The Stooges were probably the one band that you have to pull out and say they made a difference. There were bands like the Velvet Underground that impressed me and were interesting, but what Iggy brought was this incredible violence and aggression and energy, violence against a society that wasn't working for me as a teenager.

"I didn't like what I was seeing in the world, and here was someone else who didn't like it and who was roaring against it. To get up every morning and put on *Raw Power* filled me with energy, there was this great scream of aggression and somehow it gave me a very positive feel that you can say something about what's going on, despite everything. Fight back and kick back."

Iggy had spent many years pondering that same equation, living out a musical career that was part soap opera, part disaster movie, before landing his body in a psychiatric hospital, and his reputation in the toilet. "The name Iggy Pop was synonymous with shit," Pop confessed. "The guy who'd be tied up in a bag and thrown out of a window two floors up at a Deep Purple gig. The guy whose girlfriend ran off with Robert Plant. The guy who Ian Hunter said would never make it because he had no talent."

David Bowie disagreed. A fan before the two men met, it was Bowie who persuaded the Stooges to record *Raw Power* under his aegis, and Bowie whose uncompromising remix of the band's original vision that gave the finished record its defiant sound. The Stooges claimed to hate the way the record sounded, and lost few opportunities to damn the few days that an unsupervised Bowie spent working on their master tape. But even they missed the point. What Bowie created was a record that was further ahead of its time than any of his own music. When people said they hated it, what they meant was they hated the future. A future that had now arrived.

Iggy hung over the British punk scene like a predatory bat; indeed, he'd been a part of the local pop psyche for so long that his past self-destruction was part of the language. The Damned had already recorded "I Feel Alright" for inclusion on *Damned Damned Damned*; the Sex Pistols cut their own take on "No Fun." French imports of the first two Stooges albums, the only available pressings for six years or more, were now racked up in the Virgin store on New Oxford Street; *Metallic KO* was omnipresent. A hastily repackaged, budget-priced reissue of *Raw Power* was imminent.

Now a new album, *The Idiot*, was on its way, and tickets for the week's worth of shows that Iggy was playing

Ticket stub for the second of Iggy's London shows.
Author's collection

around the country flew out of the door. Bowie was one of Pop's sidemen, tucked away stage left on the piano, but scarcely anyone even cared. The opening night in Aylesbury notwithstanding, two nights at the London Rainbow in March 1977 marked Iggy Pop's first live performances since the death of the Stooges three years before, and his first UK gigs since 1972. Even the presence of his unobtrusively chainsmoking pianist couldn't have raised the demand for tickets any higher, and Pop rewarded the ensuing full houses with performances that matched every description of his stagecraft the audiences had ever dreamed of.

OK, so there was no onstage bloodletting, no graceful swan dives from the top of the speaker stacks, no danse macabre with oozing candle wax. But the possibility of all those things hung heavy over Iggy's every action, and the murky-but-magnificent tape that Jake handed me a week or two later captured the sound of a crowd on the edge of their seats, and Pop on the edge of insanity.

The set was, sensibly, oldies heavy. *The Idiot* was only touched upon, with a sinister "Fun Time" and a seething "Sister Midnight"; in its place, the opening "Raw Power" was followed by a blistering "TV Eye," a lascivious "Loose," a frenetic "1969" . . . you could run out of superlatives with a show like this, but the band not only hit the expected highs, they even ushered in a few brand-new numbers.

"Turn Blue" and "Tonight," neither of which would hit vinyl until *Lust for Life*, later in the year, were premiered, while "Gimme Danger" spiraled and "No Fun" glowered, and Bowie smoked and smoked and smoked, scarcely able to believe that this was really happening. "I Need Somebody," "Search and Destroy," "I Wanna Be Your Dog" . . . things really don't get any better than this.

The rich and the powerful flocked to the shows, and two nights at the London Rainbow were wall-to-wall somebodies. Howard Devoto was there, handing Iggy a copy of the Buzzcocks' *Spiral Scratch* with the words, "I've got all your records, now you've got all mine." The Adverts were there, just gazing in disbelief and cursing the fates that placed the Vibrators, and not them, on the bill alongside Iggy; and Johnny Rotten was there, so enamored by the occasion that when he paused to talk with the knot of kids that hung around the Rainbow backstage door at the end of the evening, he neither looked nor sounded like the hunchback of so much past renown.

"Do you know him?" an onlooker asked me as he walked away.

"Who?" I asked.

"That was Rotten, you idiot," Cassie hissed beside me. "And you didn't even recognize him."

Iggy Pop bleeds for you. *Author's collection*

Then Iggy himself emerged, and the crowd parted before him, struck dumb by the proximity—not of a legend, but of a God. Without Iggy Pop's example, punk might never have happened. Without Iggy Pop's example, we might *still* be listening to the Eagles. Former manager Tony Defries later described Pop as the most important artist he ever worked with, which probably pissed David Bowie off somewhat. But Defries was correct. He was. I don't think Iggy was even asked to sign an autograph as he walked toward the tour bus. It seemed enough just to provide him with a guard of honor.

Even deities need some downtime, though, and before Iggy left London for the rest of the tour, he decided to take in some of the local sights.

Gene October was standing outside the Roxy when a limousine pulled up and Iggy emerged.

October recognized him instantly. "Are you going in?"

Iggy looked him up and down. "I dunno, should I?"

"Yeah, you should."

Iggy stared at him for a moment, and then things got weird. "Iggy says, 'Why? You got a problem!?' I said, 'No, I'm just saying you should come in,' and he said, 'Well, come on then,' and he offered me out for a fucking fight!"

20

Long Hot Summer

EARLY APRIL 1977

SOUNDTRACK

"Cave Man Skank"	Ranking Trevor (Disco Mix)
"Daughter of Zion"	Bagga (Matumbi)
"Dirty Pictures"	Radio Stars (Chiswick)
"Don't Call Us Immigrants"	Tabby "Cat" Kelly (Tank)
"England's Glory"	Max Wall (Stiff)
"Erotic Neurotic"	The Saints (Harvest)
"Grip"	Stranglers (UA)
"I Don't Care"	The Boys (NEMS)
"In the City"	Jam (Polydor)
"In the Flesh"	Blondie (Private Stock)
"Listen"	Clash (CBS/*NME*)
"No Man's Land"	Cornell Campbell (Joe Gibbs)
"One Chord Wonders"	Adverts (Stiff)
"Party Time"	Heptone (Island)
"Peasant in the Big Shitty"	The Stranglers (UA)
"Rock to Sleep"	Horace Andy (International)
"Smokescreen"	Desperate Bicycles (Refill)
"Television Screen"	Radiators From Space (Chiswick)
"We A Socialists"	The Youths (Youth Man)
"You're So Cold"	Tyronne Evans (Clocktower)
"You're So Dumb"	Skrewdriver (Chiswick)

The Roxy was running out of time. "It was a good place to go for about a month, and the rest of the time it was a pain." Eater's Dee Generate spoke for many people when he confessed his disillusion with the place. "I think it became a sort of goldfish bowl, and punk-related headlines provoked a mass of people to come to either gawp at the oddities, cause trouble, or just look bemused. It was all about being an instant punk, getting a uniform.

New Victoria Theatre
WILTON ROAD, S.W.1
Telephone No. 834 0671/2

Peter Bowyer for
Cream International Artists
presents

LOU REED
in Concert
Evening 8.00
WEDNESDAY
APRIL   27

CIRCLE £1.50
N⁰ W 10

No ticket exchanged
nor money refunded
This portion to be retained
NO RE-ADMISSION

April 1977 was a great time to be a Velvet Underground fan . . . first John Cale performed at the Roundhouse, opening the tour that climaxed with him beheading a chicken onstage; then came Lou Reed, promoting *Rock 'n' Roll Heart* with a show that . . . well, frankly, it was tiresome. *Author's collection*

"You started to see clones of Rotten and Joe Strummer. It became all commercial and uncreative, and most of the real original punks had moved on to other looks. That stereotype spiky hair, leather jacket, and tartan pants was a fan uniform, it had nothing to do with punk. That was about difference, creativity, and self-expression. In fact, very quickly there was nowhere to go in London, so everybody stayed in and the scene was really over, because it had become part of the business."

Nils Stevenson agreed. "What was fascinating at the beginning quickly turned into this horrible look. It really was interesting the way it shifted when the word 'punk' was put on everybody. It turned into something other than what it started out to be, wanting to do one thing and turning into something else."

Of course, that was an inevitable conclusion. No movement whose popularity grows larger by the day, fed both by the support of the musicians and the ferocious opposition of the tabloids and the government, could ever retain its original beauty. By the end of March, if not even sooner, the Roxy's early exclusivity had been trampled beneath the stylized booties of a full-grown fashion monster, to become one of the premier hangouts in London. Even my now-habitual outfit of jeans and a vaguely relevant T-shirt, all that I could afford on my record store wage, looked hopelessly out of place there.

But the weekly rent had skyrocketed to £600, while Czezowski and Jones were still reeling from a daring raid at the end of January, when a gang posing as Scotland Yard's Vice Squad bundled them into the club after a sold-out Stranglers show, and made off with the night's takings. Not every night at the Roxy turned a profit; even at its height, some were dismally empty. They needed the big-name headliners to play, just to keep their heads above water. But with record deals now flying fast and furious, and every other venue in town finally opening its doors to the punk-shaped clatter of the cash register, the former uniqueness of the club was long gone. Soon Czezowski and Jones would be joining it, thrown out of their own

Roxy handbill for the month of April, published before the change of ownership and, therefore, subject to considerable disruption once everyone found out what had happened. *Author's collection*

club for nonpayment of rent. The dream had lasted precisely one hundred days.

No, that's not true. Under new, and infinitely less visionary management, the Roxy would soldier on for another twelve months, and would still host a handful of names worth noting. But it would broaden its horizons, too, begin hosting rock 'n' roll nights and disco evenings, and start booking bands that would never have dared venture down there before. A lot of the old crowd stopped going altogether; others were just a lot more selective about when they'd give it a go. The true spirit of the place really did die when Czezowski cashed in his chips. As Cherry Vanilla put it, "There were only one hundred nights, and I'm glad to say that I was featured on one of 'em."

Alan Lee Shaw agrees. Although he never played the Roxy during its heyday, "it was all pretty jaw dropping just to be there and feel part of all that was new, vibrant, expressive, and cutting edge."

But the last words must go to Wayne County. "The Roxy? What a place! Punk? What a time! Who would have ever thought that, one day, those times would be the 'good ole daze'? Long may the history and memory remain. To me, punk was not just a form of music or an attitude. It was also a space in time! Let the history be told!"

Even without that faithful subterraneous to retire to, however, things continued coming together. Musicians I'd been following for months on end, watching as not much appeared to be happening, were suddenly stepping into the limelight.

Roogalator were on the verge of a major label deal. The Tom Robinson Band, too. Adverts' "One Chord Wonders" was Single of the Week in both *Sounds* and *Melody Maker*. And with that glorious tumult still fresh in the ears, there came the news that producer Larry Wallis was not the only Pink Fairy flexing his muscles in time to the new punk beat. Twink, the Fairies' founder and drummer, too, was back on the warpath, hacking off his trademark waist-length hair (Wallis, typically, retained his) and uniting with that wild two-man show called the Maniacs to launch his musical comeback.

With former Pink Fairy Twink resplendent in curls, and Maniacs Latter and Shaw looking newly shorn and moody, the Rings take Ted Carroll's motor for a spin. *Courtesy of Alan Lee Shaw*

Twink and the Maniacs went back a long way. They first fell in with one another when all three lived in Cambridge in 1971, shortly after Twink returned from a sojourn in Morocco. Since that time, he'd jammed with Steve Peregrin Took and formed a band with the post–Pink Floyd Syd Barrett—the night Shaw saw the MC5 play, February 24, 1972, he also watched Twink and Barrett's Stars stumble through their second, and final, live show. A few months later, Twink invited Shaw and Rod Latter into a new group, ZZZ, who played a few gigs opening for Hawkwind before fizzling out when Twink split

for London. But the trio remained in touch and now Twink was looking to get back into music. Would the Maniacs be interested?

"Sure," Shaw replied. "Twink wanted to form a band and we
needed to move on from being a duo. So I said OK, let's give it a
shot." Latter's bedroom was commandeered for the new group's
rehearsal room, at least until the complaints from the neighbors
forced proceedings to move into the kitchen. There they cut their
first demos, a clutch of Shaw originals, a couple of Twink creations,
and a healthy dose of the Fairies' own legacy—"Do It," "The
Snake," and "Teenage Rebel." Twink came up with a name for the
band, the *Melody Maker* classifieds delivered bassist Dennis Stow,
and the Rings were up and running.

The band's debut gig, at Dingwalls, brought Chiswick's Ted Carroll—a long-time Fairies fan—into the frame, signing the Rings for a
one-off single, with Martin Gordon producing. They shot a fabulous
photo session using Ted Carroll's vintage Cadillac, and another outside the Rock On store. More gigs started coming in. Rings played
the Red Cow with XTC, and when the Music Machine was born
within the shell of an old BBC studio in Mornington Crescent, Rings
were the first to perform, opening for the Heartbreakers and
Siouxsie and the Banshees.

But the media regarded them askance. Older journalists recalled
Twink from his free festival days, and still carried their past percep-
tions with them; younger writers thought his presence in a punk
band completely undermined the notion that the new music had
come to sweep away the past, irrespective of how that past may have
been at odds with whatever the mainstream of the day was.

Within their own time and place, after all, the Pink Fairies were
as great an irritant to the establishment as the Sex Pistols. But unless
you possessed the musical grounding to appreciate that, what were
they but another gaggle of hairies who had ground around the hippie
circuit, smoking dope and preaching free love? When journalist Jane
Suck wrote an especially dismissive review in *Sounds*, it became clear

to Shaw what was going on. "They had it in for Twink and could not stomach his hippie past."

Not that Twink went out of his way to illuminate his punk credentials. Every night when the spitting started, he would scamper behind Latter's drum kit, and continue the show from there. The first few times he did it, it was funny, but it was only a matter of time before somebody started to make a big deal out of it, maybe sniped some more in the music papers, maybe called him an old fart to his face.

"Talk about losing face," Shaw shuddered, although he also admitted, "I couldn't really blame him, because it was a crap idea spitting on the band. But you had to front it out."

So far as I was concerned, Chiswick Records was fast shaping up as the label to look out for. Stiff was more consistent in terms of quality releases—a second Damned single, and the debut by Elvis Costello had joined the Adverts on the must-buy shelf—but there was a maddening idiosyncrasy there that rendered every new release a crap shoot. Chiswick, on the other hand, had completely shaken away the pub rock vibe that hung over the label's catalog the previous fall, replacing it with a gorgeous eye for more reliable, adrenalined talents.

The no-longer-Hammersmith Gorillas, Jesse Hector's long-running grudge against the major labels that refused to acknowledge his genius. The Radiators from Space, the first Irish punks to make it over to London, cutting a single ("Television Screen") that *Rolling Stone* would one day describe as the best punk record of all time.

The label picked up the Blackpool-based Skrewdriver, and that despite Cock Sparrer's Steve Bruce cautioning, "The first time Skrewdriver came to one of our gigs, they looked like a bunch of long-haired hippies." Johnny Moped followed, Roxy regulars whom other companies wouldn't have touched with a bargepole, and whose guitarist, Slimy Toad, used to work a milk round with Dee Generate's stepfather. Chiswick even grabbed Motörhead, at a time when no other label in the land would touch them and even Lemmy was considering knocking the whole thing on the head. Together, they conspired a self-titled single that made an earsplitting mockery of the newly discovered twelve-inch single craze by spreading a mere three minutes of thrashing brain damage across the disc. The grooves were wide enough to drive a truck through, but the record was deafening even with the volume set at zero.

The best of the Chiswickian bunch, though, was "Dirty Pictures," the song that Martin Gordon and Andy Ellison had brought to the label six months before. It was time to make everything formal. On March 2, Gordon quit Ian's Radio; on March 3, he exchanged contracts with Chiswick. All that remained now was for the group to come up with a name. Ted Carroll had already been assured that they had a shortlist of five possibilities; he had even managed to get a copy of the list from Gordon.

But Gordon knew that picking a name is never easy, not if it's something you intend living with for any period of time. The road to stardom, after all, is littered with gallant attempts at being clever or comical that can backfire horribly the following morning. TV Smith, for instance, was still at school when his first group was casting around for names, flicking through textbooks in search of whatever appealed. They found an article on the first-ever transatlantic telegraph experiment, and were intrigued by the sentence "Adolf Slaby witnessed the transmission." Slaby Witness would regret the discovery for the remainder of their short life.

Gordon and Ellison had no intention of making the same mistake, so Ted Carroll made it for them. Panicked by a phone call coming in from the *Melody Maker*, asking what the pair's new group was called, he pulled the first name off the list that caught his eye. According to Gordon, "the first we knew about it was when it appeared in *Melody Maker*'s Raver column, 'ex-John's Children and Jet man Andy Ellison resurfaces in Radio Stars.'" But he also conceded that the fates must have been smiling down on them that day. Other names on the list included the Red Rats, Teeth, and the Wurst.

"Dirty Pictures" drew closer. There may have been very little money spent on the actual recording, but the picture sleeve was worth a million dollars. Gordon had always been struck by "this great photo sequence of the Goons comedy team up against a wall, eyes right, and actress Barbara Goalen standing there looking slinky. First Spike Milligan cracks up and crawls towards her, then the others do, and this goes on in sequence until they're all lying on the floor together. I thought that was great, so I got my girlfriend of the time, Kelly St. John, to tog herself up in suspenders and naughty bits, and we did the sleeve as an homage." St. John was one of Britain's top models, and one of the bevy of topless beauties who filed through the *Sun* national newspaper's daily "Page 3" feature. She fit the bill perfectly.

Radio Stars, with drummer Gary Thompson joining the core of Ellison, Gordon, and guitarist Ian McLeod, were in Karlsruhe the day "Dirty Pictures" was released, preparing to launch their very first tour, two weeks around Germany, supporting UFO. It was an incongruous start to any career, but after so many years of inactivity, anything was better than another night at home.

Radio Stars refined just eight songs for their live show and, mindful that German UFO fans probably weren't the most adventurous ears they could try things out on, they kept all eight short and sweet. Invariably, the biggest applause was for the two songs the audience had a dim hope of recognizing, Chuck Berry's "Talking About You" and the Beatles' "Dear Prudence," and the group shed few tears when the final night of the German tour was canceled, and they headed home to celebrate with a gig far more to their liking, a one-night stand at Mill Hill Girls School on May 14. And it was there that they earned their very first encore.

"I suddenly figured out how to do it," Gordon celebrated afterward. "I nicked all the good bits of UFO's stagecraft, and realized that, if it was done properly, you could get an audience to respond as you wanted them to. Well, more or less."

A fresh repertoire was falling into place almost effortlessly, and would continue falling as the band rehearsed through the remainder of May, in readiness for their next major test—a John Peel session on May 17, followed by a full UK tour supporting Eddie and the Hot Rods.

Many of Radio Stars' biggest tunes were written long before. Like "Dirty Pictures," "Johnny Mekon" was an unheard Jet number; "Horrible Breath" dated back to Ellison's days alongside Marc Bolan in John's Children; and "No Russians in Russia" immortalized one of accident-prone President Ford's most memorable gaffes. The Soviets, the sweet old chap once insisted, were *not* in control of Eastern Europe.

Old songs, old melodies, old jokes. But it was strange how the sensibility of the tunes collided so seamlessly with that of the day, and only the tempo and the brevity of the arrangements changed. "We got faster and shorter," Gordon laughed, but he had no complaints about that. It just spurred him to greater excess.

"It meant that you used your songs up quicker, so I had to come up with more, and took influences from wherever I could find them. I recall hearing some tune on the radio, couldn't make the words out exactly, but it sounded like 'Eric, Eric, Eric!' What a great chorus, I thought. It turned out not to be Eric at all, it was a po-faced rant about solidarity with the masses, but I nicked it anyway, and it became one of our biggest live favorites."

Audiences hastened to the group's side, intuitively aware that a Radio Stars show was never, ever likely to be dull. "People began turning up in large numbers as soon as they figured that the *Sun* Page 3 girl from the front of the single might show up at the gigs. She did, of course, and she stood obtrusively by the side of the stage during most performances."

She was the only one who did remain in one place. Ellison in particular was a madman, prone to climbing the highest speaker stack, indulging in whichever gymnastics took his fancy at that moment, and then leaping, knees first, back down to the stage. Audiences not only responded in kind, they also began dressing for the occasion. Elsewhere, musicians grumbled to themselves about how punk uniforms had become so standardized—bondage trousers, mohair sweaters, leather jackets. Not at a Radio Stars concert, they hadn't. Their crowd turned out in shorts and T-shirts, because that was the only dress capable of sustaining you through the sweatbox that each gig would become.

"The punks adopted us early on, probably because we were on Chiswick Records," Gordon reasoned. "I guess Andy's past with John's Children helped out in this respect, and we began wearing leather jackets and tight jeans. There was no conscious decision to do this; it was merely what everyone who didn't work in a bank did. Plus, the fact that you couldn't get a decent satin jacket for love or money any more. I used to scour Kensington Market regularly, but those times had come and gone.

"So there we were. The audience were gagging for it, gobbing away, but mostly at Andy; clothes were removed. Brevity was good, speed was better, the girls were fast, and the music was loud. It was the best of times."

21

Where Monsters Dwell, Where Creatures Roam

EARLY MAY 1977

SOUNDTRACK

"Baby Baby"	Vibrators (CBS)
"Black Skin Boy"	15, 16, 17 (Morpheus)
Bowi EP	Nick Lowe (Stiff)
"Chinese Rocks"	Heartbreakers (Track)
"City of the Damned"	Rikki and the Last Days of Earth (Oundle Roc Soc)
"Cranked Up Really High"	Slaughter and the Dogs (Rabid)
"Do the Standing Still"	The Table (Virgin)
"Fall Out"	The Police (Illegal)
"God Save the Queen"	Sex Pistols (Virgin)
"I Wanna Be Free"	The Rings (Chiswick)
"I'm Still in Love with You"	Marcia Aitken (Belmont)
"Jah Forgive Them"	Leroy Smart (Micron)
"Lost Johnny"	Mick Farren and the New Wave (Ork)
"Natty BSc"	Dillinger (Black Swan)
"Peaches"	Stranglers (UA)
"Pickney Have Pickney"	Well Pleased and Satisfied (High Note)
"Remote Control"	Clash (CBS)
"Satta in the Place"	Big Joe (Micron)

"Sheena Is a Punk Rocker"

"Sister Suzie"

"Six Dead and Nineteen Gone to Jail"

"South Africa"

"Thinking of the USA"

"Young Savage"

Ramones (Sire)

Cock Sparrer (Decca)

Big Youth (Observer)

Mighty Travellers (Travellers)

Eater (The Label)

Ultravox! (Island)

The rumors were flying throughout early May; the Sex Pistols were about to sign their third record deal in six months, this time with Richard Branson's Virgin Records, a company that McLaren had, in fact, publicly insisted he'd never join just a few short weeks before. "Bollocks, man. We went to Virgin Records before we went to EMI and they didn't want to know."

Virgin originally denied the reports, consigning them to the same dustbin of rumor that insisted the label was also picking up Roogalator and the Motors. "We haven't signed any of these people," Virgin press spokesman Al Clark wearily teased. "But we might." And they did, although Roogalator, at least, could not see the point. One moment, the label heads were raving about the band's debut single, "Love and the Single Girl"; the next, everything else went by the board as Virgin threw all hands on deck to fight the Pistols' corner.

In the two months since the short-lived hilarity of the Pistols' A&M interlude, signed and dropped within under a week, CBS had browsed, but passed on by, and there was a moment when it looked as though the Sex Pistols would need to go abroad in order to get their music heard. The French label Barclay was expressing an interest in signing them, and McLaren was seriously considering their offer. Then Richard Branson stepped in and nothing, now, was going to hold them back.

The timing was, to put it mildly, ideal.

Away from the Roxy, away from the streets, away from every-thing that had anything to do with punk rock, British life meandered on. The Grunwick strike was still in full flow, and now the mainte-nance crews at Heathrow Airport had gone out as well. The govern-ment was pledging to convert the entire country to metric measurements within ten years (in fact, it would take them closer to twenty-five), and the European Economic Community was trying to finally confirm the conditions under which British and Icelandic fish-ermen would abide, in a bid to end the so-called Cod War.

But most people had stopped looking at the newspaper headlines long ago. The rest of the world was presumably still revolving around the sun, but Britain was in tight orbit around Her Majesty the Queen.

All year long, Britain had been gearing up toward what promised to be the biggest shindig the country had seen in a quarter of a cen-tury, because that's how long it was since the last time royalty invited everyone to a party. In June 1952, Queen Elizabeth II acceded to the throne. In June 1977, she would be marking her Silver Jubilee, no matter that the country was in the grip of recession, that the Interna-tional Monetary Fund was sick of being pestered to bail the country out yet again, that the government was limping from one crisis to another, and that the only alternatives in sight were the shrill pro-nouncements of Margaret Thatcher, prime minister elect two full years before the next scheduled election. We had a Jubilee and that was all that mattered.

Now, planning for the big day was moving into the final stretch. Four weeks, three weeks, two weeks, and each one jingled to the sound of cash. The amount of money being poured into celebrating twenty-five years of Queen Elizabeth II was boggling, and the official expenditure was only the tip of the iceberg.

Private citizens, too, were digging deep into their resources to fund the party of a lifetime, colored bunting, flags and banners, sou-venir mugs and biscuit tins, and street parties that seemed to devour entire towns. Great bonfires awaited ignition on hills across the nation—viewed from the air, it was said, the entire British Isles would be visible, picked out in a ring of fire.

Nobody mentioned that the last time that happened was when the Luftwaffe was bombing the place, because why would they? The country was happy for the first time in years, and it didn't matter where you went, there would be somebody singing the national anthem, "God Save the Queen . . .

". . . she ain't no human being." The Sex Pistols' new single, their own "God Save the Queen," was originally scheduled for release by A&M back in March, and nobody had paid much attention back then. It would have come and gone long before the celebrations got underway. Now it was back on the listings, only this time it would be in the stores just a week before Her Majesty's big day, and nobody wanted to miss the chance to get the first blow in.

Less than a week after Virgin announced they'd signed the Sex Pistols, the workers at the factory making the pressing plates for the 45 announced that they were refusing to handle it. Hours later, the printers working on the picture sleeve came to the same decision. Both disputes were ironed out that same day, but not before McLaren began worriedly wondering whether Virgin could abandon the traditional vinyl pressing plants altogether, and have the single released as a flexidisc.

The following day, the first ban came into force, as the Pistols' attempt to place a thirty-second commercial into the next broadcast of Bill Grundy's new television magazine news program was rebuffed. And then the pantomime began in earnest.

Rotten insisted that the song was serious. "We never wrote anything trivially, everything is about content and deliberateness. You cannot forget that these are not casual songs, they are full on content. You cannot ever forget that."

No. But you *could* misinterpret it. The lyrics to "God Save the Queen" circulated the nation's newsrooms like a plague, and every journalist who read them came away with their own radical impression of what was said, few of which bore any resemblance to the words themselves. "The Sick Song that Calls the Queen a Moron!" screamed the headlines.

One line insisted that the monarchy's only purpose was to keep the tourist trade alive. Another described Britain's youth as the flowers in her regal dustbin. A third even accused Britain's government of being a fascist regime, oddly overlooking a fact that Virgin records felt was intrinsic to the argument. "If this country *isn't* [a fascist regime], which is clearly the case for most people, then one of the first principles of democracy is that the band should be free to sing that line on radio and TV."

But the BBC rejected "God Save the Queen" for any airplay short of John Peel's late-night niche spot, and independent radio quickly arrived at a similar decision. On the High Street, the chainstore Woolworth's was the first to announce that the Sex Pistols were not welcome in its record racks and that it would not even stock the record. WH Smith and Boots, fellow giant retailers with an influential finger in the record-selling waters, agreed.

There was the suggestion that EMI might demonstrate its continuing anger at the Sex Pistols—or, more formally, its support for Her Majesty and its outrage at the insult—by banning "God Save the Queen" from its HMV retail arm. Ultimately, they didn't, but there was certainly a moment when it looked as though the only major retailer carrying the single might be Virgin's own growing nationwide chain of stores.

But when Virgin's reps took the first advance copies around the record stores, packaged in plain blue sleeves to match the all-black covers that bedecked "Anarchy in the UK," they almost unanimously returned to the office with tales of the fabulous sums they'd been offered to part with a copy.

After what happened to "Anarchy in the UK" (deleted after little more than six weeks) and the A&M 45 (scrapped with just a few hundred pressed), nobody wanted to take a chance on missing out on this one as well, and it was only later that we discovered that it wasn't the record that was going to be a collector's dream, it was the sleeve that the salesman was carrying it around in! Finished editions came with a suitably amended photo of Her Majesty on the front.

The record's release was still a week away, and you could smell the revolution in the air. Even more acrid, however, was the stench of counterrevolution. Polite society had already established the boundaries within which the next days would be lived. You either loved the Queen, or you didn't.

The punks didn't, that was already certain. In fact, they didn't like a lot of things. And, as the Jubilee countdown continued to click, so the tabloids began to examine them as well. What other bastions of civilization were these wretched, foul-mouthed yobbos preparing to dismantle?

The police force? That went without saying. People were losing count of the number of times the fearless boys in blue were called upon to wade into another crowd of unruly punk rockers, and drag the ringleaders off for a little readjustment.

Marriage? Johnny Rotten had already written off sex as a couple of minutes of squelching, so that was clearly off the punk agenda, and now this Tom Robinson character was trying to convince everybody that homosexuality was somehow acceptable as well.

How about God, then? Even punk rockers, raised in the nurturing arms of the state-enforced Church of England, had to believe in God, didn't they?

Apparently not.

The plot, if such it was, was breathtaking in its audacity and mind-boggling in its possibilities. A decade earlier, at the height of the Vietnam War protests in the United States, a march through Washington, DC, paused outside the Pentagon, the heart of the nation's military complex. Up to 150,000 people, representing the combined might of some 150 different protest groups, then joined hands and encircled the building to stage an exorcism, while the cops and the National Guard looked on in bewilderment.

What happened? According to the official reports, nothing. Led by Ed Sanders, the lead singer of the Fugs, the crowd chanted "Out, demons out" until it grew bored, and then the march continued. According to the organizers, however, the Pentagon rose thirty feet into the air, turned orange, and vibrated.

Imagine if Buckingham Palace did that.

Who were the pagan punks who were planning this outrage? Nobody knew for sure, although everybody seemed to have encountered somebody else who did know. It was the classic "friend of a friend" affair, granted credibility by the sheer weight of outrage that would descend upon its perpetrators should their identities ever be known.

"Witchcraft" was no longer illegal in the UK. The last statutes were swept away in 1951, when the postwar government realized that such legislation had no place in an enlightened society in the last half of the twentieth century. But the tabloid press continued to delight in relaying the salacious evils that surely attended these people's rites—the blood sacrifices, the sexual orgies, the invocation of Lucifer. Oh yeah, and reciting the Lord's Prayer backward. That was the big one.

The people I knew who claimed to practice this outlandish religion did none of those things—or, if they did, never when I was around. Occasionally, I thought of trying to catch them out— "Amen, ever and forever, glory the and power the," I would consider murmuring softly, just to see whether anyone would accidentally continue the mantra. "Kingdom the is thine for . . ."

But what would be the point? They were nice people, fun people, caring, cautious, and intelligent people. They would no more sacrifice an unborn fetus to the powers of darkness than I would go to a John Denver concert; and besides, if they were right about even half of the prejudices that they feared would devolve upon them should their "secret" be revealed, they were in an even worse bind than the rest of us—blacks, punks, and black punks—put together.

So, Buckingham Palace. Thirty feet in the air, turning orange and vibrating. Why not?

One evening, a new face joined the whisperers. His name was Rikki Sylvan, although his closest friends knew him as Nick Condron, and if there was any such thing as a hierarchy within the local Wiccan community, he was pretty high up on the totem pole.

His collection of magical literature was, from all accounts, amazing, all the more so given that there was so little material around that was readily available. If you wanted to read more on the subject than could be gleaned from a handful of Dennis Wheatley paperbacks, you needed a lot of patience, some serious money, and, more often than not, a gift for Latin and the like. His wardrobe apparently bristled with ceremonial robes and regalia—again, at a time when you couldn't simply walk into the local New Age store (because such things did not exist) and pick up all that you needed. And his conversation, politely delivered in a soft but so determined voice, hinted at a knowledge that soared way above the rest of our heads.

He also had a band.

By day, Sylvan was a tape operator at the CBS Studios in London, although he was rarely content to lurk behind the scenes. A graduate of the same Beckenham Arts Lab that spawned the prefame David Bowie, he was a vociferous songwriter and a dramatic visionary, too. Punk rock intrigued him from the outset, as a musical force, but also as a force for change.

For a few years now, he'd been toying with a Moog synthesizer at a time when such instruments were still a novelty to any musician beyond the well-heeled prog rockers and the arty types who wished they were Brian Eno. Condron was neither, and so his dreams of pushing ahead seemed doomed to failure. Even Ultravox!, the only contemporary group with whom his visions had anything in common, had been forced to let the synths take a backseat when they finally landed a record deal. Condron wanted to go further than that, and punk, with its ferocious ethic of "do it yourself," might be the vehicle that would allow him to push forward.

Rikki Sylvan, a bottle of vodka, and a synth the size of Connecticut.
Courtesy of Steve Wilkin

Sylvan and guitarist Valac Van Der Veene ran their first *Melody Maker* ads in November 1976, but even gathering a band together was slow going. It sometimes felt as though these so-called punks were even more set in their ways than the old farts they claimed to be replacing. Guitar, bass, drums? That's not reactionary, that's retrogression.

Nevertheless, the duo's first acquisition was a bassist, a Warrington lad named Andy Prince, who had scarcely even heard of punk before he'd moved to London a few weeks earlier, and was still unclear what it was until he witnessed the Pistols on *Today*.

"I remember going to the Hope and Anchor one night, and I saw someone sporting winklepickers, what looked like an old man's suit from the early sixties, and a vivid red homemade looking Ziggy-style haircut. I just thought he was some sort of eccentric until, a few weeks later, I happened to be watching the Sex Pistols being interviewed on TV by Bill Grundy (with my parents!) and I realized something new was afoot!"

The next time Prince went through the *Melody Maker* classifieds, looking for bands that needed a bassist, he kept a special eye open for the word "punk" to appear. It was astonishing just how many of them there were and, even more eye-openingly, how unchallenging a lot of them turned out to be, too many would-be musicians picking up an instrument for the first time in their lives, and thinking that the ability to thrash and make a noise was somehow all they needed to do. Well, for a few weeks, maybe they were right. But Prince wanted more than that, and when he answered Sylvan's *Melody Maker* ad, he knew he'd found it.

"I was interviewed by Val, the guitarist, and Rikki's photographer friend, Robin. We then moved on to the old TPA studio in Denmark Street where I met Rikki for the first time; which was also the first time I'd been in a proper recording studio."

With an East London drummer named Nigel and keyboard player Nick Weiss, the team busied themselves rehearsing the material that Sylvan had already composed months before any kind of band came into view, but something wasn't gelling. They lost count of how many hours a week they spent sitting around their cold brick rehearsal space on Tooley Street (just a few appropriate doors away from the London Dungeon tourist attraction), while Sylvan patiently talked them one more time through a song, or wrestled with the synthesizer, convincing it to make the same sounds today as it uttered yesterday. And without work, they were without money. "We weren't that well off," Prince mourned one day. "I was on the dole and crashing on Val's floor, or our roadie Steve's mum's place in Mile End."

I first met Sylvan in early May, around the same time as one of his friends introduced his band to a new drummer, the impressively named Old Etonian Hugh Inge Innes Lillingstone. In the meantime, of course, the precise scenario that Sylvan had been dreading not only unfolded, but also became the norm. Punk rock had already established its image. Now it had cemented its sound, the relentless barrage of an army of identical warriors, all armed with the most basic instrumentation imaginable. Sylvan sounded almost nervous as he invited a bunch of us down to see the band play and apologetic that he couldn't put us all on the guest list, to save us spending good money on what he was presenting. He knew just how far removed from the norm his baby was; he warned that a lot of us would probably walk out.

Rikki and the Last Days of Earth, as Sylvan portentously named his bandmates, made their official live debut at the Man in the Moon, on the edge of the King's Road's World's End tip, on May 28, the first night of what became a Thursday night residency. It was a discerning venue; X-Ray Spex squawked out their infancy there, and a few onlookers visibly smirked when the lineup was introduced onstage. Rikki and the Last Days of Earth? What sort of name was *that*? Even Ed Banger and the Nosebleeds sounded monosyllabic by comparison.

Rikki and the Last Days of Earth, on the other hand, were positive overachievers. A none-too-inaccurate rumor insisted that the quintet boasted no less than thirty-two O-Levels and six A-Levels between them—although quite what difference that made in the prevailing economic climate was never discussed. What were they *supposed* to do with all those qualifications? Maybe it did seem a little strange hearing Sylvan's clearly well-educated vocals enunciating the Rolling Stones' "Street Fighting Man," but a lot of rich boys were having the same problems as poor ones back then. Why *not* sing in a rock 'n' roll band?

Rikki and the Last Days of Earth. Imagine meeting them in a darkened alleyway . . .
Author's collection

Sylvan's songs dealt in death, despondency, and decay. His calling card was a motorized overture proclaiming "These are the last days of Earth," and there was no way of knowing whether he was referring to his band, or to some unimagined apocalypse that he alone knew was about to befall us. But sitting through the show that these black-leather-clad demons were touting around the clubs, it wasn't hard to guess which one *he* thought he meant. The world was about to fall apart, and Sylvan was here to orchestrate the final overture, seizing upon the moods spilling out of the Roots reggae arena, and upping the temperature even further.

Where other contemporary doom-mongers, even the Doctors of Madness at their most maggoty pessimistic, couched their dire predictions in understatement and (comparative) subtlety, Sylvan painted his in mile-high neon. There was nothing unequivocal about "City of the Damned," "Outcast," "Twilight Jack," and "Victimized." From start to finish, Sylvan's world was one of unrelenting psychopathology, a cult of demented loners who straddled social strata like a chainsaw-wielding colossus. Even their instrumentals only unified these disparate themes. "Imagine Roxy Music's 'Out of the Blue' played by the Hitler Youth Marching Orchestra," marveled one critic. "That's Rikki and the Last Days of Earth."

"Audience reactions varied, some people got it, some didn't," reported Andy Prince. At one show, following the skinhead hordes of Sham 69 onto the Vortex stage, "I managed to catch a [flying] pint glass, but Rikki got the contents of one right in the face and walked off in disgust!"

Most of the group's earliest gigs were at private parties, and you really needed to know the right people in order to land an invitation. Hell, you needed to know the right people to even get a copy of their first single! "City of the Damned" was recorded at the band's TPA Studios base and pressed up not for regular release but as the price of admission to their next concert, organized by a friend of drummer Lillingstone at the exclusive and historic Oundle Public School, near Peterborough, the day after the Chelsea show.

But when they did break cover, you went along because you knew that they were something special. They looked great, dripping leather from every limb and never pictured with anything less than their Sunday-best scowls in place, while their live show had to be heard to be believed—a seething, hissing, icy blast, a wall of synthesized menace that sounded like a million dollars and probably cost that much as well. But when you asked Sylvan how he was ever able to afford it all, he'd simply smile and say he had his means.

You bet he did. Sylvan was serious about his message, and serious about his motives too. He'd read Aleister Crowley as a youth, studied him as a teen, and if he didn't exactly live him as an adult, he could at least engage you in a conversation that made it plain that he knew exactly what he was talking about, and it wasn't all gleaned from pop-culture exposés of the self-styled Master Therion—the Great Beast.

In and out of pop culture for the past sixty years, but all the more so since the 1960s hippies rediscovered a few of his more bizarre writings, Crowley's name and reputation—the wickedest man in England—was enjoying a revival that even he would have considered magical. Around a corner off Kensington Church Street, an occult bookstore owned by Led Zeppelin's Jimmy Page did a roaring trade in Crowley reprints, and you'd often see a few punks in there, browsing through books that they may or may not buy, making notes and taking note of what other customers might be saying around them. Of course, you'd see hippies and straights doing much the same thing, but if you were a newspaper journalist hungry for a particular angle, such incidentals were barely worth noticing.

There was more. Offstage and on, Rings' frontman Alan Lee Shaw wore a badge the motto of which was pulled straight out of Crowley's lexicon, *Do what thou wilt*. When he met Patti Smith, at the Roundhouse a year before, the pair of them went deep into conversation on the subject of Crowley; maybe Shaw even told her about the song he'd written about the man, the unequivocally titled "Great Beast." Shaw was not a Crowley disciple himself. But he knew a great subject when he saw one.

> *I got the lowdown from a very good friend of mine*
> *He told me things you would not believe*
> *Blazing torrents that roar into the night*
> *Streams of molten tongues that hiss as they lick*

"The Great Beast"

Shaw was adamant. "Crowley was a selfish, manipulative, hedonistic, sex and drugs addict feeding on the insecurities of those in his thrall. In other words, perfect rock star material."

Sylvan, who had composed his own ode to the idol, "Aleister Crowley," agreed with him up to a point. But he also knew that there was more to Crowley than the sensationalism the old beast himself had encouraged to swirl around his reputation, speaking knowledgeably not only of the man's life and work, but also of the principles behind the work—the means, in other words, whereby magic could be taken out of the pages of some dusty old books and translated into something tangible and real.

Such posturing, if that's what it was, amused some people, intrigued others, and terrified others still. Which is where things started to become interesting. In an age when the Church of England remained inviolate, and in a climate where any subculture that stepped out of the norm was ripe for a hysterical kicking, even the gentlest pagan practitioners risked more than their reputation by publicizing their beliefs.

Jobs could be lost as employers vented their God-fearing wrath. Homes could be vandalized by modern-day witch-hunters. Children could be taken into care by the authorities. It had happened in the past, it would happen in the future, and even if the idea of a few dozen pagan punks exorcising the Queen's official residence was little more than another ill-informed rumor, shot through with a little wishful thinking (it really would have been cool to try!), one thing was certain: if the media were to add it to all the hysterical equations that now bounced back and forth off punk's carapace, nobody would question its authenticity.

Thirty feet.

Turning orange.

Vibrating!

The word was out and with it the whispers, percolating first through the conspirators' own private grapevine, and then out into the wider world, further and further until they finally landed, or so it was said, on the desk of a tabloid journalist at precisely the moment he was in search of something especially meaty to write about.

Again, ignorance clouded any competent evaluation of the facts. Which journalist was it? Nobody knew, but in the days when "Our Special Correspondent" and "Exclusive to" still collected as many bylines in the papers as any named author, that was no surprise. Which newspaper, then? Probably the *Sun*, maybe the *Mirror*, but it could as easily have been the *Express* or the *Mail*. Each of them had long since proved itself happy to put the newsprint boot into both punks and pagans, particularly when they knew that the repercussions would themselves become even more newsworthy.

When would the story be running, then? Well, it had to be in the run up to the Jubilee, because . . . well, just because.

Satanic Punk Cult Menaces Queen!

You could see the headlines already.

Not Just Rotten But Evil Too—Pistol Punks Curse Jubilee

Because the Pistols had to be mentioned in any story like this, regardless of whether or not they were in the room.

Back From The Grave—Great Beast Crowley Threatens Liz's Big Day

At one point, I was checking the headlines every day to see which of the papers had broken the story. I wasn't the only one either. And then—nothing. Not a sausage. Bugger all. It was as though the whole thing had just vanished into thin air. Like magic!

The Jubilee grew closer, it was less than a week now, and even the most dedicated media scaremongers were diverting attention away from all the things that *could* go wrong to examine instead everything that was going right.

Uplifting tales about the war veteran in Northumberland who spent his entire life's savings on Jubilee souvenirs as a legacy for his children. Humorous asides about the woman in Dorset who dyed her poodle red, white, and blue. Admiring gasps for the village in Rutland that was claiming to have built the biggest bonfire in the entire country.

Nobody mentioned, because nobody was aware of, the two London witches who took a National Express coach up to Lancaster to camp out on Pendle Hill, the beauty spot where, three hundred years before, the last great British witchcraft trials and executions had been enacted.

There, amid a summer storm that broke out of nowhere and rolled across that desolate site, they performed a ritual designed to honor the spirits of the condemned so-called witches, and to preserve their descendants and successors from ever undergoing such trials again. Trials such as those that would surely have been uncaged had even a whisper of the Jubilee stunt leaked out of one of the newspapers.

Nobody witnessed the proceedings; nobody recorded the couple's words. So the newspaper story never appeared, and if the plot was ever mentioned again, it was in the knowledge that it had all been forgotten.

The Jubilee was right on top of us. And so were the Sex Pistols.

22

Oh Shit, There Goes the Charabanc

JUNE 1977

SOUNDTRACK

"Alison"	Elvis Costello (Stiff)
"Calling on Youth"	The Outsiders (Raw Edge)
"Chain Gang"	Matumbi (Matumbi)
"Counter Attack"	Revolutionaries (Channel One)
"Exodus"	Bob Marley and the Wailers (Island)
"Fall Out"	The Police (Illegal)
"Fascist Dictator"	Cortinas (Step Forward)
"Flat Foot Hustling"	Dillinger (Observer)
"Freeze"	The Models (Step Forward)
"Groovy Situation"	Keith Rowe (Upsetter)
"His Majesty"	In Crowd (Cactus)
"Mony Mony"	Celia and the Mutations (UA)
"Motörhead"	Motörhead (Chiswick)
"On a Saturday Night"	Christine (Observer)
"Pride and Ambition"	Leroy Smart (Channel One EP)
"Questions"	Suburbans Stud (Pogo)
"Right to Work"	Chelsea (Step Forward)
"Sick of You"	The Users (Raw)
"Slave Master"	Gregory Isaacs (Thing)

"The Last Time"	Wayne County and the Electric Chairs (Illegal)
"The Youth"	Burning Spear (Spear)
"Three Piece Suit"	Trinity (Belmont)
"Tricked"	Ansel and the Meditations (Bam Bam)
"War in the City"	Bob Andy (Jamrock)
"You're So Dumb"	Skrewdriver (Chiswick)

Masterswitch, the band that Steve Wilkin fell in with once he broke away from his jazz-rock buddies, was one of the first groups to feel the whip of Jubilee-fired disapproval. The group had been gigging tentatively all year long, with frontman Jimmy Edwards defiantly disregarding a musical background that could be traced back to the late-1960s skinhead combo Neat Change, and who was now earning a crust producing would-be teenybop sensation Flintlock.

In between times, he soundtracked the movie *Groupie Girl*, worked A&R for the Dawn label (it was Edwards who signed Kilburn and the High Roads to the company), and cut a few singles, while still scouring the classifieds in *Melody Maker*. He hooked up with Wilkin in fall 1976, and Masterswitch debuted at the Fulham Golden Lion a few days before the Tom Robinson Band played there.

They had been gigging steadily from thereon in, but they rarely made headlines. They simply suffered through the same web of incompetent agents and uncooperative promoters that every band of the age was encountering.

"We had some horrible out of town gigs," Wilkin shuddered. "Agents would send you to the most unlikely venues. Airbase dances where they'd be horrified you didn't do covers, and complained violently about the volume. I remember us driving to Ipswich one night to discover the venue was a disco at the top of a multistory complex. Getting inside, it had no stage, but a series of podiums scattered round the room, presumably constructed for go-go dancers. They

Masterswitch—Mark P called them the Genesis of Punk, and the funny thing was, the band didn't disagree. *Courtesy of Steve Wilkin*

were only big enough to take one person on each. We left, the venue manager threatening, of course, that we'd never work again."

Even that experience paled before the one that now awaited Masterswitch, however. Back out into the wilds beyond London, they arrived at the designated venue, only to discover that what they assumed would be a regular rock club was, in fact, a local dance. A very polite local dance.

"But the organizers were nice enough, they made us a pot of tea, brought out on a tray complete with cups and saucers, biscuits, and so on." And all was going well until somebody asked what sort of music Masterswitch played.

"Oh, we're known as a punk band," Edwards answered.

It was a contentious allegation, even the musicians admitted that. As Wilkin explained, "We just did what we did. Obviously, any musician's work will reflect to some degree the climate in which they are enveloped, but we never tried to be a punk band *per se*. Somehow we were absorbed into it, just by virtue of being a new band that was evidently not part of the early 1970s rock scene." He recalled the shock with which people would respond when they heard Masterswitch's music, as opposed to simply reading about their reputation, and when *Sniffin' Glue* credited Masterswitch with their own special place within the punk hierarchy, it came with a very distinct qualification.

"Mark P called us the 'Genesis of Punk.' Jimmy wrote very direct songs with minimal chord changes that we would flesh out in rehearsals. I, on the other hand, would try deliberately not to use obvious chord progressions when writing, and these would become familiarized, as it were, by the addition of Jimmy's vocals across the top. So, while I was never particularly fond of Genesis, I interpreted the remark as recognition that we had some material which was a little outside the obvious, and had a bit more scope musically than many of our contemporaries."

Not that such an explanation held much water at the dance party. Edwards's confession was scarcely out of his mouth before the atmosphere nose-dived. The previously polite tray-bearing lady vanished, only to primly return armed with an invoice for refreshments. Once garrulous conversationalists were replaced by pinchy-faced matriarchs, while thunder-browed Alphas patrolled the perimeter, to repel any further punky interlopers. Masterswitch performed that night to a very smartly dressed crowd who absolutely detested them; and, just to round off the evening, the musicians were still packing away their gear when they were surrounded by a flock of local drunks, determined to provoke them into a fight.

They resisted the temptation, then returned to London to discover that what they had witnessed in microcosm was now exploding across the city.

Possibly, people genuinely *were* outraged that these punk rockers were standing up against Her Majesty the Queen. Maybe they really *did* feel that youth had gone too far this time, and needed to be smacked back to a degree of respectability. Perhaps they truly believed that these young ruffians deserved the short, sharp shock of a good public beating.

Or maybe they just read what it said in the papers, and didn't want to miss out on the fun. But somewhere along the line, somewhere around the middle of May, some bright spark in one of the tabloids realized that a story was unfolding beneath everybody's noses, and might well explode nationwide if it was only given the exposure.

Scratch Teds versus Punks. How about Patriots versus Anarchists?

Punk's colors were already nailed firmly, if not necessarily accurately, to the superdistorted antimonarchism of the Sex Pistols' mast. What could be more natural, then, than for Her Majesty's most loyal supporters to take matters into their own hands and give these disrespectful whippersnappers the thrashing they deserved?

The headlines would hover around the biggest-name victims. Beginning at the end of May and marching into June, sundry Sex Pistols were beaten and slashed around London, the Adverts were mugged in a Shepherds Bush subway, and so on and so forth. But the real carnage took shape away from the spotlight, restaging Cassie and Joe's misadventure on streets the length of the land.

Patrolling the alleyways and side streets, keeping a sharper look out for passing punks than they ever had for, say, worthwhile employment, or a decent meal for their kids, these patriots haunted the corridors in the tube stations and the shadows beneath the railway bridge. They mapped out the darkness on the edge of the Roxy

Club, and lurked in doorways with their breath held tight. And such was the feral grace with which they operated that even the police would look the other way, rather than try to stand in the path of a pack of rampaging thirty-somethings, pursuing a lone spiky top down a pedestrian-packed city street.

Martin Gordon looked on nervously. He never ran into these mobs himself, but "it was clear that if you went to Shepherd's Bush late at night and were wearing 'provocative' clothing, there was a good chance that you would get jumped on. So the answer, it seemed, was, don't. I was pally with Glen Matlock, we would meet in a pub in Maida Vale, and he'd tell the latest stories of mayhem and violence."

Not every reported beating was as serious as it sounded, of course. Damned fans were outraged when they learned that Dave Vanian had been set upon by skinheads during the band's latest tour, and suffered a dislocated wrist as a consequence. In fact, the injury was sustained under somewhat less sinister circumstances; namely, when he clambered into a pram at the top of a flight of boarding-house stairs, and invited Adverts' drummer Laurie Driver to give him a push. All the way down to the reception area.

* * *

Jubilee Day dawned with all the pomp and circumstance that the occasion demanded, unimpeded even by the rain that swept across the country, washing out street parties and dampening the bonfires. So many events, so much happiness, so many news stories. Even the Sex Pistols couldn't spoil the party, as they chartered a pleasure boat and chugged down the River Thames, while the law patiently waited at the dock where they'd be landing, and an army of onlookers kept pace with their transit, charging down the Embankment and cheering every note.

It was the Pistols' first "live" appearance in Britain since a one-off back in March, and the chaos that accompanied it could not have been better orchestrated if McLaren had planned it with military precision. Plus, there was that magical moment when the boat (the *Queen Elizabeth*, what else?) passed the Houses of Parliament, and the Pistols launched into a feedback-drenched snarl through "Anarchy in the UK."

Echoing tauntingly from the buildings on either side of the river, tormenting the now itchy-footed cops on dry land, it sounded fabulous. It sounded better than fabulous. If we'd been grown men, we'd have wept. As it was, we simply watched in amazement as the *Queen Elizabeth* finally hove in at the dock and the boys in blue swept onto the boat, to round up anyone they could lay their hands on. Offenses recorded that evening ranged from "obstructing a policeman" (Vivienne Westwood) to "assault" (there were a few of those) and onto Malcolm McLaren's ferociously denied "using insulting words likely to provoke a breach of the peace." If the Empire was striking back, it was doing so in a remarkably pedantic manner.

Besides, the real action that night was taking place at the Roundhouse, where the Ramones had returned for another night of triumph, and they didn't give a hoot for the petty affairs of state. A year had passed since their last visit to these shores, and another LP, their second, had materialized, bearing with it a *bona fide* hit single, the surf's-up exuberance of "Sheena Is a Punk Rocker."

If you wanted to be ruthless about it, *The Ramones Leave Home* was little more than a carbon copy of its predecessor, the same number of songs shoehorned into the vinyl, the same blink-and-you'll-miss-it running time. Somebody pointed out that a Ramones album lasted the same amount of time as the average television sitcom, with a break for commercials in the middle when you turned the record over, and Joey laughed loudly at the comparison. "Yeah. We're the Archie Bunkers of Punk."

It was a night to remember, a night to cherish, a relentless parade of glue-sniffing Nazis, homosexual murderers, bat-beaten brats, and,

The Ramones hit the UK chart for the first time, but who still has a complete copy of the twelve-inch picture sleeve today? Cut out the coupon on the back, and mail it in to the record label, and you would receive this limited edition "Ramones in the UK" T-shirt. *Author's collection*

reaching into the soul of American carnival legend, the ultimate "Pinhead" chant: "Gabba gabba, we accept you, we accept you, one of us." Corralled into the Roundhouse, two thousand sweat-and-leather-drenched pinheads shouted right back.

Work backward from the Ramones' arrival onstage . . . the deejay filling the gaps between sets with a selection of recent punk rock singles, then ending his set with "God Save the Queen" and the entire auditorium erupting into joyous pandemonium. Outside, in cities, towns, and villages the length and breadth of the nation, Straight England was partying fit to burst. But inside the Round-house, the venomous snarl and the behemoth guitar chords could never have found a more appreciative audience.

New Yorkers Talking Heads appeared before the Ramones, and were greeted with more curiosity than applause. Feted by the critics long before a note of music had percolated over, Talking Heads had one hell of a reputation to live up to, and they didn't make a very good job of it.

About six weeks before the Roundhouse show, I caught XTC at the Hope and Anchor. Danny Adler recommended them, described XTC as one of the very few bands with whom he felt any serious musical empathy. And when they took the stage, you could under-stand why.

The music began, and then halted deliberately. It twitched, it fiz-zled, it skedaddled around the half-filled bar, and pulled faces at the barmaids. Listen to "1967 (She's So Square)," which was actually maddeningly circuitous; or "Refrigeration Blues," with a chorus you could cook baked beans on. Or watch them dismantle "All Along the Watchtower" with such painstaking precision that you could see the ghosts of your Patti-hating hippie neighbors spontaneously com-busting around the three-minute mark. The bass lines burbled at a hundred miles an hour, the guitars were encased within a tin full of bad-tempered scorpions, and as for Partridge's vocals . . .

The singer raised his hands in plaintive surrender. "It was a very desperate, 'Here I am, please notice me, I'm very distinctive' vocal." All tight pants and strangulation, it was the sound of someone "who really didn't know whether they'd ever get to have another chance. You think you're only going to get one shot at it, so you decide 'I'm going to be remembered.'"

Aside from the fact that their songs weren't half as good, Talking Heads sounded a lot like that, and singer David Byrne moved like it as well, a skinny schoolteacher with his veins popping out, jerking behind his acoustic guitar while his colleagues tried to lend rhythm to his yelping. A couple of catchy songs, a lot of art school twitching, a chemistry lesson with a test tube full of songs. XTC without the ecstasy. Forget them, and bathe instead in the memory of the evening's openers. The Saints.

Eight months had passed since I first heard "I'm Stranded," and so much had changed in the interim. Back then, the Saints sounded like Armageddon on a motorcycle. Today, they sounded like just another punk group. A good punk group, mind you, but just another one all the same. Live, however, all comparisons burned to ash.

The Saints arrived in London less than a week before the Ramones show, and they were looking for trouble from the outset. Asked what he thought about the punk scene in London, Chris Bailey didn't even pause for thought before declaring that the Sex Pistols sounded like a bad Alex Harvey cover band. The music press had its headlines, and the Saints had notoriety. The two ran hand in hand from thereon in.

"I was never terribly fond of the punky rock scene in England," Bailey admitted, even though he acknowledged that it certainly served its purpose. "If it hadn't been for that scene, I'd probably still be working in an abattoir in the antipodes, so I suppose I should be grateful to it, because it did get us a bus ticket to the other side of the world. But when the band were still impressionable teenagers, and we were living in a very parochial part of a very parochial country, I think we took it all very seriously.

"It was the end of the Vietnam period [Australia, unlike the UK, sent troops to fight in that conflict], the height of that idealistic 'we're not going to sell out, bah humbug' thing, talking revolution and all that kind of thing." Australian youth was blazing with anger, dreaming that one day it could help change the world. Punk, the Saints believed when they read about it from afar, shared those same wide-eyed principles. "And you only had to spend two days on the Kings Road to realize that wasn't true."

He was right. It wasn't.

Summer was here, but so was the end of the road. Nobody had planned it and the groups that rose (and would continue rising) from the punk métier were scarcely likely to admit it. For them, the journey was still beginning. The Damned, the Stranglers, and the Clash had debut albums out, but the Sex Pistols were still only two singles old, and the Jam, the Buzzcocks, and the Adverts had just one to their name.

Everybody else—Generation X, Chelsea, Siouxsie and the Banshees, the Slits, Masterswitch, XTC, whoever—was still awaiting their chance. In their eyes, punk, or whatever they chose to call the musical explosion that allowed them to escape the rehearsal room and discover an audience that wanted to listen, was still vibrant and vital, still billowing beneath them, pushing them inexorably forward to fame and glory.

But when the last bedraggled souvenirs of the Jubilee came down, they were joined in the bin by a lot more than mere memories.

"Punk rock was our generation's equivalent of the London Blitz," mused Martin Gordon. "It was an excuse for one lot of people to get together in a bunker and sing 'Knees Up Mother Brown,' while another lot flew over their heads and tried to blast them out of existence." And, just as the Blitz ended when Hitler turned his attention to the Russians and decided to give Britain a break, so punk ended when the newspapers realized that it was too late to strangle the thing at birth, and moved on to other shock-horror controversies.

On June 20, just two weeks after the Pistols threatened to destroy the monarchy forever, Anglia Television broadcast *Alternate 3*, a spoof documentary that discussed a secret plan hatched by the British and American governments to transport the world's greatest scientific brains to a colony on Mars to protect them from an imminent global cataclysm.

In fonts at least as large as those that followed the Sex Pistols' appearance on *Today*, the following morning's headlines (and those for several days after) documented the storm over TV's spoof and out they came again, the horrified viewers who had nothing better to do that evening than call in their protests to the press. Nobody seems to have kicked in their television screen on this occasion, but still it was difficult to suppress a very weary sense of *déjà vu*.

Cut off from the air supply of disapproving publicity, the punk bands found they needed to start appealing on other levels instead—musical ones, which is why the Pistols followed the acerbic one-two of "Anarchy" and "God Save the Queen" with the power-pop harmlessness of "Pretty Vacant," a gobsmacking chorus in search of a song, and so deliciously innocuous that even the BBC couldn't be bothered to ban them any longer. Without a broadcast supporter in the land, "God Save the Queen" topped the UK chart. Even an appearance on *Top of the Pops* couldn't shove "Pretty Vacant" into the Top Five.

Malcolm McLaren had hoped to formulate a movement that would rise up as one and change the world. Instead, it had smashed into so many shards that even the biggest pieces were no longer visible.

Decay was everywhere, punk was shattering. When Stiff Records launched Elvis Costello with the intriguing "Less than Zero," people looked at his photo, all spindle and spectacles, and wondered why they'd dressed him up like Danny Adler.

When the Lurkers emerged from darkest Fulham, journalists called them the English Ramones, and then announced they were bored with the American Ramones as well.

Sniffin' Glue folded with its tenth issue in June, when Mark P decided to pump his energies instead into his own band, ATV. Their first single was sticky-taped to the cover of the magazine, a moping antisex song called "Love Lies Limp." It was probably really good if you enjoyed going to art school.

Bands were being singled out for death or glory on a more or less hopelessly random basis, and the worst thing was, with no media beyond the music press to inform or incite, audiences were going along with those pronouncements, regardless of any evidence to the contrary.

Add the violence that only increased as the months passed by, but seemed ever more meaningless as even the thugs forgot what they were fighting for, and suddenly a lot of the fun had gone out of things.

But if the symbolism had died, the spirit was still alive, and a few final acts were still to play out before whatever kind of future lay in store could take shape.

Chelsea was about to release "Right to Work," an almost impossibly brilliant slice of didacticism that had Gene October in raptures. "I hope to instigate something if I can. I wanna take [punk] away from the rough side that it's got, and I wanna add a bit of smoothness to it, a bit of polish, a bit of style. There's too many of these punk groups being looked on as thickos."

The Adverts were signing to Anchor Records and preparing to record "Gary Gilmore's Eyes," a song inspired by convicted American murderer Gilmore's insistence that he be executed, and that his eyes be donated to medical science for transplant ("I don't think the heart will be any good"). Larry Wallis was again the producer.

Rikki and the Last Days of Earth were working toward the release of one of the most confident LPs of the age, one that would set the stage for the synthesized future of the early 1980s.

Eater had its first LP in the pipeline, the Damned were preparing their second, and Radio Stars were recording an EP. Rings was breaking up, but Shaw and Latter would re-emerge as the Maniacs and pick up where the old band left off. The Tom Robinson Band was signing to EMI, amid promises that not one of the songs that meant the most in their repertoire was going to fall by the wayside. Roogalator would have an LP out in the new year, Ian Dury would be a superstar by the end of the decade, and while a Heavy Metal Kids reunion ultimately proved disastrous, Gary Holton would go on to become one of Britain's best-loved television stars, before his ongoing drug problem finally ended his life in October 1985.

And Bob Marley was playing the London Rainbow, just one month before the two sevens clashed.

Oddly, reggae never really took off at the shop. Even among the kids who had otherwise devoted themselves to the punk rock lifestyle, festooning their school uniforms with tiny symbols of allegiance, or asking the barber for a more extreme haircut, there were now so many punk records appearing that even the biggest Jamaican hits of the day found it difficult to take root on the Hertford Road. Even worse, on those occasions when a certain song *did* capture the imagination, procuring a copy was a lot easier said than done.

The supply lines between the Jamaican studios and the London market stalls were fraught with difficulties. Even with a growing coterie of local labels competing for the Kingston producers' wares, and major labels Island and Virgin sweeping up the cream of the crop, still it could be weeks and even months before a record made it over in sufficient quantities to satisfy everybody who wanted a copy. By which time, they might not want it any longer.

The sound systems got their hands on them, of course, the mobile discos that touched down in clubs and basements alike to fill the night with sound. Before there was even a UK reggae industry, the sound systems had made it over from Jamaica, and their descendants were still hard at work: Fatman Hi-Fi, Lloyd Coxson, Jah Shaka, Silver Camel. Reggae Nights at the 100 Club every Thursday. Catch them on a good evening and every record was a winner. But try to find those records.

Salvation! Every Saturday morning, a record stall on Portobello Road would fill up with boxes of cassette tapes, stuffed with sixty, even ninety minutes of new sounds. Not every one was correctly labeled; some weren't labeled at all, so you never knew until you got home whether you'd just bought much the same compilation as you picked up the week before. But you'd sit with a few back issues of *Black Echoes*, then scour each lyric for a title in the chart, and if it wasn't the same as owning the vinyl, at least you now knew what the records sounded like.

Except once, there was a song that defied all investigation. For a start, it was little more than an acoustic ghost, a guitar strumming just hard enough to accentuate the beat, and a voice that sounded enough like Bob Marley to make you think it was probably somebody else, half-singing, half-scatting a half-complete lyric. "Ex-o-dus . . . movement of Jah people."

I asked about it the following week, and I wasn't the only person who did so. But the Rasta behind the table didn't know, or, if he did, he wasn't about to tell me. A friend of a friend of a friend of a friend, however, reckoned he'd seen Leroy Anderson dropping off tapes to one of the other stalls a few days before—the same Leroy Anderson whose half-sister, Rita, was Bob Marley's wife; the same Bob Marley who was now holed up in a rented house on Oakley Street, Chelsea. For sure Leroy wouldn't have dropped off *this* tape; he was one of Marley's most trusted confidants. But if he was helping to stock up one stall (and *Sounds* journalist Vivien Goldman later confirmed that he was), then who knows who else in the Marley circle might be supplying some of the others?

It would be a while longer before the finished glory of Marley's "Exodus" would be premiered, onstage at the Rainbow. But that cassette tape whispered its incipient glory regardless, so loud that everything else on the compilation was forgotten long before its first few minutes wore out and the tape finally snapped from its spool.

Some great reggae shows hit London that year—Big Youth and Dennis Brown side by side at the Rainbow; Johnny Clarke and John Holt at the Hammersmith Palais; and, in the same week as the Marley concerts, Dillinger, Leroy Smart, and Delroy Wilson, also at the Palais. The morning after that one, Joe Strummer awoke to scribble down the first lines of what became "White Man in Hammersmith Palais," destined to become the Clash's greatest-ever record; on another occasion, singer Joe Jackson would remember being at the Big Youth gig, "and there were only about ten white people in the audience." Neither could have been paying attention to their surroundings. Two years before the term became a multiracial marketing slogan, the audience at all three gigs was truly two-tone.

Marley, however, was the big one, a working week of concerts that sold out within hours of the box office opening to a serpentine queue that draped itself up and around the Seven Sisters Road. Hemmed in by the venue's wall on one side, and the watchful cops on the other, Jah People were moving very slowly that morning.

Exodus was an album of the moment, for the moment. The impassioned ferocity of "Exodus" itself was everywhere, an eight-minute statement of intent that crystallized all the pain and confusion that still blazed across the landscape. Summer, according to the *New Musical Express*, would not begin until "Waiting in Vain" was released as a single (it finally arrived in August), and that in turn meant that the heat that beat the streets before then was simply a forewarning of the firestorms that would erupt from the political clouds overhead.

The National Front was really flexing its muscles now. In the long-awaited local elections, leader John Tyndall scooped 19 percent of the vote in Hackney South and Bethnal Green, while the party attracted two hundred thousand votes nationwide. New recruits, too, seemed plentiful. An ill-advised attempt to line up alongside the Sex Pistols prompted Johnny Rotten to dismiss the Front as "loathsome slugs." But the skinhead movement had no single definable leader and, unlike the punks, no immediately identifiable credo. The Front found plentiful pickings there, and while nobody has ever published a reliable estimate of exactly how many skinheads were drawn into the National Front's ranks, even if it was just a couple of percent of the organization's overall force, who would be the most visible figures on the Fascist frontline? An army of middle-aged men in jeans, suits, or donkey jackets? Or a handful of skins with shaven skulls, braces, and boots?

Exodus served up the soundtrack to the resistance. As Rock Against Racism battled the fascists in the country's city centers, Marley's music would rise above the sounds of destruction—the clarion call of resistance.

From the moment the Rainbow shows were announced, the media previewing the shows, and the cops policing them, were primed to expect trouble, one with the salacious anticipation of newsmen chasing a Reggae Race Riot exclusive, the other with the more sinister motives of protecting society by crushing its roots. "Kill it before it grows," a line from "I Shot the Sheriff," rang with special resonance at the Rainbow.

The simple positioning of police vans and the flying phalanx of lawmen who would dive into the crowd at preordained intervals to emerge with another struggling innocent in bondage suggested something more than mere crowd control. It was divide and conquer, setting brother against brother, skin against skin. The Rainbow's own security was edgily aggressive, sending a fresh wave of tangible emotion out across the crowd.

By the time the Wailers appeared onstage, an audience gathered in that state of peaceful union for which Marley fought so hard had long since fractured into glowering factions, through which the police passed like an avenging angel, smiting anybody who even looked like trouble. That most of the arrests that night were for marijuana possession only exacerbated the law's total lack of understanding of the situation.

From the stage, Marley took in that same situation with a glance. Talking to the press later, he condemned the police, condemned the bouncers, and condemned the handful of kids who attended the shows looking for trouble or worse. But he praised the audience that ensured that they didn't find it. Through a set dominated by *Exodus* (the album) and crowned by "Exodus" (the song), Marley first steadied, then utterly salved the troubled waters lapping to the lip of the stage. And, by the time "Jamming" came around, that's exactly what was happening, a seething partylike celebration of release, relief, and joy that drew and then threw the anger aside. Even the cops were dancing. Well, some of them were.

Rock Against Racism was out in force that night. You could barely walk a yard outside the venue without running into another tireless volunteer staggering beneath the weight of a sackful of *Temporary Hoarding*. Rock Against Racism had launched its monthly fanzine in April, and it had already established itself as crucial literature for everybody who realized that the guiding principles of the organization would remain inviolate long after all the other punk tenets had come crumbling down. It was already apparent that unemployment, poverty, and hunger wouldn't be swept away by electric guitars, and maybe racism would not be destroyed. But the culture of ignorance that was its most fertile breeding ground was certainly given less raw material with which to work.

"Before Rock Against Racism got going," Gene October reminded me, "if you were white, there were parts of town you simply didn't go into, because the blacks would kick the shit out of you, not because they were racist, but because you might be. The black kids wanted to mix and later, after punk happened and Rock Against Racism got going, they could. You'd walk past a bunch of Rastas and they'd be fine, 'How you going, mate?' You'd get black kids at punk shows, punk kids at reggae shows. That simply couldn't have happened a year earlier. That's how much Rock Against Racism changed things."

Marley at the Rainbow was, quite possibly, the first major reggae concert where black and white could mix together without fear of one another's intentions. Just two weeks later, and less than a year since the nightmare of Reading, the Stonehenge Free Festival turned that triumph around to stage the first major rock event where the same could be said.

Rumor insisted that the Sex Pistols, unable to find a single legitimate gig to play anywhere else in the country, had earmarked the Stonehenge Free Festival as a suitable venue for their next onstage outrage. Ever ready with a quotable comment, Virgin PR man Al Clark dismissed the story the moment it surfaced, insisting, "The likelihood of the Pistols appearing at Stonehenge is comparable to that of [middle-aged crooner] Vince Hill doing a season at CBGBs." But, once uncaged, the beast was free, and even the traditionally sensible *Guardian* newspaper picked up on the story. Except that they called it a threat.

Of course, the Pistols didn't show, but it didn't matter. As Cassie and I milled through the weeklong campsite, thronging with black and white, punk and rocker, gay and straight, male and female, reveling in the freedom, worshiping amid the stones and dancing to the

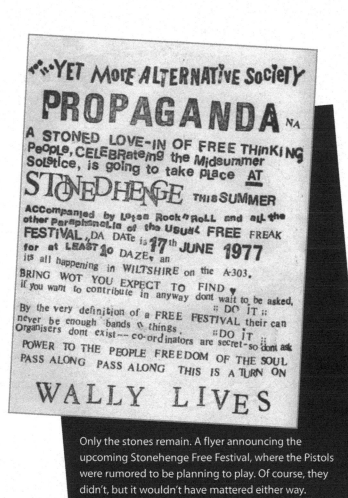

Only the stones remain. A flyer announcing the upcoming Stonehenge Free Festival, where the Pistols were rumored to be planning to play. Of course, they didn't, but it wouldn't have mattered either way.
Author's collection

music, one song lyric became so repetitive in my head that several times I had to look around to make sure that the Adverts hadn't suddenly turned up to play instead.

The song was called "New Day Dawning" and I clung to its lyrics like the credo they were, confident that they would get us through the rest of the month . . . the rest of the year . . . and into the future ahead of us.

> *Don't be a hero because we don't need one*
> *Be a panther or a poet*
> *Someone to light the beacon*
> *And I wonder . . . is a new day dawning?*
> —"New Day Dawning"

ePiLoGUE

The Two Sevens Clash

JULY 1977

Back in the spring, while Marley's *Exodus* sessions were still taking shape, you would occasionally see one of the Wailers out and about around London. Marley himself was rarely spotted; he and Cindy Breakspeare, Jamaica's first Miss World, were sighted at the super-exclusive Tramps disco one evening, but tramps like the rest of us had never been in there, and probably wouldn't know what to do if we were. Another time the word went out that he'd visited the London headquarters of the Twelve Tribes of Israel, in St. Agnes Place, Kennington—a Rasta stronghold that was destined to become the longest-occupied squat in the whole of London. But it was a private audience, the details of which passed on to the grapevine by whisper and rumor alone.

St. Agnes Place was an amazing bolthole. An entire street of tall, dark brick houses had been left to decay by the local council, in such maddening defiance of the housing crunch that even the locals were happy to see them being taken over. The first squatters arrived in 1969, pushing open the barely bolted front doors and making the houses their homes. More and more followed, happily renovating the more tumbledown buildings, fixing roofs and windows that had been open for years, transforming a slum into a vibrant neighborhood.

There'd be parties there, wild and loud and late into the night, with Dennis Bovell or Don Letts in occasional attendance to make sure the music was never turned down, and the air so thick with smoke that even stepping outside for a breath of fresh air left you feeling as though you'd just downed a whole joint.

But they were moody, uneasy parties as well, where the black guys eyed the whites suspiciously, while the white kids felt like interlopers at best, invaders at worst, knowing they were welcome but certain that every move they made, even picking up a can of Red Stripe, might be construed as some form of threat. Even talking to the girls was to take your life in your own hands, and it was only later that you learned that the Jamaicans found the whole thing hysterically funny. "Let me tell you," my friend Winston once told me. "If you weren't welcome there, they'd have slit your throat before you got through the door."

So when Winston and Margarita asked whether Cassie and I were interested in catching a poet they knew, performing at a house around the corner from the squat, we didn't think anything of it. Well, maybe the term "poet" rang a few alarm bells, but that was about all. I certainly don't remember looking at the calendar, on which we'd long ago circled the date in black felt-tip, and thinking "Oooh, we ought to stay indoors today." It was Thursday, July 7, 1977. The day that the two sevens clashed.

In fairness, a lot of the foreboding had gone out of the date by the time it finally arrived, certainly among the people we ran around with, and further out of our orbit as well. A year earlier, so many people had their own opinions of what was going to befall that day—looking back from two decades hence, for the benefit of a friend too young to have shared in the terror, I described it as our generation's Y2K, and that's exactly what it turned out to be. But even before we knew that, so much else had happened over the past twelve months that one more day of disappointment or disaster, and that included the end of the world, really wasn't worth worrying about. Either it would happen, or it wouldn't, and we'd just have to get on with our lives in the meantime. Grin and bear it!

We arrived at the party, and there, too, the once-portentous date appeared to have slipped everybody's mind. Or maybe they just had more important matters to commemorate. The house had a history. Michael X, the black revolutionary, was said to have lived there twenty years ago. . . . He was Michael de Freitas back then, but according to Winston, who told us the story as we walked the few blocks, he was as charismatic then as he ever was once he turned to direct action, leading the resistance against the white boys who stormed Notting Hill in 1958, confronting the slumlord mafia, and pretty much single-handedly leading the British black civil rights movement into the twentieth century.

But then things started to go wrong. He gave a speech urging the shooting of any black woman seen with a white man, and got eighteen months in jail for that; he was released, and walked straight into an extortion racket. By the time he fled back home to Trinidad, he'd already lost a lot of the local support he could once rely upon.

He established a commune, but though he claimed to have abandoned violence, he seemed to have gone even further overboard, committing one murder and looking like the chief suspect in another. They hanged him in Port of Spain in 1975, and a lot of the older folk around the Hill weren't too sorry to hear that. A few of them, though, remembered him before he went off the rails, when he was genuinely working toward a good cause, and tonight was their tribute to that man.

It was strange. Twelve months ago, I'd only ever set foot in Notting Hill on a handful of occasions, and never strayed far from the main shopping area. Now I felt as though I'd known it my whole life and, more important, that it knew me. At least half a dozen different people spoke or nodded to us as we threaded our way through the crowds on the pavement outside Michael's place, and though I knew they were Winston and Cassie's friends, I recognized half of them. I didn't understand everything they said to me, of course, but I knew that would come as well. Anyone who survives five years at a boarding school on the edge of Thomas Hardy country has to have a pretty good handle on accents, or he'd still be in the first form, trying to decipher his own name during roll call.

The entire house had been given over to the event, though it was long ago converted to private flats. Everybody living there simply threw open their doors to all comers, while someone had festooned the place with wire and loudspeakers, so there wasn't a corner of the building, or the street outside, that wouldn't be able to hear what was going on.

There was a schedule of sorts, readings mostly, from X's writings, with a handful of big-name writers from the black press coming down to add either their own voices or their own words to the proceedings. "And don't worry if you can't understand what they're saying," Margarita assured us—a little unnecessarily, I thought, although it turned out that she was right. "Follow the rhythm and the meaning will become clear."

"I smell shit." A voice, unpleasantly close, sounded in my ear. I turned and found myself staring into a gaunt black face, its owner rolling his eyes back and baring his teeth. "I see shit, too."

Instinctively, I reached for Cassie's hand. She clasped it, but didn't move closer. Another figure had drawn up alongside her, effectively blocking us from one another. "So white girl thought she'd crash our party?"

"She brought her boy along to watch," the first one murmured. "Maybe we oblige her, maybe we just slit their throats and throw them to the pigs."

"Cassie?" I croaked. I wasn't quite sure what was going on . . . or, rather, I knew *exactly* what was going on, but had somehow managed to forget what she told me all those months before at the carnival, about how it wasn't only the Front and the cops we had to watch out for. Some of the islanders were hostile as well.

"Stand your ground," I heard her hiss. "Winston or one of the others has to be around here some place. In the meantime, don't let them see you're frightened."

Don't let them see I'm frightened? What the fuck? We're not talking about a mad dog here, you know. But I felt as though I was addressing one anyway. "We're here with friends," I spoke softly and slowly. "We're not looking for trouble."

"No, but you found it anyway." They stood on either side of me now, each one breathing heavily in my ear. Something sharp pricked against my skin, through the thin lining of my T-shirt and denim jacket. Christ, they're going to disembowel me here and now, and all Cassie can do is stand there telling me not to panic. And I was just about to do just that, when I heard her scream at the top of her lungs.

"Winston! Margarita! For fuck's sake, help!"

A silence fell over the room, maybe even the entire building. The two guys beside me certainly froze; they may not have known who Cassie and I were, but they certainly knew whom she'd just called to, and when I turned my head, I saw them both simply staring at one another. One of them turned to run; a foot shot out from somewhere, and sent him sprawling. People who, just a moment ago, had seemed content to simply stand and watch while the pair of them cut us to shreds, had suddenly executed a complete somersault, and were now doing their best to slow the pair down.

Winston wasn't even in sight, but when I heard a thud and a groan beside me, I knew that someone else had taken down one of the pair, and as I turned, it was to see two hefty black guys hauling an insensible body across the linoleum, pausing at the top of the stairs, and then hurling, *literally hurling*, it down to the floor below. It was Linton at the bus stop all over again.

There were some cries, some scuffling . . . presumably people getting out of the way of the missile . . . and then a sickening thump as it hit the ground. A few seconds later, a second similar thump was accompanied by an almost animal cry of pain, and then my own world was suddenly lost in a thick wall of perfume, as Margarita enfolded us both and held us tight, while she gently asked whether we were all right.

I freed myself from her grip when there was a sudden, loud boom of the sound system. I was so grateful it hadn't started up a few minutes earlier. The last words I heard before the very air turned to sound was Margarita only half-jokingly telling me, "A lot of good you turned out to be. Don't you white boys stand up to anything any more?"

Yes, we do.

It just needs to be a fight worth fighting.

Index

Dave Thompson is one of rock 'n' roll's leading experts. In 1999, he was ranked among the top five rock biographers by *Mojo* magazine, and he received an ARSC "best research" award in 2003 for his encyclopedia *Reggae & Caribbean Music*. More recently, former Rolling Stones manager Andrew Loog Oldham proclaimed Thompson "Sherlock Holmes with the facts," while celebrating his refusal to allow preconceptions to bog down his opinions. Thompson's first book, the U2 biography *Stories for Boys*, was published in 1984. He relocated to the United States in 1989, shortly after being proclaimed the most published English music biographer under the age of thirty. Among Thompson's other titles are biographies of David Bowie, Deep Purple, the Red Hot Chili Peppers, Gothic Rock, Genesis, Depeche Mode, the Cure, ZZ Top, and KISS. His 1994 biography of Kurt Cobain, *Never Fade Away*, was an international best seller, while *Wheels Out of Gear*, his study of British music and politics at the end of the 1970s, was elected one of *Uncut* magazine's top twenty-five rock books for 2004.

Born in Devon, England, Thompson got his start writing and publishing a fanzine during the punk explosion at the end of the 1970s. A regular contributor to the weekly music paper *Melody Maker* throughout the 1980s, he has also written for *Record Collector*, *Rolling Stone*, *Mojo*, *Q*,, *Spin*, *Alternative Press*, and many others. He is currently a columnist for the record collecting magazine *Goldmine* and a contributor to the All Music Guide.

Thompson is also the author of a number of well-received titles in other fields. These include the English soccer trilogy *Those We Have Loved*, biographies of actors John Travolta and Winona Ryder and television's *Doctor Who*, plus a groundbreaking history of the development of erotic film, *Black and White and Blue* (2007).